PORTLAND

Fairgoers appear ghostlike due to the long exposure time required for this 1905 photo of the Lewis and Clark Exposition at night. Courtesy, Oregon Historical Society (OHS)

PORTLAND

GATEWAY

—TO THE—

NORTHWEST

CARL ABBOTT

Pictorial Research by Ted Van Arsdol

Produced in Cooperation with
Portland State University

American Historical Press
Tarzana, California

© American Historical Press
All Rights Reserved
Published 1997
Printed in the United States of America

Library of Congress Catalogue Card Number: 97-74096

ISBN: 0-9654754-3-3

Includes Selected Reading
Refer to page 261 for Negative Numbers
of photos from Oregon Historical Society

Facing page: Skidmore Fountain has been one of the city's favorite landmarks since its completion in 1888. Increasing numbers of people have visited the fountain on S.W. First Avenue since the opening of the Saturday Market and restoration of the New Market building, both nearby. Courtesy, Barbara Gundle

Endpapers: Portland in 1861 enjoyed a lovely and active riverfront according to this lithograph "drawn from nature" by Grafton T. Brown. Courtesy, Amon Carter Museum, Ft. Worth, Texas

CONTENTS

Willamette Falls, fifteen miles above Portland, was a barrier to transportation on the Willamette River. The Hudson's Bay Company established a trading post at this popular fishing place in 1829. A townsite was laid out in 1842. (OHS)

PROLOGUE: GATEWAY TO THE NORTHWEST

Our great-great grandparents were quick to give full credit to divine providence for the growth of their cities. The Creator, said one early Chicagoan, had marked the inevitable destiny of that city by rolling back the waves of Lake Michigan. The great bend of the Missouri River seemed a heaven-sent guarantee for the success of Kansas City. Armchair geographers were confident that the falls on the Mississippi assured the future of St. Paul.

In the case of Portland, the general idea was clear enough. There seemed to be no doubt that a major center of commerce would develop *someplace* along the lower valley of the Columbia River between the Cascade Mountains and the Pacific Ocean. The only problem was exactly *where* that place would be. It was not until 1843 and 1844—after fifty years of Anglo-American exploration and thousands of years of occupance by Native Americans—that a permanent settlement was founded at what has now become the middle of downtown Portland.

More than any of its West Coast rivals of Seattle, Tacoma, San Francisco, or Los Angeles, Portland is indeed "the city that gravity built," to repeat the phrase of historian Glenn Quiett. It lies at the center of a great lowland crossroad that the forces of geological change have stamped into the mountains and plateaus of western America. From north to south, more than two-

thirds of the population of the Pacific Northwest and all but one of its major cities are found along a 500-mile trough between the volcanic peaks of the Cascades and the string of coastal mountains that extends from the redwood country of northern California to the spine of Vancouver Island. South of the Columbia, the Willamette River flows through the heart of the trough. Further north, the Cowlitz River extends the lowland through Washington State to Puget Sound and the Strait of Georgia. The string of cities runs from Eugene, Salem, and Portland in Oregon, through Olympia, Tacoma, Seattle, and Bellingham in Washington to Vancouver and Victoria in British Columbia.

The Columbia River crosses the lowland axis after breaking through the Cascade range 160 miles from the Pacific. East of the mountains, the river drains an Inland Empire that is larger than all of New England. As soon as the Columbia's existence was known, it entered the dreams of eastern Americans as the sure route to the western coast—the "North American road to India," in the words of Missouri Senator Thomas Hart Benton.

Later boosters talked as if the divine hand not only had pointed out the general location for the metropolis of Oregon but had actually staked the exact site. In sober fact, as we have said, it took explorers and pioneers half a century to hit on the precise spot for Port-

land.

The English-speaking discoverer of the Columbia River was the American trader Robert Gray, who entered the mouth of the river in May 1792 but showed no interest in venturing upstream into the interior. It was left to Lieutenant James Broughton of the British navy, sailing with Captain James Vancouver on the expedition that first mapped Puget Sound, to become the first European actually to explore the lower Columbia. In October 1792, he took the 135-ton *Chatham* across the dangerous Columbia bar and spent three weeks exploring the river in small boats. He reached the Sandy River and claimed the region for England. Although he noted the confluence of the Willamette, he was more interested in enjoying the scenery and bestowing the name Mt. Hood on the region's most prominent peak.

A decade later, Meriwether Lewis, William Clark, and their handful of companions on their famous transcontinental expedition of 1804-1806 missed the mouth of the Willamette River not once but twice. On their way downstream to the Pacific in November 1805, they recorded several islands along the south shore of the Columbia but failed to notice the mouth of the Willamette. On its return after a winter at Fort Clatsop near present-day Astoria, the expedition reached the Quicksand (Sandy) River before Clark doubled back with a Cushook Indian guide to find the "Moltnomar" or "Multnomah" river, his term for the Willamette. On the morning of April 3, he paddled as far as the bluff now occupied by the University of Portland, where the river turned east-southeast to swing around Swan Island. As Clark recorded in his journal, he turned around in a thick mist "being perfectly satisfied of the size and magnitude of this great river which must water that vast tract of Country between the western range of mountains and those on the sea coast."

One reason that Clark and other explorers failed to remark on the site that was to become the heart of Portland was because the location was relatively unimportant to Native Americans. When European and American fur traders began to arrive in the Pacific Northwest at the end of the 1700s, Chinook-speaking peoples dominated the lower Columbia west of the Cascades from its mouth to the falls at The Dalles. The Lower Chinooks, among whom Lewis and Clark spent the winter of 1805-1806, lived around the wide Columbia estuary. The Upper Chinooks lived in small bands along the middle stretch of the river. Their greatest concentration was on Sauvie Island and along the adjacent Oregon shore, an area dominated by a subgroup known as the Multnomahs. Lewis and Clark counted 2,400 people on the island and

Captain Meriwether Lewis, shown here circa 1810, and Captain William Clark headed the army exploring party down the Columbia River past the mouth of the Willamette in 1805. This was the first recorded visit of an American to the vicinity, although trading ships had stopped along the coast. (OHS)

another 1,800 nearby on the south shore. Six years later, British fur trader Robert Stuart reported a population of about 2,000 for the island itself. By piecing together the reports of different travelers, we can now locate more than fifteen separate villages on Sauvie Island and immediately across the Columbia, the Willamette, or Multnomah Channel.

Twenty-five miles up the Willamette were other Indians who also spoke Chinook dialects. The Clackamas groups were the largest, with perhaps a dozen villages. Smaller bands included the Cushooks and Chahcowahs, who clustered below the falls at the present Oregon City, where it was easy to take salmon out of the Willamette and Clackamas rivers. Above the falls to the south, the

Willamette Valley was occupied by the Kalapooias, a people distinct from the various branches of Chinooks. They were divided into at least a dozen bands with defined territories. Closest to present-day Portland was the Tualatin band in what is now Washington County.

Compared to Native Americans in many other parts of the continent, the Chinooks along the lower Columbia lived a relatively rich and easy life. Lewis and Clark remarked on the special fertility of the Columbia Valley in the vicinity of Portland. The Multnomahs, Clackamas, and other groups in this Portland basin fished for salmon, sturgeon, and smelt; hunted migratory birds and deer that thrived in the riverside woods and clearings; gathered nuts and berries; and dug wappatoo roots out

Captain Robert Gray of Boston discovered the mouth of the Columbia River in 1792, as depicted here. The Willamette River and other important tributaries of the Columbia remained unknown. Courtesy, Oregon State Transportation Department

of the mud of the marshes with pointed sticks. The abundance of wappatoo on Sauvie Island gave the island its first name and supported an especially dense population that was quite possibly larger than is found there now. Cedar logs washed loose from the mountains provided the materials for dugout canoes, cooking utensils, and longhouses made of planks lashed to a framework of poles and posts. Usually erected over a shallow pit, the plank lodges might reach 100 feet in length, with woven tule mats subdividing the interior space.

For travel to seasonal hunting and fishing grounds, the Chinook bands used temporary shelters of poles covered with mats and hides.

Chinook settlements ranged from clusters of a few small houses to substantial villages with hundreds of residents. Each village was an independent entity, bound together by complex kinship ties and represented by one or several headmen. Although the Chinook-speaking villages acknowledged some common connection, each was closer to an extended family than a unit within

an organized tribe. Villages were built to last for years, not for decades or centuries, for the abundance of resources made it easy to move from one spot to another within a band's general territory.

In the economy of the Chinook bands, the centers of trade were the mouth of the Columbia and the future site of The Dalles, where Celilo Falls marked a break in navigation on the river. Where the Columbia met the sea, they traded with other coastal tribes and, after the visits of Robert Gray and James Broughton in 1792, with European and American sailing ships. The Dalles was the dividing point between the lush coastal lands and the dry ranges and plateaus of the interior. It was also the boundary between the lifestyle of the northwest coast and that of inland tribes such as the Shoshonis, Paiutes, and Nez Perce. Both before and after the arrival of British fur traders, the break in navigation on the Columbia made The Dalles a natural market, as well as "a general theater of gambling and roguery" in the critical view of one trader. The Multnomahs and other tribes near the lower Willamette lived along the artery of trade but controlled neither of the key points of exchange.

The Chinooks were natural trading partners for American and British fur companies. The initial commerce was carried on by both "King George's men" and "Boston men"—English and American merchants who took two years to make a round-the-world circuit

with stops at the northwest coast, the Hawaiian Islands, and China. The heyday of maritime commerce to the Columbia lasted from 1792 until the War of 1812. Thereafter attention was focused on transcontinental trade. New Yorker John Jacob Astor organized the Pacific Fur Company in 1810 and planted the trading post that evolved into the city of Astoria at Point George on the south bank of the Columbia. Three years later, he sold out to the North West Company, a Montreal-based firm that renamed the post Fort George and dominated the fur trade of the Columbia Basin until 1821.

In turn, the North West Company was absorbed by its powerful rival, the British Hudson's Bay Company. Fort George was soon reduced to a lookout post to report on possible competition,

Left: *Hall J. Kelley predicted "shipmasters might find secure and commodious harbors" in the Willamette River. Kelley, a strong proponent of American settlement in the Oregon Country, visited Fort Vancouver near present-day Portland in 1834 but got a cool welcome from the Hudson's Bay Company. (OHS)*

Far left: *Alexander Ross, who arrived on the Columbia River in 1811, was involved in the fur trading business. He led a party that conferred with Indians on opening up the Willamette region. A book by Ross,* Fur Hunters of the Far West, *was published in 1855. (OHS)*

and the Hudson's Bay operations moved to Fort Vancouver, built in 1825 on the north shore of the Columbia seven miles upstream from the Willamette. Under the leadership of Dr. John McLoughlin, chief factor for the Hudson's Bay Company in the Oregon Country, it was the focal point of a Columbia Basin trading network extending hundreds of miles into the interior.

Fewer than thirty years after the Lewis and Clark expedition brought back reports of the Chinooks and Kalapooias and less than a decade after the building of Fort Vancouver, disease vir-

tually exterminated the population of northwestern Oregon. The spread of the Anglo-American trading system opened the possibility of both immediate economic gains and ultimate catastrophe for the Indians. The "Cold Sick" or "Intermitting Fever" appeared in the Chinook and Kalapooia villages in 1829 and raged for the next three years. Circumstantial evidence suggests that the disease may have been malaria brought in from the tropics by traders, although a form of influenza is another possibility. The disease was at its worst around Fort Vancouver and Sauvie Island. Eu-

Parts of old Fort Vancouver, headquarters of the Hudson's Bay Company in the Northwest, have been restored at Vancouver, near Portland. Among these is the blacksmith shop, where tools similar to those of frontier times are made for the nearby trader's store. Courtesy, Ted Van Arsdol

ropean observers estimated death rates that ranged from 50 percent to the appalling 90 percent reported by John McLoughlin of the Hudson's Bay Company. Observed from the outside and in retrospect, the Cold Sick was a tragedy whose human cost we can scarcely reckon.

The first Caucasian settlers who filled the void left by the virtual destruction of the native population also ignored the site of Portland. Fort Vancouver continued to be the major British settlement in the Portland area and hummed with activity that deeply impressed occasional visitors. Fort William, a rival trading post built on Sauvie Island by the independent American fur trader Nathaniel Wyeth, lasted only two years, from 1835 to 1837, before the Hudson's Bay Company took over the abandoned site

as a dairy farm. Hall J. Kelley, an eccentric New Englander who dedicated his life to fervent boosting of the Oregon Country, proposed to the general public the establishment of a "commercial town . . . about two miles square" at the juncture of the Willamette and Columbia. According to his crudely sketched plat, the city was to run across the North Portland peninsula from Smith Lake and the Columbia Slough to the St. Johns neighborhood of present-day Portland. We are scarcely surprised that the proposal sank without a trace, since Kelley had picked the site years before his own brief and highly unsuccessful visit to Oregon in 1834 and 1835.

Early traders and settlers who followed the Willamette upstream from Fort Vancouver in the 1830s or early

1840s had their eyes on the falls or the interior valley beyond. Their diaries and reports usually ignored or dismissed the first few miles of the river, where Portland was eventually to be built. The banks were either low and swampy, or else too thickly wooded for quick and easy cultivation. Philadelphia physician and naturalist John Townsend summed up the common reaction when he wrote that "there is not sufficient extent unincumbered, or which could be fitted for the purposes of tillage in a space of time short enough to be serviceable; others are at some seasons inundated, which is an insurmountable objection."

Indeed, the first large European settlements along the Willamette itself were both upstream from the site of Portland. Retired employees of the Hudson's Bay Company, mostly French Canadians, had begun to settle and cultivate the "French Prairie" in 1829. By 1840-41, the community had grown to more than sixty families who could worship in a new Roman Catholic church and sell their surplus wheat to Fort Vancouver through a small warehouse and landing at Champoeg, twenty-five miles above the Willamette Falls. A second settlement formed at the base of the falls where John McLoughlin and Methodist missionaries contended for control of what seemed to be the natural location for a major town. Rival development efforts started in 1840 and 1841. By the winter of 1842-1843, the new community of Oregon City had made a significant impression on the wilderness, with more than thirty buildings, a gristmill, and a growing competition for building lots. It was the first destination for most of the participants in the swelling American migrations that had brought over 800 new settlers to Oregon in 1843 and about 1,200 more in 1844.

Into the early 1840s the history of Portland is, in short, a story of near

misses. The Chinooks preferred to live at Sauvie Island and the falls of the Willamette and traded at the mouth of the Columbia and The Dalles. The Hudson's Bay men operated out of Fort Vancouver with a satellite settlement at Champoeg. Missionaries followed the Indians into the Willamette Valley and up the Columbia, while American settlers made Oregon City their first real town. The site of Portland, meanwhile, remained at the start of 1843 what it had been before—a small clearing of an

A somewhat fanciful 1846 illustration shows sailing ships at the great river of the West, the Columbia. Vessels sometimes encountered difficult conditions crossing the river bar before proceeding upriver to Fort Vancouver or into the Willamette, where several towns were vying for prominence. Courtesy, Reverend C.G. Nicolay's The Oregon Territory

acre or so made by trappers and Indians traveling between Fort Vancouver and Oregon City. It served as a sort of early rest area where travelers could rest or cook a midday meal on the thirty-mile trip. Jesse A. Applegate later described the site he had visited as a boy in 1843:

We landed on the west shore, and went into camp on the high bank where there was little underbush . . . No one lived there and the place had no name; there was nothing to show that the place had ever been visited except a small log hut near the river, and a broken mast of a ship leaning against the high bank. There were chips hewn from timber, showing that probably a new mast had been made there . . . . We were then actually encamped on the site of the city of Portland, but there was no prophet with us to tell of the beautiful city that was to take the place of the gloomy forest.

Lieutenant Henry J. Warre of the Royal Engineers, on a reconnaissance of Oregon for the British, sketched the new American settlement at Oregon City. He arrived with Lieutenant Vavasour in 1845 and started on the return trip in the following spring. (OHS)

CHAPTER I
STUMPTOWN

The Pacific Northwest was an international trouble spot in 1845. Political control of the Oregon Country—what is now Idaho, Oregon, Washington, and British Columbia—had been in dispute since the eighteenth century. England and the United States had pushed Russian claims north to Alaska and Spanish claims south to California in the first quarter of the nineteenth century and had then settled down to a diplomatic marathon that lasted from President to President and Prime Minister to Prime Minister. Along the lower Columbia, both sides traced their claims to the 1792 voyages by Gray and Boughton.

Tension had mounted rapidly with the Presidential campaign of 1844, when the issue of American control of Oregon helped to put Democrat James K. Polk in the White House. The growing American settlements along the Willamette and Columbia rivers were upsetting the delicate balance of commercial interests worked out by the men of the Hudson's Bay Company, and the British government correctly feared that Polk would cancel the joint occupancy agreement that had given citizens of both nations free access to Oregon since 1818.

The Northwest was a North American hot spot with its own set of spies and agents. The British military command in Canada dispatched Lieutenants Henry Warre and M. Vavasour from Montreal in 1845 for a military reconnaissance of Oregon. They traveled openly under the joint occupancy agreement in the guise of "private individuals, seeking amusement." Their real job was to spy out possibilities for coastal defenses, sea batteries, and river fortifications in case Britain decided to hold the territory against the Americans. Their report from Fort Vancouver in October 1845 counted the surviving Chinooks, Kalapooias, and Klickitats; described the American settlements; and suggested that a small British force stationed at Oregon City "would overawe the present American population" of 300. The only other settlement they noted on the lower Willamette was one family at Linnton.

Warre and Vavasour's second report on June 16, 1846, mentioned a new town. "Since the summer," they wrote their superiors, "a village called Portland has been commenced between the falls and Linnton, to which an American merchant ship ascended and discharged her cargo, in September." After struggling with their canoes through high water and willow swamps and camping on muddy beaches for more than a year, the two British officers were impressed by dry land. "The situation of Portland is superior to that of Linnton, and the back country of easier access. There are several settlements on the banks of the river, below the falls, but the water, covering the low lands during the freshets render them valueless for cultivation, and but few situations can be found adapted for building on."

Neither the British travelers nor the handful of Portlanders knew that exactly three days after Warre and Vavasour sealed their second dispatch, the United States Senate would make their mission

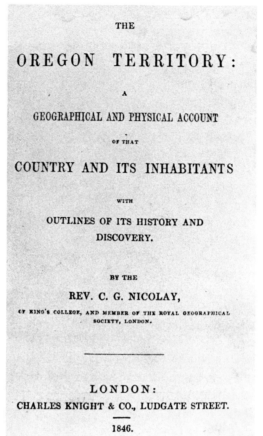

THE

OREGON TERRITORY:

A

GEOGRAPHICAL AND PHYSICAL ACCOUNT

OF THAT

COUNTRY AND ITS INHABITANTS

WITH

OUTLINES OF ITS HISTORY AND
DISCOVERY.

BY THE

REV. C. G. NICOLAY,

OF KING'S COLLEGE, AND MEMBER OF THE ROYAL GEOGRAPHICAL
SOCIETY, LONDON.

LONDON:

CHARLES KNIGHT & CO., LUDGATE STREET.

1846.

Far left: Peter Skene Ogden *was prominent among Hudson's Bay Company leaders when Great Britain claimed the land on the north bank of the Columbia, opposite today's Portland. Ogden led hardy groups of traders from Fort Vancouver to the Snake River country to trap and trade for furs.* (OHS)

Left: Books and articles *helped build interest in the relatively unsettled Pacific Northwest in the decade or so before Portland was established. This book reported that the Willamette settlement was flourishing, and begins "to wear some little appearance of civilization." Courtesy,* The Oregon Territory

irrelevant by ratifying the Anglo-American Oregon Treaty. The compromise boundary was the 49th parallel from the Rocky Mountains to Puget Sound, and from there around the south end of Vancouver Island and through the Strait of Juan de Fuca to the open Pacific. The future states of Idaho, Washington, and Oregon became the undisputed territory of the United States.

Portland was two and a half years old when the new treaty officially made it an "all American" town. The burgeoning settlement was the result of a bright idea by a drifter named William Overton. Overton had spent two years off and on in Oregon before he spotted the clearing along the west bank of the Willamette. In November 1843 he showed the site to Asa Lovejoy, an Oregon City lawyer, and the two became co-owners of the 640 acres that would become

downtown Portland when they filed a claim with the settlers' provisional government at Oregon City early in 1844. Lovejoy took a half-interest in the property when he agreed to pay the 25-cent filing fee with the provisional government. The men were claiming presumptive title, awaiting official acquisition of the territory by the United States and a procedure for distributing land to Oregon pioneers.

Portland's founding fathers quickly lost interest in their land speculation. Overton left Oregon to try his fortunes in California and, in the spring of 1844, sold out to Francis Pettygrove, a leading Oregon City merchant, for a $50 grubstake. Later that year, Pettygrove and Lovejoy hired a man to enlarge the clearing at the Willamette and build a cabin; he soon complained that the mosquitoes were so thick he couldn't work outside and that fleas made the inside of the cabin just as intolerable.

The next year brought the property both a name and a survey. But for the toss of a coin the town would have been called Boston, not Portland. Co-owner Asa Lovejoy was from Massachusetts and held a degree from Amherst College; he liked the idea of owning half of "Boston." Pettygrove hailed from the state of Maine and wanted to name the town "Portland." They "snapped up a copper," to use Lovejoy's words, and Pettygrove won the toss. That same year the speculators hired surveyor Thomas Brown to stake out blocks and lots so they could sell their property to new settlers. The original plat was two blocks deep and eight wide, bounded by Front, Second, Washington, and Jefferson streets. There were eight 50-by-100-foot lots on each small block.

Though Portland seemed well on its way to becoming a real community, Lovejoy, like his former partner Overton, soon lost interest in the townsite. Beckoned by a career in politics, Lovejoy decided in November 1845 that his future lay at Oregon City, the territorial capital, and sold his half interest to Benjamin Stark, cargomaster on the bark *Toulon*. Stark had traded with Pettygrove in the New York-to-Portland trade. Since Stark spent most of his time sailing back and forth to Oahu, finally settling down to a prosperous life in San Francisco, Pettygrove found himself responsible not only for the name but for the future of Portland.

What historian Eugene Snyder has called "Portland's Pettygrove period" lasted for two years of steady but unremarkable growth. Before the summer of 1846 was over, about sixty residents lived in Portland's first dozen or fifteen houses. James Terwilliger shoed horses at First and Morrison. Daniel Lownsdale's tannery was out of town to the west, where a creek flowed from the hills past the present site of Civic Stadi-

Asa Lovejoy, one of Portland's founders, arrived in Oregon with Dr. Elijah White in 1842. He rode east with Marcus Whitman during Whitman's efforts to save the missions in Walla Walla Valley and at Lapwai in Idaho. Lovejoy also served in the Oregon legislature. (OHS)

um. The center of town was Francis Pettygrove's store and wharf at the foot of Washington Street. A rough and rutted wagon track ran from the wharf past Lownsdale's tannery to the "Twality Plains." Other settlers in this first year of city-building included merchant J.L. Morrison, physician and teacher Dr. Ralph Wilcox, sawmill operator John Waymire, and shingle-maker William Bennett.

By the next summer of 1847, the town had grown to about 100 inhabitants. J.Q. Thornton, an early Oregon judge, described the place as having "an air of neatness, thrift, and industry." Sophisticates from larger towns like Oregon City were not always so kind. Although the trees had been cleared from rights of way to show where the streets had been surveyed, many of the stumps remained. Some were whitewashed to prevent nighttime wanderers from tripping. It was hard for outsiders to resist the nickname "Stumptown."

California's Gold Rush brought both crisis and opportunity for Stumptown. The news of James Marshall's discovery of gold at Sutter's Mill near Sacramento arrived in Oregon in August. Thou-

primarily wheat, for the California market. The supplies were sent by ship down the Willamette and Columbia rivers, then down the coast to San Francisco. On one day in midsummer 1849, twenty ships were loading in the lower Willamette at the same time. The volume of Oregon exports increased by fivefold in that year.

One summer of trade does not make a city. "Why Portland?" was the question that every smart investor and newly arrived merchant should have asked at the beginning of 1850. Stumptown would only grow if it was based on a successful business foundation. Two "generations" of Portland promoters— Overton and Lovejoy, Pettygrove and Stark—had already given up on Portland to seek greener pastures. Half a dozen rival settlements along a fifty-mile stretch of the lower Willamette and Columbia offered serious competition, and fortunes changed fast on the frontier. Would Portland or Milwaukie be the metropolis of Oregon? Milton City or Oregon City? St. Johns or St. Helens or some site still unnamed?

The competition between Portland and its rivals in the early 1850s is a fairly typical chapter in the familiar story of American townsite promotion. As settlement moved west in the nine-

Left: "Beaver" coins, five- and ten-dollar gold pieces, were produced by pioneers in 1849 at Oregon City, and were circulated for several years along the Willamette River. They helped eliminate bartering and the use of gold dust as money. Gold for the coins came from California. (OHS)

Below: Daniel Lownsdale, who occupied land in what is now downtown Portland, was involved in a townsite venture with Stephen Coffin and William Chapman. Lownsdale, who arrived in Oregon Territory in 1845, also established Portland's first tannery. (OHS)

sands of Oregonians caught gold fever. They hurried south to reach the Sierras before the snows and to get a jump on the expected hordes of prospectors from the East. Among the gold-seekers were dozens of families from Portland. According to popular lore the town's population was reduced to a grand total of three people. Francis Pettygrove bartered his half ownership of Portland to Daniel Lownsdale, Portland's first tanner, for $5,000 worth of leather, and liquidated his other assets in Oregon before sailing to San Francisco early in 1849. There he sold Lownsdale's leather to '49ers at a healthy profit. People who stayed in Portland also made good money by supplying lumber and food,

teenth century, speculators rushed to claim every promising harbor, ford, and dry stretch of riverfront. A cynical British observer had previously described the process in the Mississippi Valley:

A speculator makes out a plan of a city with its streets, squares, and avenues, quays and wharves, public buildings and monuments. The streets are lotted, the houses numbered, and the squares called after Franklin or Washington. The city itself has some fine name, perhaps Troy or Antioch. . . . All this time the city is a mere vision . . . five hundred miles beyond civilization,

probably under water or surrounded by dense forests and impassable swamps.

This ambitious platting of towns occurred across the young United States. The towns that managed to attract more than a handful of settlers plunged into a struggle for reputation and trade. There were half a dozen aspiring Toledos in northwestern Ohio in the 1830s. Chicago had to contend with the ambitions of Waukegan. At the same time that Portland was scrambling for its future, Kansas City was fighting Atchison and Leavenworth to be the metropolis of the Missouri. A few years later, Den-

Because early businesses faced the Willamette River, the street parallel to the water was known as Front. Wagons carried loads along the muddy street in this 1850s scene showing a washhouse, the Union Hotel, and a foundry. (OHS)

ver would have to battle the claims of Auraria, Highland, Mountain City, Arapahoe City, and Golden. Closer to home, Portlanders would soon be able to watch Tacoma, Seattle, and Everett competing to be the major city and chief port on Puget Sound.

In Oregon, the ostensible issue in 1850 was the location of the "head of navigation," the point of closest access by ocean shipping to the agricultural riches of the Willamette Valley. As every sailor knew, there was actually no such definitive point. The head of navigation varied with the season, the length of the wharf, the type of ship, and the courage or foolishness of its captain. Every town could legitimately advance some claim to the title. The real question was which town had the most *push*—a wonderful word that meant ambition, boosterism, and canny entrepreneurship to our great-great grandparents.

Portland eventually took the prize, beating out its rivals to establish itself as the head of navigation, because it

had the most skilled and persistant promoters. Daniel Lownsdale had divided his share of Portland with two new partners during the course of 1849. Stephen Coffin of Maine, an energetic building contractor who had come to Oregon City in 1847, and William Chapman of Virginia, a lawyer who had made money in the California Gold Rush, provided ideas, energy, and capital. In the short space of 1850 and 1851, Portland's triumvirate provided three essentials that assured their town's permanent growth—dependable steamship service to California, the Great Plank Road across the West Hills, and promotion of the town in the form of the purple prose of the *Oregonian* newspaper.

A newspaper on the nineteenth-century frontier was vitally important, serving as a sort of urban identification card. Like a post office or a county courthouse, even a four-page weekly was accepted proof that a townsite was a going concern. It rankled and grated the city's leadership in the early months of 1850 that Portland merchants had to advertise their wares in Oregon City's *Spectator*. Chapman and Coffin remedied the situation by recruiting an unemployed editor with a battered hand printing press from San Francisco. Thomas Jefferson Dryer arrived in November, his equipment a month later. The first issue of the *Oregonian* appeared on December 4, 1850.

Dryer ran the paper for ten years. He advocated the Whig and then the Republican party, boosted the city of Portland, and used every printable insult in the language in feuds with Salem's *Oregon Statesman* and Portland's second newspaper, the *Democratic Standard*, which was published from 1854 to 1859. The typical weekly issue of the *Oregonian* in the 1850s was a combination of newspaper, *Reader's Digest*, and telephone yellow pages. The first page

Thomas J. Dryer founded the weekly Oregonian *in 1850. Ten years later he turned it over to Henry Pittock, who had started work there in 1853. Despite serious competition over the decades,* The Oregonian *survived as a daily and became Portland's main newspaper. (OHS)*

carried short fiction, jokes, articles copied from Eastern papers, and the equivalent of today's wire service filler. The back page and one of the interior pages carried business cards and advertisements from firms in Portland, Oregon City, and more distant towns like Albany and Olympia in the Oregon Territory. The listings, which scarcely varied from month to month, functioned as a business directory. The other inside page contained editorials and "Latest News by the Mail" from San Francisco.

If the *Oregonian* gave Portland equal standing with Oregon City as an information center for the territory, then a few miles of unfinished plank road were enough for Portland to gain victory over the town's nearest rivals. At the start of the 1850s, Americans throughout the Midwest and South were seized by a mania for plank roads—highways with a surface of sawed planks spiked to wooden stringers. They were touted as

"the farmers' railroad," easy for amateurs to build and almost as cheap as dirt in the states around the Great Lakes and in the Northwest where lumber was virtually free for the cutting.

The territorial legislature chartered the Portland and Valley Plank Road Company in January 1851. The organizational meeting was held in Lafayette, but Portland's "Big Three"—Lownsdale, Coffin, and Chapman—signed up to buy a third of the stock and the construction started southwestward from Portland. The route led up the ravine of Tanner Creek, over the Sylvan hill, and on to its final destination of Hillsborough. Work on the roadbed started in late summer. The first planks, from Portland's own steam sawmill, went down with great fanfare and suitable oratory on September 27, 1851. The company ran out of money after planking only a few miles of this first version of Canyon Road, but even the rutted track that continued into the rich agricultural lands of the Tualatin Valley made Portland the most accessible port for Washington County farmers, who shipped their abundant wheat to San Francisco.

Portland's plank road doomed the already fading hopes of the nearby town of Linnton. Its founders were Morton McCarver, a "compulsive town promoter" in the words of historian Malcolm Clark, Jr., and Peter Burnett, a frontier lawyer who had come to Oregon ahead of his creditors and who eventually became the first governor of the State of California. They had staked out the town in 1844 at the end of an old cattle trail that the Hudson's Bay men at Vancouver had used to move their cattle to summer pastures in the Tualatin country. The developers planned to turn the cattle trail into a real road, but in fact never did, and few farmers bothered to ship their wheat through the Linnton warehouse. The

Peter H. Burnett promoted Linnton, northwest of Portland, as a future great commercial town in 1844 and 1845. Burnett, who helped organize the Oregon legislature, moved to California in 1848 and was elected governor there in 1849. (OHS)

California Gold Rush took Linnton's last residents as they headed south to seek their fortunes, and the Portland plank road killed any hopes of the town's revival.

Cazeno or Baker's Landing or Springville—it took a while to settle on a name—was a slightly more successful town located a mile upstream at what is now the west end of the St. Johns Bridge. Washington County cut a road through the hills in 1852 to give wheat farmers and stockmen on its northern edge an alternative route to the Willamette. One result was a new community that grew up around the warehouse at the Willamette terminus of the road. This small settlement of Springville helped to fill ships that sometimes left Portland half empty. We have no population count, but it was important enough to be made a post office around 1860. By the early 1870s, however, the warehouse had burned and the town and its road had fallen out of use.

Milwaukie and St. Johns, located on the Willamette's east side, were on the wrong side of the river to profit from the development of Washington County agriculture. James Johns had claimed a square mile of land and laid out a town

directly across the river from Springville at the end of the 1840s. By 1851 his town of St. Johns had a dozen families, but it was too isolated to prosper. There was more uncleared forest than farmland on the east side of the river and therefore little business for the town. The "ferry" to Linnton was a rowboat. The settlement would have a renaissance as an independent port and city around 1900 but it was not a serious contender in the competition among the region's towns in the early 1850s.

The other east-side town of Milwaukie had been founded by Lot Whitcomb in 1848. Whitcomb built sailing ships to carry lumber to the California market at great profit, and published the *Western Star,* whose first issue went to press two weeks ahead of the *Oregonian.* He also built a side-wheeled steamboat named for himself. The *Lot Whitcomb of Oregon* went into service in February 1851 on a regular run to Portland, St. Helens, the mouth of the Cowlitz River,

Left: *Joseph Kellogg operated a shipyard at Milwaukie, a rival of Portland for preeminence on the Willamette. Milwaukie, on the river's east bank, began trading with California as gold fever began rising. Today, Milwaukie is a suburb of Portland. (OHS)*

Below: *Milwaukie had big hopes of developing into Oregon's leading city. The community was served by a pioneering newspaper, the* Western Star, *and the steamboat* Lot Whitcomb, *named for one of the town developers. (OHS)*

Left: *The* Multnomah, *pictured in 1853 at the waterfront, was built in the East in 1851 and shipped to the Pacific Coast in sections. The boat, traveling as far up the Willamette as Corvallis, was called "a barrel boat"; it was built of stavelike timbers.* (OHS)

Below: *Sea captain John Couch and his wife Caroline posed for this photo circa 1865. Couch visited the Willamette River in the 1840s and with George H. Flanders in 1846 took up a donation land claim, provided by an act of Congress, in the vicinity of what is now Old Town.* (OHS)

Cathlamet, Astoria, and back. The steamer had a 140-horsepower engine and made an impressive fourteen miles per hour. It was also painfully expensive to operate. By June, Whitcomb was forced to sell his namesake to a syndicate of Oregon City investors.

Milwaukie was a good place to load lumber but, like St. Johns, was isolated and inconvenient for Washington County wheat growers. Ships reached Milwaukie without trouble during the spring floods. During the winter of 1850-1851, however, one after another scraped bottom or bent a propeller on the Ross Island sandbar that lay between Portland and Milwaukie.

Captain John H. Couch, the New England seaman and merchant who had made Portland his base of operations in 1849, announced to the public that the river at Ross Island ordinarily had "only about four feet of water." He had himself ridden across on horseback at Ross Island and did not think that Milwaukie would ever overcome the handicap created by the shallows. Most embarrassing of all for Milwaukie, the editor of the *Western Star* (who had gained ownership when Whitcomb ran out of cash) moved his business to Portland, where he printed the first copies of the *Oregon Weekly Times* on June 5. "In removing from Milwaukie to Port-

land," he announced, "we have been guided by those considerations which govern all business men."

Portland's promoters matched their rivals sawmill for sawmill, editor for editor, and boat for boat. Coffin and Chapman had rounded up more than editor T.J. Dryer in San Francisco. They had also found the steamer *Gold Hunter,* which arrived in Portland from California on the first day of December 1850 after they convinced the captain to sail to Portland with the idea of selling an interest in the ship. The San Fran-

25

cisco owners wanted $60,000 in order to transfer control. Several citizens of Portland decided to invest in the steamer, with Coffin taking the largest share. The *Gold Hunter* was a side-wheeler like the *Lot Whitcomb*. It was only twelve feet longer but much broader, displacing 510 tons to the 300 displaced by the pride of Milwaukie. Most important, the *Gold Hunter* ran not just to Astoria but to San Francisco, giving Portland a sort of presumptive equality with the metropolis of the West. The *Gold Hunter* made only four round trips before past debts and old creditors surfaced in California and squeezed out the Portland owners.

Though the *Gold Hunter* was a financial failure it was a speculative success because its service from San Francisco prompted California merchants to say "Portland" when they meant "Oregon." This helped fend off Portland's last and potentially most serious rival, St. Helens. Historian Eugene Snyder has summarized the situation by stating that Portland fought two battles with St. Helens and its satellite of Milton City: "one battle was fought over the wagons; the other battle was for the ships." St. Helenites built a road over the Cornelius Pass in 1850, but Portland countered successfully with the Great Plank Road. In February 1852, the Pacific Mail Steamship Company announced that its California-Oregon service would terminate at St. Helens. Portland had not been chosen as terminus since the company was concerned about the sandbar at Swan Island, which threatened to hamper navigation at Portland just as the Ross Island bar had done at Milwaukie. Two years later, however, Portland's population of a thousand, and its plank road, proved too much for tiny St. Helens. And, with Portland still served by sailing ships and occasional steamers, the Pacific Mail found it hard to make full cargoes in St. Helens. At the start

of 1854, Pacific Mail advertised to San Franciscans that its Oregon service would terminate at Portland.

With transportation by land and water and a newspaper editor to tell the world about its increasing success as a trade center, it was time to turn the settlement of Portland into a city. The territorial legislature issued Portland's municipal charter early in 1851, incorporating 2.1 square miles of fir forest, stumps, and houses as the city of Portland. In the city's first election, held the same year, Portland's male citizens chose Hugh O'Bryant as mayor and five other residents as city councilmen to serve the fledgling metropolis. Their main function seems to have been to keep the city in business. During their first months in office they established systems for assessing property, collecting taxes, recording city finances, selling business licenses, recording their own deliberations, and conducting elections. The first bill paid from the city treasury came to $29.65 (three brass candlesticks at one dollar each and a box of whale oil candles). In 1854, the territorial legislature created a separate Multnomah County with Portland as county seat.

By the time such recognizable names as Josiah Failing and William S. Ladd begin to appear on the list of mayors (elected in 1853 and 1854, respectively), the city had started to keep the peace and to lift the residents out of the mud. There were ordinances for abating nuisances, licenses for vehicles, and a town jail. Ordinance No. 20 required that "all male persons over the age of 21 years" devote two days a year to work on street improvements, or pay an equivalent tax. A start was made at planking the most heavily used streets, which one visitor had described as mud and water mixed to "a very good batter." Wooden sidewalks prevented pedestrians from miring down alongside

Facing page, right: *Douglas firs, shown here in an illustration about 1855, were thick at the mouth of the Willamette River and in other places, reported surveyors for a Pacific railroad. Woods had to be cut away to make room for early Portland. Courtesy,* Report of Explorations and Surveys for Pacific Railroad, 1854-55, VI

Facing page, far right: *Josiah Failing opened a Portland store with his son Henry in 1851. The elder Failing, elected mayor in 1853, was also a promoter of schools and active in the Baptist Church. (OHS)*

look. Another woman commented tersely that Portland was "rather gamey."

Over the next decade, Portland's population nearly quadrupled, increasing from 805 to 2,874. Oregon grew even faster as immigrants filled the Willamette Valley and explored the mountains with an eye toward a mineral bonanza like that of California. The city's mix of population set it apart from the rest of the territory. The typical Oregonian in

the horses and wagons and let the ladies keep their skirts out of the deepest mud.

The town that Mayor O'Bryant and his successors tried to govern was more like a giant fraternity house than a real community. Three quarters of the 805 residents recorded in the 1850 census were male. Nine-tenths of all Portlanders in their twenties were men, attracted by jobs in road and building construction. When young Elizabeth Miller and four other schoolteachers from New England passed through town in 1851 on the way to new posts in Oregon City, Miller reported that "the one-sided community was exceedingly interested." She speculated that the entire population must have crowded the wharf for a

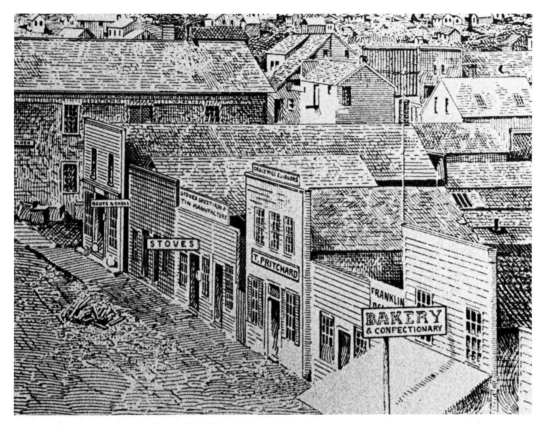

Left: *Plentiful trees near Portland provided timber for the first businesses and homes. Substantial stone and brick structures were to come later than 1854, the date of this drawing. Courtesy, The Oregonian Souvenir*

Below: *This sketch by Charles B. Talbot shows the log-cabin style of the first post office, established at S.W. Front Avenue and S.W. Washington Street in 1849. Thomas Smith was the first postmaster. (OHS)*

the early 1850s had come from states like Missouri, Illinois, Kentucky, and Indiana in the heart of the Mississippi Valley. In Portland, a much larger proportion hailed from New England and from New York, the number one state of origin. Together, Yankees and New Yorkers constituted more than a quarter of Portland's total population in its early decades. The states of the Northeast also supplied a disproportionate share of the city's business leaders, many of whom began their careers in the early 1850s as agents or correspondents for New York and Boston mercantile companies.

Portland served as the depot and general store for the growing Oregon population. Visitors usually began their descriptions of the city by tallying the number of businesses—eighteen "stores" in November 1850, thirty-five "wholesale and retail stores" in 1852, and a hundred shops by 1858. The census of 1860 counted 146 merchants,

ranging from local retailers to prosperous agents for large Eastern wholesalers such as Henry W. Corbett or the Failing family.

Portlanders strung their town along the river. In the first few years of development, any building more than 200 yards inland was likely to be hidden in the trees. Daniel Lownsdale had expanded the original survey with more than a hundred additional blocks in 1848, reserving two blocks as public squares between Third and Fourth streets and setting aside a narrow strip of eleven park blocks along the western edge of the city. In the long term citizens have been grateful for his foresight, but the earliest Portlanders continued to build on Front, First, and Second. If we can trust a view of the city drawn in 1858, woodcutters and sawmill owners had cleared the forest about half a mile back from the waterfront, leaving the straggling town exposed on bare ground between river and hills.

Business centered on the docks, warehouses, and waterfront stores. Four floors was the maximum and two floors the norm for the commercial buildings. The usual materials were locally sawed wood and white paint. Successful merchants followed the lead of Vermonter William S. Ladd, who had arrived in Portland in 1851 and who put up the city's first brick building to house his

Above: *Portland presented this view in 1858 as seen from the east bank of the Willamette. The gold rush to the Fraser River in Canada boosted business that year but the biggest gold excitement east of the Cascades took place in the 1860s. (OHS)*

Left: *Henry W. Corbett opened a general merchandise store in Portland in 1851. Later he entered the wholesale hardware business, became a financier, served as president of Willamette Iron and Steel Works and president of Portland Hotel Company, boosted street railway construction, and served in the U.S. Senate. Courtesy, H.W. Scott's* History of Portland, Oregon

mercantile business in 1853. Residents lived in old log cabins or new frame houses. The modern survivors of the first building boom are the Hallock and McMillan Building, erected in 1857 at the corner of Front and Oak, and the 1859 Delschneider Building half a block west on Oak, now handsomely restored.

In a city with few families, tax-supported schools were a hard sell to unmarried male voters. Transplanted New Englanders succeeded in organizing a public school district in 1851 and offered classes for two years, although *Oregonian* editor Dryer fulminated against spending a thousand dollars "for pedagogueing some dozen or two of children." The first schoolmaster not only taught school, but also unloaded ships, worked on the streets, and fought the shaking ague between terms. In 1854 the major educational institution in the city was the Methodists' Portland Academy and Female Seminary, but a reorganized district opened again in 1855 in rented space. Future mayor and Oregon governor Sylvester Pennoyer

taught in the new public school for six months until he established a law practice in Portland. There was another gap in public education in 1856 and 1857, but the first public school building, Central School, opened in 1858 at Sixth and Morrison, the present site of Pioneer Courthouse Square. By 1860, 272 students crowded into the three rooms of Central School, while an equal number attended several private schools.

Like every ambitious town on the Western frontier, Portland looked on every new building as a step from the log cabin to the metropolis. Portlanders were proud of public structures like the Central School and the city jail. Culture came to Portland in 1858 when the Willamette Theater opened on Stark Street. Traveling troupes of second-rate actors from San Francisco could now play to audiences of up to 600 rather than making do with second-story lecture halls or the Multnomah County Courthouse. Drinking, fighting, and horse racing were also high on the list of amusements.

Beards for men and lace collars for women were the vogue in the 1850s. One of the earliest pictures of the town's residents shows the first organized choir of the First Congregational Church in 1857. (OHS)

More proper citizens in the 1850s could join the Sons of Temperance and pledge total abstinance from alcohol. They could attend Sunday services in a new Taylor Street Methodist Church after 1850, a new Congregational church in 1851, and a Roman Catholic church in 1852. Presbyterians and Episcopalians built their churches in mid-decade and Baptists at the beginning of the 1860s. The city's hundred or so Jews organized Congregation Beth Israel in 1858 and finished a synagogue in 1861.

By the end of the 1850s something about Portland set it apart from the rowdiest of the West's instant cities. There was money to be made here, but with none of the bonanzas of Nevada's Virginia City or Colorado's Leadville or the overnight fortunes of San Francisco. The New Englanders and New Yorkers who dominated the city's economy cannot be called complacent or sober, but they did treat their business lives as se-rious business. They also propped open the door of opportunity for anyone who could help the city grow, whether U.S. born or immigrant from Europe. For example, Jewish immigrants like Bernard Goldsmith and Philip Wasserman started prosperous businesses in the 1850s and each later served two terms as mayor.

Few of Portland's city-builders wanted the life of Daniel Boone or Jim Bridger. They were true conservatives who wanted to reconstruct the society they had left behind while reserving a place for themselves at the head table. By the end of the 1850s, when the town was poised for a new surge of growth, Portlanders had organized a typically American community of churches and schools, government, politics, and fraternal organizations. To most visitors, Portland was a little island of New England on the western margin of the continent—handsome, energetic, steady, and homelike.

George H. Himes arrived in Portland in 1864 and became well-known as a printer. He kept a voluminous diary, started in 1866 as the longtime secretary of the Oregon Pioneer Association, and served as the curator and field secretary of the Oregon Historical Society beginning in 1898. (OHS)

CHAPTER II
ON THE EDGE
OF THE WEST

Portlanders have always lived on the edge of the West. The "real West" of Zane Gray and Louis L'Amour begins seventy-five or one hundred miles inland at The Dalles or Redmond and stretches across another 1,000 miles of sagebrush, and dry gulches, and Rocky Mountains to the high plains. The Oregon pioneers of 1844 and 1845 hurried through this area in their covered wagons heading for the green vision of the Willamette Valley. The Western interior is also the territory to which Portlanders turned back in the 1860s and 1870s to make their fortunes secure. Portland's success story is a chronicle of valley dwellers who learned to tap the wealth of the dry country without leaving the drizzle of their metropolis.

After the boom created by the Gold Rush to California, new discoveries of gold in the interior of the Northwest gave Portland its second and most essential spurt of growth. The boom of 1848-1849 and the benefits of victory over river-town rivals in 1850-1851 had faded by the middle 1850s. A national depression compounded problems at the end of the decade. Portland in 1860 was still economically dependent on San Francisco, prospering when Californians wanted Oregon wheat and suffering when the demand declined.

Mining booms in Idaho, Montana, and the interior of the Columbia River Basin provided Portland a strong impetus for growth. A gold strike along Ida-

ho's Clearwater River in August 1860 was as fortuitous for Portlanders as it was for the prospectors. During the next four years, miners fanned out from Idaho's Orofino and Pierce City diggings to the Salmon River and Boise Basin, the Owyhee River on the present Oregon-Idaho border, Bannack City and Gold City in western Montana, and the Kootenay River just over the border in Canada. The old trading center of Walla Walla, Washington and the new town of Lewiston, Idaho were the final outfitters for the mines, but Portland was the supply base and jumping off point during these frenetic boom years. More than 15,000 people passed upriver through Portland in 1861, 24,000 in 1862, and 22,000 in 1863. The *Oregonian* reported gleefully that "rents are up to an exorbitant figure, many houses contain two or more families, and the hotels and boarding houses are crowded almost to overflowing. The town is full of people ... buildings are going up ... wharves stretching their proportions along the levees, and a general thrift and busy hum greet the ear."

Portland monopolized the growing business of the Inland Empire of the Pacific Northwest because of geography *and* because of the Oregon Steam Navigation Company (OSNC)—Oregon's first "millionaire-making machine" in the words of one early employee. The company's leading figure was John C. Ainsworth, a former Mississippi River

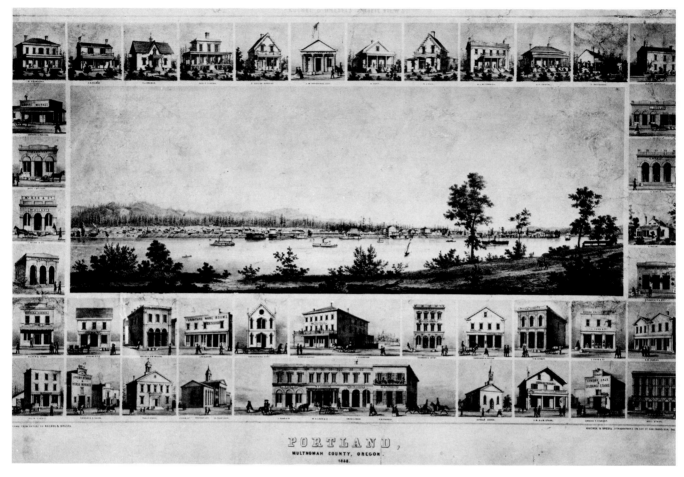

Above: *This 1858 lithograph by Kuchel & Dresel shows a wooded Portland sporting a few stone structures amid the wood-frame buildings. Courtesy, Stokes Collection, New York Public Library*

Left: *The Willamette Theater was bedecked in the national colors during somber rites for Brigadier General Edward R.S. Canby, commander of the Department of the Columbia. He was killed by Modoc Indians in 1873. An honor guard stood at attention in front of the building. (OHS)*

steamboat captain who had been the first master of the Milwaukie steamship, the *Lot Whitcomb*. He knew that navigation on the Columbia was interrupted by rapids at "the Cascades" and again by Celilo Falls at The Dalles. If Portland were to profit from the river, there would have to be something better than crude portages around both barriers. In 1860 Ainsworth formed the OSNC to unite the various businessmen who operated segments of the Columbia River route. The new corporation controlled improvements at both bottlenecks, operating a six-mile railroad on the north bank of the Columbia that carried traffic around the rapids at

what is now the town of Cascade Locks and a fourteen-mile road that bypassed Ceiilo Falls at The Dalles. OSNC investors Simeon Reed, Robert R. Thompson, William S. Ladd and others who put up large chunks of capital learned the value of conservative management as they put profits back into the business, expanding and improving service. OSNC operated Columbia River steamers, wagon trains, stage lines, and connecting boats on the Snake River, Lake Pend Oreille, and the headwaters of the Missouri, establishing, within a few years, a powerful transportation monopoly.

Few residents of eastern Oregon,

Below, left: Steamboats from Portland could not pass the Cascades of the Columbia River, but a railroad provided a link to other craft just above the rapids. The river business bolstered Portland's prosperity. This ad is from the 1877 Portland Directory. (OHS)

Below: J.C. Ainsworth was a key figure in steam navigation development on the Columbia River. Courtesy, Portland, Oregon, Its History and Builders

OREGON
team Navigation Co.

The Oregon Steam Navigation Company's Steamers

ONEONTA" and "EMMA HAYWARD,"
(CAPT. JOHN WOLF).
leave PORTLAND Daily (Sundays excepted), at 5 A. M., connecting
with the
CASCADE RAILROAD,
—AND—
Steamers 'DAISY AINSWORTH' and 'IDAHO,'
Capt. JOHN McNULTY,
Arriving at the DALLES at 4 P. M. same evening.
s. 'YAKIMA', 'TENINO', and 'ALMOTA',
leave CELILO on TUESDAY and SATURDAY (on arrival of the Morning
Train from THE DALLES) for UMATILLA and WALLULA, proceed-
ing as far as LEWISTON during high water in the Snake River.
FOR KALAMA AND ASTORIA,
Strs. 'DIXIE THOMPSON' AND 'BONITA',
Captains J. W. BABAGE and GEORGE A. PEASE,
leave PORTLAND at 6 A. M. daily, arriving at ASTORIA the same
day at 6 P. M.

eastern Washington, or Idaho had a kind word for the OSNC monopoly. They paid high tariffs on every cargo they imported or shipped out via OSNC. (Customers who paid in gold received a 30- to 50-percent discount over those who used paper money.) Rumor had it that the company paid for a new steamer with the profits from a single trip upriver from Portland to the gold mining country. Through the OSNC, pioneers and prospectors indirectly paid for the growth of Portland by generating the Ladd and Ainsworth and Reed fortunes. These investors would provide much of the capital for the city's railroads, factories, utilities, and real estate development.

The OSNC made Portland the true gateway to the Northwest, but the city would remain a second-class citizen in the commercial world as long as the latest news and mail arrived twice a month by steamer from the Golden Gate. In 1860 the California Stage Company cut the time in half when it signed a contract to carry the mail overland from Sacramento to Portland. Service began in September. The running time was seven days during an optimistically defined dry season from April through December. In mid-winter running time was twelve days as drivers contended with hub-deep mud, landslides, and sudden snows in the Siskiyous. By 1866, when Portland's Henry Corbett took over the route, the time in good weather was down to five and one-half days. In the years before railroads began to creep south, the stage line was essential in making Jackson and Douglas counties seem an integral part of Oregon.

In 1864, the telegraph replaced the creaking and bouncing stagecoach as the source of essential information. The California State Telegraph Company built a telegraph line north from Sacramento and Maryville to Yreka in

As one of the leading officials of Oregon Steam Navigation Company, Simeon G. Reed gained a fortune when the organization was sold to the Villard syndicate. He and his wife bequeathed money to fund a college, which was named in their honor. Courtesy, Portland, Oregon, Its History and Builders

Northern California in 1858. W.S. Ladd, S.G. Reed, H.W. Corbett, and A.L. Lovejoy incorporated the Oregon Telegraph Company in 1862 to make the connection to the California company. The Portland company's first load of wire sank in a shipwreck while being transported from San Francisco, but the company was able to string its line southward through Aurora, Salem, Corvallis, Roseburg, and on to California in 1863. The first dispatch from San Francisco arrived in Portland on March 8, 1864, with news that had been dispatched from New York just twenty hours before. The mayors of Portland, Oregon, and Portland, Maine exchanged congratulatory messages. Other lines connected Portland to Seattle, Walla Walla, and Boise before the decade was out. The rate for ten words to the east coast was $7.50—enough to feed a Portland family for a week or educate a public school pupil for a year.

Rails followed the roads and wires. Railroad building south from Portland confirmed the city's dominance in Oregon. It also shook the conservative Port-

land establishment by introducing them to Ben Holladay. An unscrupulous but highly successful businessman, Holladay had built the Overland Mail into the country's largest stageline in the 1860s. He had sold his company to Wells Fargo for $1.5 million in 1868 and turned his attention to railroad building in the Pacific Northwest. Proper Portlanders were fascinated by his success and repelled by his style of life. They whispered that he had populated his house with high-priced prostitutes and competed to find the right adjectives to describe him: vulgar, low, haughty, dictatorial, dishonest, and immoral were some of the favorites.

Holladay used the money from the sale of the Overland company to plunge into a struggle between rival railroad companies that wanted to build from Portland to California on opposite sides of the Willamette. The west side line was the Oregon Central Railway Company, backed by the Portland establishment of Reed, Corbett, and Ladd, who wanted to make sure that Willamette Valley trade poured directly into the city and added to the business of the

Above: *Smith's stage operating between Portland and Vancouver was typical of nineteenth-century transportation. Stagecoaches were displaced rapidly in Oregon when railroads were constructed. The rail lines also hurt steamboat business, but steamboats endured into the early 1900s. Courtesy, The Columbian*

Left: *Ben Holladay had already built a transportation empire in the West when he entered the railroad business in the Portland area in 1868. His methods aroused the ire of competitors and others. One typical critic described him as "rampaging, rapacious, ruthless." (OHS)*

Above: *Before building started, East Portland was a pastoral land, a semi-wilderness. Roads were poor and steamboats along the Willamette River were the easiest way to move in and out of the Portland area. (OHS)*

Left: *At Oswego, south of Portland, the Oregon Iron Company was the first plant on the Pacific Coast to manufacture pig iron in a blast furnace. Production started about 1867 and continued sporadically for a few years. The community is now Lake Oswego, a Portland suburb. (OHS)*

Oregon Steam Navigation Company. Holladay took them on by buying control of the east side line, which he named the Oregon and California Railroad Company in 1869. At stake were not only freight and passengers, but also a federal land grant of twenty square miles for every mile of track. It would go to the first railroad that finished twenty miles of operational track. His enemies later reported that Holladay spent $35,000 to bribe the state legislature to rescind a premature declaration in favor of the Oregon Central. However, he also had the drive and money to finish the necessary track and win the grant. By 1870, his Oregon and California Railroad bought out the defeated west side line.

As the Oregon and California Railroad (eventually absorbed into the Southern Pacific system) pushed slowly southward, Holladay put together a tottering transportation empire in Portland. He owned docks, warehouses, and steamships. He monopolized the local transfer of passengers and freight. Expecting that an east bank railroad would shift the city's economic center across the river and that a growing city would require the level lands of the east side, he built two hotels, grabbed a large chunk of the Northwest Portland waterfront, and laid out Holladay's Addition to East Portland in the present Lloyd Center area.

Portlanders tolerated Holladay's presence until 1874, when he came up nearly $500,000 short in interest payments on money borrowed from German investors for construction costs. Eastern

Left: *Construction began in 1869 on a post office and district court building, which opened in 1875. The building, once considered too far out of downtown, was surrounded in later years by businesses. Today it fronts on Pioneer Courthouse Square. Courtesy, Harper's Weekly*

Below: *This much traffic might not have been seen on the Willamette River on a typical day in 1882, but this illustration was good for promotional purposes for Portland. West Shore magazine artists recorded the city frequently before the advent of photography. (OHS)*

banker Henry Villard, a German-born newspaper man who was gaining a reputation as a shrewd businessman, investigated the viability of their investments for the German bondholders. In 1876, Villard bought Holladay out and laid the foundation of his own railroad kingdom. The Oregon and California Railroad was completed through Medford to California in 1883.

The growth of Willamette Valley farming was less spectacular than the Idaho gold rushes and less exciting than Ben Holladay's full throttle railroad career, but it provided a solid foundation for Portland's progress. Between 1860 and 1880, Oregon's improved farmland acreage increased by 150 percent; the production of wheat rose by 800 percent. Portland merchants began to ship grain directly to Liverpool, England at the end of the 1860s. Portland's foreign exports, mainly farm products, totaled $500,000 in 1870-1871 and reached $4 million by the end of the 1870s. The frontier was changing rapidly. One of the shrewdest observers of the mid-century American West was Massachusetts newspaper editor Samuel Bowles.

Bowles' 1865 account of his journey west, *Across the Continent*, is a classic description of the last frontier between the Rockies and the Pacific; his account of Portland summed up the city's expanding economic base:

Portland, by far the largest town of Oregon, stands sweetly on the banks of the Willamette . . . Ships and ocean steamers of highest class come readily hither; from it spreads out a wide navigation by steamboat of the Columbia and its branches, below and above; here centers a large and increasing trade, not only for the Willamette Valley, but for the mining regions of eastern Oregon and Idaho, Washington Territory on the north, and parts even of British Columbia.

Portland's population was growing as fast as its trade. The 2,800 Portlanders of 1860 more than doubled by 1864; the census included 700 "floaters" in hotels and boardinghouses. In the Pettygrove and Coffin eras, everyone who counted in Portland knew everyone else. By 1863, however, the city was big enough to need the first annual city directory, published by former mayor S.J. McCormick. The population continued to grow to 8,300 in 1870 and 17,600 by 1880.

Railroads and steamers made Portland a center for ideas as well as commerce. At the end of the 1870s readers in the city and the greater Northwest supported a score of periodicals ranging from daily newspapers to scientific journals. Portland citizens dissatisfied with the weighty *Oregonian* could read the daily *Bee, Standard,* or *Telegram.* The weekly *Sunday Mercury, Sunday Welcome,* and *Sunday Call* (out of East Portland) supplemented the dailies. The *Pacific Christian Advocate* carried news to northwestern Methodists, the month-

ly *Columbia Churchman* to Episcopalians, and the weekly *Catholic Sentinel* to Roman Catholics. There was a weekly *Willamette Farmer*, a monthly *Medical Journal*, and a semi-monthly *Journal of Education*.

The magazine *West Shore* (1875-1891) was the epitome of nineteenth-century geographic boosterism. Editor L. Samuel served up lavishly illustrated articles on the progress and possibilities of Portland and the Pacific Northwest. Stories of economic growth and pictures of new buildings and bridges had a wide appeal up and down the coast. The publication's subscription list grew from 9,000 in 1880 to 37,500 in 1890 before overextension put it out of business.

The founder and editor of the weekly

newspaper *New Northwest* (1871-1887) was Abigail Scott Duniway, who advocated women's rights, woman suffrage, "Eternal Liberty," and "Untrammeled Progression." The masthead spelled out Duniway's philosophy: "A Journal for the People, Devoted to the Interests of Humanity, Independent in Politics and Religion, Alive to all Live Issues and Thoroughly Radical in Opposing and Exposing the Wrongs of the Masses." Each weekly issue offered news on business and cultural events, descriptions of prisons and asylums, reports on Duniway's constant travels on the Western lecture circuit, and vitriolic editorials against the mossbacked opponents of female emancipation and social progress. There were also stories by famous writers like Mark Twain and Bret Harte and the serialized fiction that served as frontier soap operas. Duniway herself wrote seventeen serialized novels

during the paper's sixteen-year life. Behind the melodrama in such stories as *Madge Morrison: The Mollala Maid and Matron, Ethel Graeme's Destiny,* and the other stories were lessons about the problems of unloving and unequal marriages. Abigail Duniway certainly had one of the most energetic minds in late nineteenth-century Portland and quite possibly the brightest.

The Portland press served immigrants along with English-speaking residents. The *Deutsche Zeitung* after 1867 and the *Staats Zeitung* after 1877 kept alive the German language and supported Portland's German community on the Western frontier. New arrivals could put up at the *Deutsches Gast Haus* (also known as the New York Hotel), call on the German Aid Society, and drink lager brewed by a man appropriately named George Bottler. By 1880, several thousand German-Americans

Ship masts in the background denote the proximity of Willamette River business in the early 1880s. McCracken & Company, at left, was an importing and wholesale grocery business. At right is the office of Oregon Railway and Navigation Company, a major transportation firm of the era. (OHS)

supported four German-language churches and occasional stage performances in German.

The growth of Portland's black population from 16 to 147 during the 1860s was a more severe test for local tolerance than the immigration of easily assimilated Germans. In 1867, the school district and the courts refused to enter the four children of Maryland-born shoemaker William Brown in the all-white public schools. The *Oregonian* applauded the alternative—the appropriation of $800 for a segregated school that would enroll up to twenty-five black students between 1867 and 1872. But with the onset of a major national depression brought about by the Panic of 1873, the principle of segregation hardly seemed worth the cost and black students quietly enrolled in the regular schools. Black Portland staged an annual celebration of the anniversary of Emancipation in the 1870s but otherwise received little notice. They comprised only a small minority in the growing city. Judge Matthew Deady was satisfied to report in 1868 that they were "moderately thrifty and well conducted."

In fact, Deady was pleased with almost everything about his city. Writing a profile of "Portland-on-Wallamet" for the first issue of San Francisco's *Overland Monthly,* he described it as a "solid and reliable town." It would never be the center of fashion, he explained, but the blue river and the sublime Monarch of the Mountains, (Mt. Hood), glistening above the dark green forests forty miles to the east, were more than adequate compensation. Portland's good citizens, Deady told his readers, would "sleep sounder and live longer than in San Francisco." Oregon historian Francis Fuller Victor, who had lived in both California and Portland, shared Deady's assessment. She thought the Portland of 1871 "a cheerful-look-

Left: *Equal rights for women was the goal of Abigail Scott Duniway, who published* The New Northwest. *When the women's suffrage law was finally passed in 1912, Mrs. Duniway wrote the proclamation and was the first woman to register as a legal voter in Multnomah County. (OHS)*

Below: *German and Austrian culture was reflected in ads for a "chop house" and newspaper, appearing in McKenney's* Pacific Coast Directory, 1880-81. *(OHS)*

ing town . . . with handsome public buildings and comfortable, home-like dwellings." The well-to-do could pass their time with pleasure drives on the macadamized road that ran up the west side of the Willamette to the Riverside Race Course. And, wrote Victor, on sunny afternoons the "youth, beauty, and fashion of Portland" strolled the public squares opposite the courthouse to the bright music of brass bands.

One of the major functions of city government in those early years was to keep Portland pleasant for its business and professional families. One ordinance prohibited fast riding and driving "at a furious pace" anywhere east of Fourth Street and another banned horses and wagons from the sidewalks. An early version of the Oregon "bottle bill" made it unlawful "to throw, deposit, or leave any glass bottles or other glass vessels"

Brick buildings and ornate storefronts were replacing older wooden structures by the time of this parade in 1873. This view looks east on S.W. Morrison Street from S.W. Second Avenue, toward the Willamette River. A sign at the right advertises J. Kohn's "Clothing Palace." (OHS)

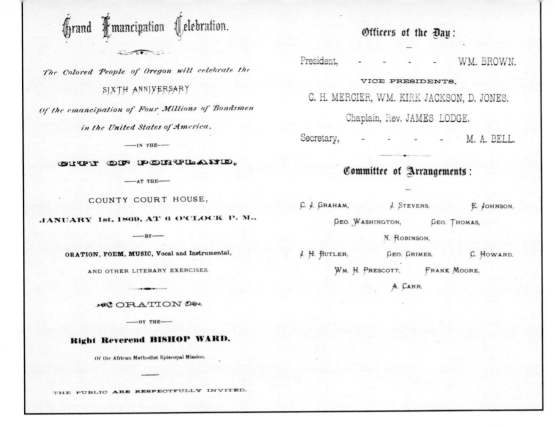

Grand Emancipation Celebration.

The Colored People of Oregon will celebrate the

SIXTH ANNIVERSARY

Of the emancipation of Four Millions of Bondsmen

in the United States of America,

—IN THE—

CITY OF PORTLAND,

—AT THE—

COUNTY COURT HOUSE,

JANUARY 1st, 1869, AT 6 O'CLOCK P. M.,

—BY—

ORATION, POEM, MUSIC, Vocal and Instrumental,

AND OTHER LITERARY EXERCISES.

ORATION

—BY THE—

Right Reverend BISHOP WARD.

Of the African Methodist Episcopal Mission.

THE PUBLIC ARE RESPECTFULLY INVITED.

Officers of the Day:

President, - - - WM. BROWN.

VICE PRESIDENTS,

C. H. MERCIER, WM. KIRK JACKSON, D. JONES.

Chaplain, Rev. JAMES LODGE.

Secretary, - - - - M. A. BELL.

Committee of Arrangements:

C. J. GRAHAM,	J. STEVENS,	E. JOHNSON,
GEO. WASHINGTON,	GEO. THOMAS,	
	N. ROBINSON,	
J. H. BUTLER,	GEO. GRIMES,	C. HOWARD,
WM. H. PRESCOTT,	FRANK MOORE,	
	A. CARR.	

Left: Some former slaves migrated to Oregon following the Civil War. They gathered in 1869 to commemorate the Emancipation Proclamation, issued January 1, 1863, abolishing slavery in the Confederate States. The black population remained relatively small in Portland for many years. (OHS)

Left, below: New Market, built for Captain Alexander Ankeny, opened in 1872, with stalls for public markets on the first floor. A theater opened upstairs in 1875. In recent years, before restoration, the building was used as a parking garage. Now, after restoration, it houses restaurants and specialty shops. (OHS)

Below: Some lawyers' businesses must have been flourishing in the 1880s, judging from the fine residences occupied by J.W. Whalley (left) and M.W. Fechheimer, his partner (right). Home construction had not started on the hills in the background. (OHS)

in the streets; residents were to pick up litter to the mid-line of the street in front of their premises. The city encouraged the growing of shade trees and spent a substantial $32,000 to buy a forty-acre nucleus for Washington Park in 1871.

But Portlanders who ventured off their front porches in the "suburbs" west of Sixth Street could find a less sedate city if they knew where to look. Many theaters catered to the popular taste with "low grade minstrels and vulgar comedy." British visitor Wallis Nash in 1877 complained in a travel book he wrote that *Othello* fell flat

Far left: *Judge Matthew Deady, best known now for his two volumes of diaries,* Pharisee Among Philistines, *(edited by Malcolm Clark, Jr.) came to Portland in 1860 as an attorney, and served on the territorial supreme court. He was appointed a U.S. judge and served in that position until his death in 1893. Courtesy, H.W. Scott's* History of Portland, Oregon

Left: *Frances Fuller Victor lived in Salem and Portland and, beginning in the 1870s, wrote a series of books. Some of her work was included in Hubert Howe Bancroft's histories. Her biography of Joseph Meek was titled* The River of the West. *(OHS)*

compared with a "half hour of screaming farce" that followed. Thousands of patrons crowded into more than 200 saloons to drink, gamble, and try out Phelans Patent Billiard Tables. The Oro Fino saloon and theater at Front and Stark Street advertised "the choicest qualities of wines and liquors, ales, port, and fine cigars." The saloon belonged to James Lappeus, Portland's city marshal from 1859 to 1861 and chief of police from 1870 to 1877 and again from 1879 to 1883.

Law enforcement efforts expanded with the city. A part-time marshal was adequate to keep the peace at the beginning of the 1860s, but by mid-decade two paid deputies were hired, and a formal police force was established in 1870. Six officers covered three beats north of Oak, between Oak and Yamhill, and south of Yamhill. The officers' biggest responsibility in these early years was to run in drunks who threatened to tear up the town. With the police chief counted in their number, saloon owners and gamblers had less

trouble than they might otherwise have had. Portland's police were not noticeably energetic about enforcing the liquor and gambling laws. Saloon keeper Edward Chambreau later recalled of this era: "The first thing I did when I took charge of this 'Hell Hole' [Chambreau's saloon] was to *fix* the policeman on my beat." Economic growth, however, brought more opportunities for creative crime, as the Police Commission noted in 1874:

The number of arrests for 1873 are about double the number of any year prior to 1871 .... The perpetrators of housebreaking and highway robbery find this too hazardous to pursue, and have changed their occupations and found encouragement in a higher role .... A number of these dangerous characters are to be seen daily about our docks and custom house, placed side by side with many honest laborers, ready always to extend the hand of friendship to the

crews of newly arrived vessels, and to tender their services to show them "the sights about town"— through the "dives" where these characters and female "pals" do dwell. The sailor is easily imposed upon generally, and becomes an easy victim. His gold is soon gone . . . and he is unable to tell by whom or how, for when it is done he is usually intoxicated, and thus the thieves escape detection and arrest. The great increase of our commerce has opened a wide field for the operations of these persons.

Portland's decision makers thought that jackrolled sailors and shanghaied crews were a small price to pay for commercial expansion. They also knew that the next necessary step in that growth was a direct transcontinental railroad connection. Hopes for such a connection rose in 1870 when the Northern Pacific decided to build down the south bank of the Columbia and engaged in a stock swap that made the Oregon Steam Navigation Company a wholly owned subsidiary. The same hopes fell with the financial crash of 1873, which drove the Northern Pacific into bankruptcy, brought the OSNC back to its original ownership, and stopped railroad construction on the Northern Pacific and other railroads for five years.

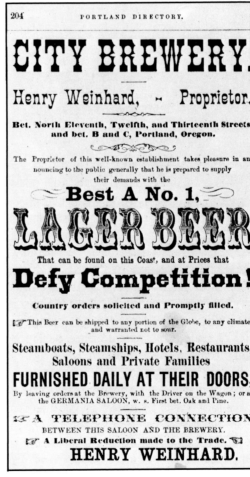

Henry Villard filled the vacuum. He controlled Ben Holladay's system of Willamette Valley railroads and steamers after 1876. In 1879 Villard bought out the OSNC and formed the new Oregon Railway and Navigation Company, which included his entire network of Oregon rail and steamship compa-

nies. Portlanders who profited from the deal included OSNC founders Ainsworth, Reed, and Ladd plus later investors with names like Kamm, Lewis, Failing, and Corbett.

But Villard's greatest coup came in 1881. Raising eight million dollars from fifty capitalists, he gained control of the Northern Pacific and made himself the transportation magnate of the Northwest. While Portland businessmen lobbied the federal government to deepen the bar at the mouth of the Columbia, Villard tried to develop the city's railroad connections to the East. The main line of the Northern Pacific was finished at the end of the summer of 1883. A corporate peace treaty had already given the Union Pacific access to Portland over Northern Pacific tracks and the Northern Pacific reciprocal use of

UP tracks into Utah. When a Union Pacific branch reached the NP at Huntington, Oregon, in December 1884, Portland gained the advantages of service by two transcontinental railroads.

Henry Villard celebrated completion of the Northern Pacific by hauling four trainloads of dignitaries from the East, and bringing another train from San Francisco and Portland to the golden-spike ceremony at Deer Lodge, Montana. The eighty VIPs on the West Coast special could wander through four Pullman cars, two dining cars, and two commissary cars. A potpourri of diplomats, New York bankers, German financiers, Congressmen, and governors watched the driving of the golden spike (actually ordinary steel) late in the afternoon of September 8, 1883. Actually, the line had quietly opened to traffic in August, but trains had moved on a bypass, leaving a 2,700-foot gap in the main line to be officially closed in front of General Ulysses S. Grant and hundreds of Crow Indians in full regalia at the Deer Lodge ceremony. It was the first step in a systematic publicity campaign that would bring investment and immigrants to the High Plains and Inland Empire through Northern Pacific agents in Liverpool, Hamburg, New York, Boston, Omaha, and Portland.

Villard, Grant, and the rest of the party pulled into east Portland several hours later than expected on the evening of September 10, 1883. The grand parade planned to celebrate the event was postponed until the following day but thousands of enthusiastic Portlanders still turned out along First Street to welcome the train. On the 11th, country people packed the ferries and crowded the roads into town. Restaurants served the throngs on double shifts at double time. The parade itself looped south on Fourth to Hall, gathered momentum back up Third to Burnside, and turned back on First to the Mechanics Pavillion where the Civic Auditorium now stands. Unlucky businessmen and their wives had to sit through the obligatory speeches, while the average Portlander got to enjoy the rest of the informal holiday in the bright sunshine. Board of Trade President Donald MacLeay expressed the reason for the excitement in one sentence: "We are now connected with the rest of the world."

Below: *The Mechanics Fair Pavilion between Clay and Market on Third Avenue was built in 1879 for exhibitions and large public gatherings. U.S. Grant was honored at a reception there in 1879, and President and Mrs. Rutherford Hayes stopped at the pavilion a year or so later. The building was empty and dilapidated in this circa 1895 view. (OHS)*

Facing page, far left: *Henry Villard, railway promoter and financier, headed several Pacific Northwest transportation companies. In 1881 he was named Northern Pacific president, and in 1883 Portland welcomed him as a hero, after the "last spike" was driven in Montana, linking Portland with the East by fast transportation.*

Facing page, left: *This was one of three arches on S.W. First Avenue in 1883 commemorating completion of most of the Northern Pacific Railroad. Although the line was finished only to central Washington Territory, it linked up with other rail lines, giving Portland access to the East. (OHS)*

"One seeing Portland for the first time will be surprised to find how well-built it is," reported Harper's Weekly *in 1889. This engraving from the well-read magazine showed imposing storefronts and busy traffic on S.W. Front Avenue. Courtesy,* Harper's Weekly

CHAPTER III
GROWING UP
AND SETTLING DOWN

At the time of its railroad revolution Portland was still a small community. With only 17,000 residents on the west side of the Willamette and a few hundred more scattered among the fir-covered ravines and knolls of the east side, Portland in 1880 was similar in size to Roseburg or Pendleton today. In an 1880 compendium titled *The Social Statistics of Cities,* which compared the development of 222 American cities, the Census Bureau reported that "the growth of Portland has been moderately steady." The tone of Portland life in that year appeared to federal officials to be that of a country town rather than a bustling city: "The population is American, with a large mixture of Europeans and Mongolians [Chinese]. Business is in the hands of men from the eastern and middle states, Great Britain, and Germany. Education is guided by Americans from New England and the northern states. The New England element has had a marked influence throughout."

Twenty years later, Portland had become a metropolis. Transcontinental railroad links facilitated immigration, boosted business, and helped to more than quintuple Portland's population to 90,000 in 1900. Portland in its first generation had been the isolated center for an "island" of settlement along the Willamette and Columbia. But during the 1880s and 1890s, the Northern Pacific and Union Pacific joined it to the rest

of the nation. In the words of historian Malcolm Clark, Jr., the transcontinental connection by steel rails "cracked Oregon's insularity, though it did not shatter it."

Portland was a diversified city at the time that it made its transcontinental railroad connection. About 1,000 workers in small factories manufactured iron products and processed agricultural goods for customers in the Northwest and produced lumber, furniture, sash and doors, and other wood products for buyers up and down the West Coast. The city directories of the early 1880s listed about a hundred merchants under the categories of dry good wholesaler, liquor dealer, grain dealer, commission merchant, grocery wholesaler, and hardware dealer. The city's middle class included lawyers, bank tellers, clerks, and retailers. A larger working class supplied the muscle power for transportation and construction work.

Portland as a small town in 1880 had a "self-help" approach to public services. Residents bought water and coal gas for lighting from private companies. The Portland Street Railway Company operated a tiny street railroad with a mile and a half of track along First Street; five one-horse-powered cars hauled 600 passengers a day for ten cents each. The city paid the bills for a variety of unsatisfactory street pavements—stone blocks, chunks of wood set grain-end up, gravel, and planks, but

The docks provided lively scenes during loading and unloading of passengers and freight. Here, the boat is the Olympian, *an Oregon Railway & Navigation Company sidewheeler built in the East in 1883. The boat ran to Ilwaco, Washington Territory, in 1886. (OHS)*

adjacent property owners were required to sweep or scrape the pavements every Friday afternoon. Householders were responsible for hauling their garbage and street sweepings to the outskirts of the city. Protection from serious fires, such as the city had suffered in 1872 and 1873, was still in the hands of five volunteer engine companies and a hook and ladder company. A paid fire chief and two assistants provided professional supervision for 400 volunteers. The city owned a police station (with jail) and several firehouses, but the mayor, city treasurer, and city attorney had so little work to do that the city didn't even provide them with office space.

The informal approach to public services and government came to an end in the decade following the arrival of the transcontinental railroad. By the 1860s the city government had increased its responsibilities to include parks, street lighting, sewers, water, and public health. The police department had been expanded and the fire department was

converted to employ full-time professionals.

Among the most important new services were bridges across the Willamette built by both private and public enterprise to open up the east side of the river to residential development. The first was the Morrison Bridge, which was the largest span west of the Mississippi when completed by the Willamette Iron Bridge Company in April 1887. By contributing to east side development, it also marked a basic change in the shape of the city. A railroad bridge (Steel Bridge) followed in 1888; it opened to wagons and streetcars a year later. Private investors built the rickety wooden Madison Street Bridge in 1891 and sold it to the city a year later. The city erected the expensive Burnside Bridge in 1894. The first three bridges have been replaced twice and the Burnside Bridge is in its second incarnation.

Portlanders could reasonably expect to walk around a city of 17,000, but

Left: *William Beck, active for years in trying to build a bridge across the Willamette, was reported to have "cried like a child" for joy when the Morrison Bridge opened in 1887. A drawbridge had eliminated objections to the span from people interested in river navigation. Courtesy, Fred DeWolfe*

Below: *Nine bridges now carry traffic over the Willamette River at Portland, but the community lacked any bridges until 1887. Ferries provided the earliest solution for travelers. The west landing of the Stark Street Ferry is pictured here, during a flood time. (OHS)*

they needed the help of mechanically powered streetcars in a city of 90,000. Between 1885 and 1895 the City Council granted dozens of franchises allowing private companies to build and operate street railways. Small steam engines on the first east-side line hauled passengers across the Morrison Bridge to the new neighborhoods of Sunnyside and Mount Tabor. Cable cars began to climb Portland Heights in 1890. The first electrified trolley ran across the Steel Bridge to Williams Avenue in 1889. By the mid-1890s, almost all the new lines and most of the old used electric power. The public transit lines covered more than a hundred miles, reaching to Willamette Heights, Portland Heights, and Fulton on the west side and to Oregon City, Lents, Montavilla, St. Johns, and the Vancouver ferry landing east of the river.

The booming city required better water than the privately owned Portland Water Company could pump out of the Willamette opposite Milwaukie. In

Left: Portland Traction Company, successor to the Cable Railway, operated an electric and cable street railway from the Union Depot to Portland Heights and the city park. Connections were made with Portland Railway Company and East Side Railway Company. Courtesy, Fred DeWolfe: Old Portland.

Left, below: *In 1890 the Portland Directory predicted the cable and electrical railway systems would soon "do away entirely with the tedious and obsolete horse car." This 1890 photo shows the cable route on to Portland Heights, still relatively wooded and untouched. (OHS)*

1885, the Oregon legislature authorized the city to issue bonds to buy out the water company and bring pure water from the mountains. A committee chaired by banker and investor Henry Failing selected the Bull Run River in 1886; Bull Run water reached the Mount Tabor and Washington Park reservoirs late in 1894 and flowed through Portland taps on January 1, 1895. The names on the Portland water committee—William Ladd, Henry Corbett, Cicero H. Lewis, Frank Dekum, Simon Rees, William K. Smith, Joseph Teal—

show the importance that major businessmen attached to good water. Combined with Portland's low density of population and its extensive sewer system, a reliable water supply helped to make Portland one of the healthiest places in the country in 1900. The death rate was far below that in most Eastern cities.

Bridges, streetcars, and Bull Run water were the keys to successful suburbanization east of the Willamette. In the 1870s and 1880s, East Portland and Albina were Portland's Jersey City and Hoboken, secondary industrial centers built around docks, sawmills, flour mills, and railroad yards. East Portland—stretching from the present Northeast Halsey to Southeast Holgate streets—had been platted in 1861 and incorporated in 1870. Albina was laid out in 1873 and incorporated in 1887; it was dominated by the Oregon Railroad and Navigation Company, whose riverfront shops employed hundreds of workers. One of those employees, D.M. McLaughlin, served as mayor from 1888 to 1891.

The east side boom arrived in 1887 with the opening of the Morrison Bridge. Speculators rushed to take advantage of improved transportation by laying out new middle-class subdivisions on higher land back from the rowdy east-side waterfront. Irvington dates from 1887; Sunnyside and Central Albina (Boise) from 1888; and Woodlawn, Kenilworth, Woodstock, and Tabor Heights from 1889. Portlanders continued to pin high hopes on real estate development in the early 1890s, years that saw the promotion of Ladd's Addition, Brooklyn, Richmond, Arbor Lodge, University Park, and Piedmont. Every developer issued special maps and colored brochures promising fine residential neighborhoods to the city's newcomers. The brochure titled *Piedmont, The Emerald, Portland's Ever-*

green *Suburb, Devoted Exclusively to Dwellings—A Place of Homes* was typical. Developer Edward Quackenbush assured potential customers that "no dwelling can be built at a cost of less than $2,000. Thus the surroundings are assured."

One result of the rapid economic and population growth brought by the railroad was the great consolidation of

The Skidmore Fountain was installed in the business district in 1888. In New York in 1887 sculptor Olin Warner posed with a plaster model of the maiden destined for the fountain. The figure was cast in bronze and shipped in 1888. (OHS)

Portland, East Portland, and Albina. After disappointing results in the 1890 census, which showed limited growth within the city limits, the Portland Chamber of Commerce began to push for the consolidation of all adjacent neighborhoods. East siders would benefit from the removal of bridge and ferry tolls, while businessmen would be able to impress outside investors with a high population total. Consolidation of Portland, Albina, and East Portland into a single city of Portland passed overwhelmingly in all three towns in a general referendum held in 1891. The area within Portland city limits jumped from seven square miles to twenty-six. Two years later the city grew by another 50 percent in area by annexing chunks of the southwest hills, Sellwood, and subdivisions east of Twenty-Fourth Street. In 1880, when it had 3,000 residents, the east side had been a neglected fringe. Twenty years later, the 32,000 east siders were an essential part of the city.

The Census Bureau's brief summary of Portland's population mix in the 1880 census—American, with a large mixture of Europeans and Orientals—was actually a preview of the segmented city that would emerge by the turn of the century. The Willamette bridges and streetcar lines not only allowed local builders to put up thousands of new homes on previously inaccessible land, they also made it possible for the city's residents to segregate themselves by race, nationality, and income. The process created a neighborhood pattern somewhat like an elongated archery target. Downtown was the bullseye, surrounded by a ring of low-income neighborhoods of immigrants and unskilled workers. Further out was a second ring of middle- and upper-class neighborhoods for more established or successful families.

Portland was, in fact, an immigrant city by the end of the century. The 1880s ushered in a thirty-year surge of European immigration to the United States, with a new influx of immigrants from Italy, Greece, Hungary, Poland,

and Russia joining the established streams from Germany, Ireland, and Scandinavia. Portland never welcomed the volume of newcomers who landed in New York or who clambered off the trains in Chicago, but nevertheless, by 1900, 58 percent of its residents—52,000 out of 90,000—had either been born outside the United States or were the children of immigrants.

By 1890 Portland's Chinatown was second in size only to San Francisco's. The Chinese had come to Oregon originally to construct the railroads, but as the railroad jobs dried up, more and more settled permanently in Portland. The city's Chinese population grew rapidly, from 1,700 in 1880, to 4,400 in 1890, to 7,800 in 1900. Their numbers

Mt. Hood rises above this 1890 panorama of Portland. Many new buildings reflected the city's prosperity after completion of railroad lines. Courtesy, National Archives

Above: *Chinatown has been a distinctive downtown area of Portland for a long time. Oriental garb was common, as shown in this 1900 scene. In earlier years, Chinatown was concentrated in the S.W. Second Avenue area. Now Chinese businesses are across W. Burnside Street, in the Northwest section. (OHS)*

Left: *Chinese formed a working class in Portland, and provided some of the best vegetables each season, a writer observed in the late 1880s. The Chinese quarter was a subject of interest for visitors, who were intrigued by the oriental customs. Courtesy, Harper's Weekly*

Left: *Many Chinese were employed on railroad construction in the Pacific Northwest in the late 1800s. Salmon canneries along the Columbia River also employed many who lived in Portland seasonally or visited there. Courtesy, L. Samuel's* Portland and Vicinity

Below: *Various ethnic groups ran their own businesses at numerous times during Portland's history. In the early 1900s, the Slavonian Bakery and Grocery catered to Eastern Europeans. The Panoff family was involved in this venture on N.W. Glisan Street. Courtesy, City of Portland*

included refugees from less tolerant Seattle and Tacoma, which drove out their Chinese residents in 1885 and 1886. The center of Portland's Chinese neighborhood was Second and Alder. Most observers agreed that the district stretched from Ash or Pine to Salmon between the river and Third Street. Portland's standard brick and cast-iron buildings were transformed to an Oriental style with wrought-iron balconies, paper lanterns, and brightly colored signs for Chinese food stores. The Chinese operated more than a hundred businesses by the late 1880s, but most worked as laborers, dishwashers, cooks, and laundrymen. Hundreds commuted seasonally to farms, lumber camps, and

Columbia River salmon packing plants. By the end of the 1890s, about 1,200 newly arrived Japanese worked on railroad construction crews with Portland as home base; early in the new century they would begin to turn to farming in the Portland area.

Meanwhile the South Portland neighborhood of Italian and Jewish immigrants developed along the streetcar line that ran south from downtown on Third, jogged on Grant, and continued on First toward the furniture and wood processing factories of Fulton. Its small affordable houses and apartment buildings attracted the growing population of immigrants. Easy access to downtown made South Portland convenient for

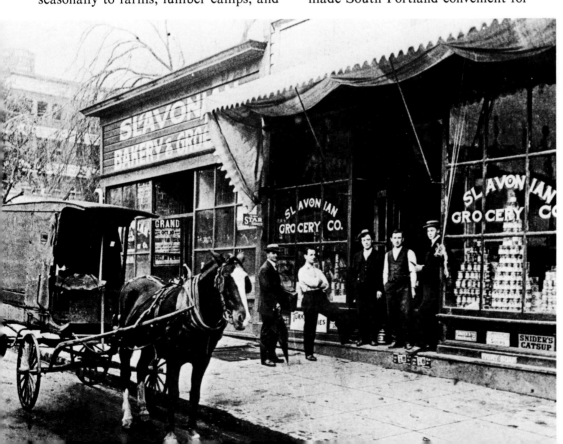

newcomers with jobs as construction workers, peddlers, and salesmen. The neighborhood was still in its formative stages in 1900, but the outlines of a classic ethnic district were clear. The commercial core of kosher markets, bakeries, groceries, and drugstores was First and Front streets between Sherman and Arthur, an area virtually obliterated in the 1960s by urban renewal and I-405. The Italians had their benevolent societies and St. Michael's Church, established in 1901. Orthodox

Jews worshipped in Shaarei Torah and later in Kesser Israel. Children from both groups attended Failing School. Women from Portland's long-established community of German Jews operated Neighborhood House, the "Industrial School and Kindergarten," located on First Street from 1904 to 1910 before moving to a new building at Second and Woods. Neighborhood House provided recreation, meeting rooms, sewing and manual arts training for children, and adult education for

Lodge buildings, churches, and social clubs helped provide a diversity of activity in and near the downtown. One of many gatherings was this children's party, at the Beth Israel synagogue in 1898. Some youngsters were probably children of immigrants who had recently come from Europe. (OHS)

Jewish and non-Jewish immigrants alike.

Only fragments survive in the present, but turn-of-the-century Portland also counted several other distinct immigrant neighborhoods. A small colony of Croatians clustered around northwest Nineteenth and Savier, in the Slabtown district close to jobs in sawmills, factories, and rail yards. The Roman Catholic Croatians replaced earlier Irish immigrants as parishioners for St. Patrick's church.

Many of Portland's 3,000 Scandinavian immigrants and their children lived in Albina, with the working men near the railroads below the bluff and the middle-class families on higher land around Williams and Union avenues. They supported a community center known as Scandinavian House on Northeast Seventh; mutual aid societies for Danes and Swedes; and Scandinavian, Swedish, and Danish Lutheran churches. The same area held a large

German population, while Polish immigrants had begun to settle a little to the north around Interstate and Failing, where St. Stanislaus Church would open in 1909. German-Russian immigrants—the descendants of Germans who had settled lands along the Volga in the 1700s—clustered a few blocks inland near the present Irving Park.

Underscoring the division between newly arrived immigrant and established Portlander was the social distinction between unattached men and family households. Through the 1880s and 1890s, there were in Portland three males to every two females. The Chinese, almost all of whom had come as single men, accounted for about half of the excess of 16,000 men at the end of the nineteenth century. The rest were European immigrants and native-born Americans.

It was easy to find men without families. All one had to do was to follow the loud music and the smell of stale beer

Part of downtown Portland developed a roistering atmosphere of which the more straitlaced residents disapproved. Saloons were the center of much of this activity. In 1892 this load of St. Louis Lager beer arrived at Louis Sechtem's Fountain Saloon on S.W. Washington Street and S.W. Second Avenue. (OHS)

to the riverfront blocks and downtown wards from Everett Street south to Jackson. The district included Chinatown, with its gambling halls, brothels, and opium parlors, and a growing skid road around Burnside Street. The onset of each rainy season brought several thousand seasonal farm, lumber, and railroad workers to winter in the city's rooming houses, cheap hotels, and the back rooms of saloons.

Portland's not unjustified reputation as a wide-open town was an important factor that pushed the respectable middle class into the new suburbs east of the river and the elite toward higher ground on the west. The increasing segregation of single men in a downtown

Above: *For twenty-one years, since its incorporation in 1870, East Portland was an independent community. The Willamette River cut the town off from Portland. Among East Portland businesses was an agency of the Studebaker Brothers Company, on S.E. Morrison Street. (OHS)*

Left: *Sylvester Pennoyer supported the Democratic party with his* Oregon Herald. *In the late 1880s he served as Oregon governor and later spent two controversial years as Portland mayor. Pennoyer was a leader in the movement against Chinese laborers. (OHS)*

district that met their needs and took their money also provided a prime target for moral reformers. The ensuing battles for temperance and clean living represented efforts to impose the standards of the native-born middle class on immigrants and workers and to demonstrate that Victorian family values had triumphed over the raw frontier.

The Chinese were the most obvious target for a police chief or mayor who wanted to prove his moral fiber. An 1851 ordinance against gambling had gone virtually unenforced until William Watkinds took office as police chief in 1883. Ignoring the thousands of white gamblers sitting down every night to faro and poker in Portland saloons, he systematically raided the dozens of fan tan dens along Second Street and made nearly 500 arrests before the year was out. His patrolmen also brought in several dozen Chinese women on charges of prostitution, continuing the pattern of racially selective enforcement of the city's 1871 anti-prostitution law. Watkinds' immediate predecessor, James Lappeus, had been more concerned about Ordinance 2073 which prohibited the smoking, buying, or possession of opium; Lappeus arrested several dozen offenders in 1879 for keeping or visiting opium houses, explaining in his annual report:

Another evil, and a rapidly growing one, is the habit of opium smoking, which is ruining the health and destroying the minds of many of our young men and girls. There are a large number of these dens, kept principally by Chinese, where men and women . . . congregate and indulge in this vile and filthy habit, and sleep off their stupor. Some of the females who frequent these places are married and have families, and young girls of the most respectable class of soci-

The wholesale grocery business was the key to success for William S. Mason. He also served as mayor in the early 1890s and won another term as mayor in 1898, when he purged the police force. He died in office. (OHS)

ety. Could their names be published society would stand amazed. . . . Some more stringent and severe measures should be taken to break up these dens of infamy.

Although Lappeus thought that several hundred white Portlanders puffed the opium pipe, their most common downfall was whiskey. In the spring of 1883, City Council adopted a prohibitive annual license fee of $500 for each of the city's 162 barrooms and saloons. Both the temperance advocates and the liquor interests focused their attention on the coming 1883 council election, which would determine if the high license fee was sustained or repealed. The *Oregonian* and the Women's Christian Temperance Union thought that the election was a contest between the "immoral, vicious, and disorderly classes" and the "decent part of the community." Local politicians saw only another power play in which the temperance cause was a screen for maneuvering by political fac-

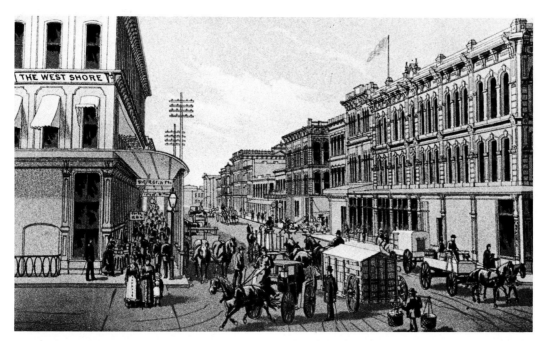

Left: *A variety of conveyances were clustered on S.W. Second Avenue north of S.W. Yamhill Street in this sketch from L. Samuel who included his* West Shore *magazine office at the left. Portland's businesses were still mainly situated near the waterfront.* Courtesy, Portland and Vicinity

Below: *Among vestiges that Portland retains of its past are some Victorian homes, such as this building on N.W. Hoyt Street used in later years by a rug dealer.* Courtesy, Ted Van Arsdol

tions. Leaders of both political parties quietly stacked the nominations with candidates who favored business as usual, and Portland awoke after the election to find operators of two saloons on its governing body.

A decade later, the Portland Ministerial Association tried an even more direct approach to fighting the liquor business. It researched and published the names of landlords of more than 200 drinking joints that operated illegal-ly or after hours. A large proportion of leading businessmen appeared on the list of property owners who profited from Demon Rum. Despite public embarrassment, there were enough members of the upper crust on the list that most owners decided to ride out the fuss and bother without evicting their disreputable tenants.

The general lack of enthusiasm for the temperance campaigns demonstrates one way in which Portland's "other

Left: *Construction of Union Station started in 1890 but financial problems delayed the opening until 1896. The depot, a cooperative venture of the Union Pacific, Southern Pacific, and Northern Pacific, was quite active until post-World War II, when freeways and airlines trimmed train business. (OHS)*

Below: *Portland of the 1870s and 1880s offered opportunities for wealth and prominence to some residents. One who rose to the top in journalism was Harvey W. Scott, Oregonian editor, called "a molder of opinion" on this statue by Gutzon Borglum at Mount Tabor Park.*

half" could defend its interests against residents of middle- and upper-class neighborhoods. Portland in the 1880s and 1890s was a city in which political party bosses mediated between working-class voters and the elite of the business community. Each of the city's wards, of which there were eight after the consolidation of 1891, elected two members to the city council. The councilmen themselves were most often businessmen or employees of large firms, yet political common sense dictated that they work to protect the interests of their constituents. The mayor had relatively little authority, and, after 1885, shared executive authority with a separate Board of Police Commissioners. The police commissioners formed a corrupt alliance with the political machine. Mayor William Mason complained in the early 1890s about his inability to force tough law enforcement: "We lack the power

OREGON

The Greatest Exposition ever held in the Northwest.   Opens in Portland September 28, Closing October 28, 1899.

A Splendid Exhibit of the Natural Products of God's Country, surpassing in Extent, in Variety and Quality anything ever before seen here, in Grains, Grasses, Fruits, Vegetables, Minerals, Etc.

INDUSTRIAL

The Music and Attractions are the best to be had.   Bennett's Renowned Military Band, with Miss Alice Raymond, America's greatest Lady Cornet Soloist.

OPENS
SEPT.
28,
1899.

CLOSES
OCT.
28,
1899.

EXPOSITION.

The FLORENZ troupe of Acrobats, direct from their great triumphs in Berlin and London; their first appearance in America.   Five Male and one Female Performers, in their wonderful Pirouette Somersaults and other astonishing feats.
The SISTERS MACARTE, their first tour of the Pacific Coast.   The most wonderful Aerial Performers in the world.   Three beautiful and fascinating artists and extraordinary exponents of equipoise.

DON'T · MISS · IT!!

FILIPINO WAR MUSEUM under supervision of Oregon's sturdy warrior, GENERAL OWEN SUMMERS.

Greatly Reduced Rates on all Transportation Lines.

ADMISSION, 25 CENTS.   CHILDREN UNDER 12 YEARS OF AGE, 10 CENTS.

to enforce the laws. . . . Our police perambulate the streets day and night and we hear of no arrests for violations." Mason's fear that the police were "the protectors, the sharers in the spoils" of a corrupt system was certainly correct in the North End, where entrepreneur and future U.S. Senator Jonathan Bourne was the political boss who called the shots.

Although bosses claimed to look after working-class interests, labor unions offered a better long-run goal. Efforts to organize Portland's skilled workingmen dated to the 1870s, but one of the first major events in local union history was a mass meeting in 1880 in which an organizer for the Knights of Labor addressed a crowd of 4,000. The following years brought the organization of several craft unions such as Local 50 of the

Brotherhood of Carpenters and Joiners. When AFL President Samuel Gompers visited Portland in the late 1880s, the city's Federated Trades Assembly had fifteen unions representing 400 members. The early union movement came to a climax in 1890, when Portlanders participated in a national drive for the eight-hour day in the building trades. Carpenters, painters, plumbers, and trimmers participating in a general strike and lockout settled by agreeing to an eight-hour day with proportionately reduced wages. In the mid-1890s, as the United States plunged into its deepest depression of the century after the Panic of 1893, Portland unionists struggled, though with limited success, to hold onto the gains of the previous years.

In the depths of the same depression, hundreds of other Portlanders marched behind the banner of the "United States Industrial Army." "Coxey's Army," as it was called, was the plan of Ohioan Jacob Coxey to bring thousands of the unemployed from all over the United States to a grand rally in Washington, D.C., when they would petition the federal government for work relief. In April 1894, recruiters for Portland's "commonweal companies" set up tables on the sidewalks of the North End and

Left: *Portland's Industrial Exposition building, opened in 1889, was reportedly capable of holding 15,000 persons "without crowding." Entertainment and exhibits drew throngs. The 1899 exposition advertised a Filipino war museum, reflecting high interest in the Spanish-American conflict. (OHS)*

Below: *Longtime real estate developer William Killingsworth called Portland the future "New York of the Pacific." He was especially active in development of North Portland. A street is named for him in "The Peninsula," the section between the Willamette and Columbia rivers. (OHS)*

directed several hundred enlistees to a camp at the mouth of Sullivan's Gulch. Attacked by the press as "herds of vagrants" and lazy tramps, and denied food by the very proper Board of Charities, the army walked the dozen miles to Troutdale, where, on April 27, they seized an Oregon Railway and Navigation Company train. Their intention was to head east, picking up recruits along the way and depending for help on the sympathetic railroad workers. They got as far as Arlington (with a festive stop at The Dalles where they were cheered on by residents) before a detachment of cavalry from Walla Walla rescued the property of Portland's most powerful investors and arrested the train's hijackers. Federal judge C.B. Bellinger reprimanded and released the 439 prisoners. A crowd of sympathizers milled angrily around the Oregonian Building

for several hours but dispersed without convincing editor Harvey Scott that the unemployed needed jobs rather than contempt.

Portlanders from overseas had to turn to each other to build their communities in the boom years of the 1880s and 1890s. Churches, neighborhoods, and benevolent societies all helped these new Americans to make their place in the growing city. Residents at the bottom of the economic pyramid—often these same immigrants and their children— also organized through trade unions and ward politics to protect their interests and battle for a share of the benefits of growth. Portlanders at the top of the economic structure had no such problems. They ran the city, and they assumed that to do so was their privilege and responsibility. *The Oregonian's Handbook of the Pacific Northwest*, a regional guide published in 1894, drew a clear-cut line between "progressive, intelligent, and cultured" citizens and "the debasing influence of foreign paupers." Editor Harvey Scott, who was confident that he spoke for the "better" sort, was scornful of those who needed help in ascending to the heights of the "first-class" citizen. From the pages of the *Oregonian* he growled against public high schools, women's suffrage, and the

reform movement of the Populist Party. He thought that the Chinese were "not very desirable people" but worth tolerating because their services in housework, wood-cutting, laundries, and construction gangs allowed for work of a more "rewarding kind for the

American."

Portland's "Americans," particularly the fortunate few, were directly affected by the emergence of large corporations that marked a change in the national economy at the end of the nineteenth century. After 1880, the *Portland City Directory* found it impossible to continue to list every new building and every incorporation for the past year. The general-purpose merchant of Portland's pioneer decade was gradually replaced by firms that specialized in fruit or hardware or men's furnishings. There was one category of insurance broker in 1880 and a dozen types by 1900. Before the arrival of the Northern Pacific, the typical factory was a small shop where the owner knew all of his six or seven employees. Though Portland still had no giant factories on the scale of Pittsburgh or Chicago at the turn of the century, its lumber mills averaged 100 workers in 1900 and 150 by 1905; its furniture factories, sash and door makers, and packing houses averaged thirty to forty hands.

Factory owners could show their wares and discover new ideas at the Portland Mechanics Fair, held every September from 1880 through 1888 in the Pavilion on the future site of the City Auditorium. The success of the Mechanics Fair paved the way for the North Pacific Industrial Exposition. A great success until attendance dropped in the depression of 1893, the Industrial Exposition occupied a vast new structure covering two full blocks at Nineteenth and Washington and included a music hall with seating for 5,000. Boosters claimed it was the largest building on the Pacific Coast.

The arrival of big manufacturing and specialized commerce required new methods to maintain common goals within the business community. The Portland Chamber of Commerce was organized in 1890 and the Manufactur-

Left: William S. Ladd, who opened Portland's first bank in 1859, was active in a variety of business and civic activities before his death in 1893. The Ladd & Tilton bank name was widely known, and Ladd left a large estate, partly in undeveloped land. Courtesy, H.W. Scott's History of Portland, Oregon

Left, below: Frank Dekum's name survived as part of the Dekum building on S.W. Third Avenue. This native of Germany came to Portland in 1853 and was involved in real estate, banking, and the Portland Mechanics Fair Association. He imported songbirds from Germany. Courtesy, H.W. Scott's History of Portland, Oregon

er's Association in 1895. Flamboyant real estate developer William Killingsworth helped to create a new Board of Trade in 1899 to attract men of "push and progress" in both commerce and the professions. Social clubs were an equally important way in which the elite set themselves apart from Portland's middle classes. The Commercial Club, founded in 1893, devoted itself to entertainment, socializing, and business promotion. The Arlington Club incorporated in 1881 and occupied an elegant new building in 1892. It was the city's most exclusive refuge for white gentile businessmen with big bank accounts. As historian E. Kimbark MacColl points out in *The Shaping of a City,* "the large banks, the utilities, the railroads, and Oregon's United States Senators were especially well represented within the Arlington Club's membership. During the 1890s the club could normally count at least four or five of its members serving in a session of the Oregon State Legislature. The direct political influence of the club reached its peak around 1900 with two successive mayors who were members."

In an increasingly segmented city, the economic upper class was eager not only to control the important decisions but also to create a life apart from the ordinary folk. The *Portland Blue Book* of 1890, published out of San Francisco, and the home-grown *Portland "400" Directory: A Residence Address, Visiting, Club, Theater, and Shopping Guide*

of 1891 imitated Eastern social registers and helped the "right people" identify one another. Elegant private parties, chronicled in the diary of Judge Matthew Deady, replaced the less sophisticated socializing of the 1860s or early 1870s. Families with leisure could follow the new fad of vigorous outdoor recreation in the 1890s by joining the new Multnomah Amateur Athletic Club and Waverly Golf Club. There were picnics on Ross Island, day trips on Portland's rivers, and weeks or entire summers to spend at the new resorts of Seaside and Gearhart, Oregon, and Seaview, Washington, where large hotels and new summer cottages overlooked the cold Pacific at the end of railroad lines. The hardiest Portlanders joined the Alpine Club, which built the Cloud Cap Inn, a resort on Mt. Hood, or the Mazamas, whose inaugural climb took 200 hardy souls to the top of Mt. Hood.

There were social strata even within the upper crust. The old-line elite consisted of influential families whose founders had arrived in Oregon in the 1850s and 1860s. By the 1890s, men like

Left: Fortunes and reputations were made with steamboats. One Portlander near the top in this field was Jacob Kamm, a large stockholder in Oregon Steam Navigation Company and Willamette Transportation Company. He was associated later with Vancouver Transportation Company and Ilwaco Railway and Navigation Company. Courtesy, H.W. Scott's History of Portland, Oregon

Below: The Jacob Kamm home, built in the early 1870s, is significant as one of the earliest Portland mansions surviving into recent years. This photo of the 1930s shows the building before it was moved to The Colony, a restoration project on N.W. 20th Avenue. Courtesy, Oregon State Library

Henry Corbett, Matthew Deady, Frank Dekum, Joseph Dolph, Henry Failing, William S. Ladd, Cicero H. Lewis, John H. Mitchell, Henry L. Pittock, Simeon G. Reed, Ben Selling, Joseph Simon, and Philip Wasserman had been accustomed to leading the city for a generation. They were for the most part merchants, bankers, and investors who, by the century's last decades, held controlling interests in the area's railroads, manufacturing, and real estate. Many had held public office and the most of the rest were like John C. Ainsworth, "willing to pull wires, and mean to do it." Newer monied arrivals in the city often shared the same outward characteristics as their more established counterparts, but they lacked some of the

Left: *The Willamette River, separating the main part of Portland from East Portland, was a threat during runoff time. Floods of 1887 and 1894 brought muddy waters into the street. Courtesy, Portland District, U.S. Army Corps of Engineers*

Below: *Sightseers were advised to "pass on, don't stand here," at a narrow boardwalk used to cross a flooded street in 1894. Seawalls were constructed later to protect the city from periodic floods of the Willamette River. Courtesy, Portland District, U.S. Army Corps of Engineers*

intricate marital alliances that united older families into economic cartels, and could not expect the respectful attention accorded to a Ladd or Corbett.

Portlanders with money were careful to pick the right neighborhoods for their increasingly palatial houses. Northwest Third and Fourth streets and the southwest Park Blocks were the favored locations of the 1860s and 1870s. By the 1890s, most of Portland's business and civic leaders had moved to the western edge of town—especially Nob Hill or "Nineteenth Street" in the northwest district. Double-sized blocks gave the space necessary for "substantial comfort and tasteful display" according to Harvey Scott. Completion of an incline and cable car line from Jefferson Street to Portland Heights in 1890 foreshadowed the next migration of the elite to the highlands in the twentieth century.

The building boom in the years around 1890 gave Portland's influential families some magnificent churches worthy of a major city. The wooden spires of Calvary Presbyterian—now preserved and restored as the Old Church—were adequate for 1882, but leaders of the burgeoning city soon preferred to worship in grander buildings. The First Congregational, First Presbyterian, First Baptist, St. James Lutheran, Grace Methodist, and Temple Beth Israel congregations all occupied new stone or brick buildings in a district located west of the business center from the Park Blocks to Thirteenth Street.

Portland's cultural institutions were as much the responsibility and prerogative of its upper class as were its economic decisions. The Library Association of Portland operated the city's main library on a subscription basis; 625 members paid $5 a year in 1895, cut from $9 because of the depression. Contributions of $10,000 each from Henry Failing and Simeon Reed, added to generous bequests, allowed the li-

Left: *Lawyer P.A. Marquam served as a Multnomah County judge and state legislator, and was also involved in real estate. His Marquam Grand Opera House at Portland was called "one of the finest specimens of architecture in Oregon." Courtesy, H.W. Scott's* History of Portland, Oregon

Below: *The old West Side High School, opened in 1885, was known as Lincoln High School shortly before World War I. The building, on S.W. Morrison Street, was known as Girls Polytechnic School in its final years. It was razed shortly before the Great Depression.*

brary to move its 20,000 volumes into a new building at Stark and Broadway in 1893. Eastern library expert R.R. Bowker called it the finest such building on the coast. The new Art Association opened a small gallery of reproductions in the Library Building in 1895. Ladd and Corbett dollars allowed the Association to graduate into a new building in 1905.

The same list of established families provided much of the support for private charity, responding to the growing problems of an increasingly complex metropolis, although still lagging behind the needs during the hard years of the mid-nineties. More often than not, they followed the leadership of Thomas Lamb Eliot, pastor of the First Unitarian Church. He was chiefly responsible for organization of the Boys and Girls Aid Society in 1885 and the citywide Board of Charities, which coordinated the city's volunteer charities, in 1889. Like the Children's Home, which dated to the 1870s, these projects were commendable but limited attempts to treat specific symptoms rather than the larger problem of economic inequality. More valuable in the long run were experimental night schools for working men and boys sponsored by the YMCA, and similar schools for working girls sponsored by the Portland Women's League. The classes were adopted by the school board in 1889 at the urging of superintendent Ella Sabin.

It was the people on top who formulated Portland's late-nineteenth-century image of livability with advantages "as a place to reside, as a place to engage in business, and as a place enjoying the requisite educational and social attributes necessary for the proper rearing of a family," in the words of a promotional pamphlet titled *Portland Oregon in 1900.* Portland meant good health statistics, pure water, clean streets, pleasant homes, and, by the early twentieth century, roses in abundance. It also meant a bustling harbor with ships jostling to take on cargoes of lumber and wheat—the favorite illustration for articles about the city. In the first decades of the twentieth century Portland would truly fulfill its promise as what Henry W. Corbett called "a modern city of great wealth, and of truly metropolitan importance."

Left: *Transcontinental railroads brought more prominent entertainers to Portland, adding to the metropolitan flavor. Jeannie Winston, touring with her own company, was a favorite in light operas in the 1880s. She frequently appeared in male roles. (OHS)*

Left, below: *Portland of earlier years was "a sober-sided town," the Reverend Thomas Lamb Eliot recalled. Eliot, pastor of the Unitarian Church, was active in philanthropic and cultural work and supported prison reform, temperance, and women's suffrage. He came to Portland in 1867. (OHS)*

Above: *Turn-of-the-century delivery men from Meier & Frank pose before their horse-drawn vans at the Meier & Frank Delivery Depot on N.W. 14th Avenue and Everett Street. Courtesy, Meier & Frank Company*

Left: *Umbrellas are always a common sight on downtown streets. Rainy weather earned the name "webfooters" for Oregon residents, and postcards such as this one from 1906 by Murray Wade poked fun at the situation. Courtesy, Webfooters Postcard Club*

Flower-decorating crews have always paid meticulous attention to entries competing for Rose Festival awards. This float, circa 1915, claimed that "human rosebuds" were Oregon's crowning glory. Courtesy, Webfooters Postcard Club

CHAPTER IV
THE FAIR AND THE CITY

In the decades around the turn of the century Portlanders loved a parade. Before movies and television, parades were a major form of entertainment, grand spectacles that brought citizens together to share the excitement of city life. In 1890, the *Oregonian's* Harvey Scott noted that "scarcely a day passes but thick or thin files of men, accompanied by drum and brass band and banners, march to and fro." There were torchlight processions for political candidates. There were parades that included hundreds of cyclists during the bicycle craze of the 1890s, and parades featuring dozens of proud automobilists in the next decade. In June 1907 Portland staged the first annual Rose Festival with three days of pageantry. The grand parade included twenty illuminated floats built on flatcars carried on the trolley system.

One of the grandest parades of that era started at the corner of Sixth and Montgomery at 10 a.m. on June 1, 1905. Mounted police and a detachment of U.S. Cavalry led off, followed by marching bands, 2,000 National Guardsmen, and more police to bring up the rear. As the marchers trooped up Sixth, their ranks opened in front of the elegant Portland Hotel to make way for the carriages of visiting Congressmen, governors, and Vice President Charles Fairbanks. Their destination was northwest Portland and the inaugural ceremony for the Lewis and Clark Centennial Exposition, where the opening-day crowd of 40,000 could listen to nearly a dozen long speeches about the

importance of Portland and its world's fair.

Visitors who drifted away from the oratory discovered 400 acres of fairgrounds planned around the shallow waters of Guild's Lake. The formal layout imitated the "White City" of Chicago's magnificent Columbian Exposition in 1893. The majority of the exposition's buildings overlooked the lake from the bluff on which the Montgomery Ward warehouse later stood. A wide staircase led downslope to the lake and "The Trail," the amusement arcade where the wonders of the world were available for a dime or a quarter. A "Bridge of Nations" connected the mainland to the United States government buildings which were situated on a peninsula in the middle of the lake. For no apparent reason, the major exhibition halls followed the "Spanish Renaissance" style with domes, cupolas, arched doorways, and red roofs. The federal building was built in a style that combined the architectural features of a railroad depot and a Mexican cathedral. The whitewashed stucco of the light frame buildings gleamed against the West Hills in the occasional Portland sun—like "diamonds set in a coronet of emeralds," according to one speaker.

From June 1 through October 15, nearly 1.6 million people paid for admission to the fair. Four hundred thousand of them were from beyond the Pacific Northwest. They could attend high-minded conferences on education, civic affairs, and the future of the United States in the Orient or partici-

Left: *"Acres of 'Rose City' heights and lawns are resplendent with the Queen of Flowers,"* proclaimed an early advertisement for the Portland Rose Festival. Parades, such as this *"Human Rosebud Parade,"* helped call attention to the city's interest in flowers and celebrations. Courtesy, Cross and Dimmitt

Left, below: *Floats and marching units enlivened the annual Rose Festival parades. In 1911 the cadets of Oregon Agricultural College at Corvallis were photographed in military array. Soldiers from Vancouver barracks and other martial units also paraded frequently in Portland.*

pate in national conventions of librarians, social workers, physicians, and railroad conductors. They could inspect the exhibits of sixteen states and twenty-one foreign nations. They could fritter their money on such carnival-like exhibits as "The Streets of Cairo," Professor Barnes' Educated Horse and Diving Elk, who plunged into a tank of water from a forty-foot ramp. They could listen to band concerts or gape at the Forestry Building, the "world's largest log cabin." Constructed entirely of undressed logs, the "cabin" stretched 105 feet by 209 feet. The visitor entered through a portico of natural tree trunks into a vast interior colonnaded with more trees. The largest foundation logs weighed in at thirty-two tons and measured fifty-four feet long and five across.

The city's business leadership gave wholehearted support to the planning and promotion of the Lewis and Clark

Exposition because its purpose was a bigger and better Portland. It was an age when every ambitious city aspired to put on a national or international exposition. The list from recent decades already included Chicago, Omaha, Buffalo, St. Louis, Atlanta, and Nashville; it would soon add Norfolk, Seattle, San Francisco, and San Diego. At the least, a well-planned and successful event would show Easterners that Portland was a mature and "finished" city rather than a frontier town. At most it could give Portland an edge in the ongoing competition with upstart Seattle and confirmed the city as a commercial center for the Pacific. When Oregonians of today speak about the importance of trade with the Pacific Rim, they are reiterating ideas that were common eighty years ago. The official title of the event was the "Lewis and Clark Centennial Exposition and Oriental Fair." The

SEE OREGON ROSES BLOOM

PORTLAND ROSE SHOW AND FIESTA

Carnival Days:
June 19-20-21-22, '07

Wednesday, June 19th

Oregon Pioneers' Day

Thursday, June 20th

Competitive Exhibit of Oregon's Rare Rose Blooms at Forestry Building. Floral Parade of 2000 school children, trained in Kaleidoscopic marching movements, by Prof. Krohn.

Friday, June 21st—FIESTA DAY

Monster parade of Floral Decorated Automobiles, Competitive Floats, Equestrian Clubs, Military and Bands, Trophy and Cash Prize Awards. Convening of Oregon Development League.

Saturday, June 22

Continuation, Oregon Development League Convention. No set public program announced for Wednesday and Saturday of Carnival Week. Special Rose Matinees at Theatres and visitors will enjoy those days going about gaily decorated Portland when acres of the "Rose City" heights and lawns are resplendent with the Queen of Flowers.
Building decorations and illuminations during the Carnival Days will follow the color scheme of Rose Pink and Leaf Green.

Above: *Organizations and communities have vied with each other to produce the most colorful and attractive floats in annual Portland parades since 1907.*

Left: *A tradition was established by the Rose Show and Fiesta in 1907. Carrie Lee Chamberlain, daughter of Governor George E. Chamberlain, reigned as Queen Flora. Parades of children, floats, and decorated cars were highlights of the first rose festivals.*

Crowds surged across the Willamette River, along with packed streetcars, headed for exposition fun in 1905. The streetcars which brought fairgoers had also been instrumental in helping to open up new outlying residential neighborhoods. Courtesy, Fred DeWolfe

motto over the entrance gate was "Westward the Course of Empire Takes Its Way." The biggest foreign exhibit came from Japan. As Exposition president Henry Goode explained, the first large international fair on the West Coast would "demonstrate to the commercial world . . . the actual inception of the era of new trade relations with the teeming millions of Asiatic countries." Even Portland's prestigious *Pacific Monthly* took time out from publishing stories by Jack London and essays by John Muir to tell readers about Portland's role in "The Coming Supremacy of the Pacific." A visiting journalist agreed that "the whole fair is a successful effort to express . . . the natural richness of the country and its relative nearness to Asia."

Civic boosters had plenty to crow about. The Exposition, in the words of *Harper's Weekly,* "marked the close of an old epoch and the beginning of a new one for Portland." The Exposition had helped launch a boom in both business and population. Skyrocketing prices in downtown real estate made speculators rich and millionaires richer. The annual value of new construction quintupled between 1905 and 1910. Portland's population passed 200,000 by

1910 and may have reached 225,000 by 1913 when the boom finally ended.

A primary reason for expansion was Portland's increasingly significant role as a trade center and port. As early as 1891, the state legislature had created the Port of Portland to maintain and improve harbor facilities. Given the city's situation as a river port, the agency's most important service was to maintain the channel in the Willamette. It also operated a dry dock and improved towing and pilotage services. Its work was supplemented by the Army Corps of Engineers, which began to improve the dangerous mouth of the Columbia in 1884. Between 1903 and 1917, the Corps deepened the bar channel to thirty-seven feet and maintained a minimum depth of twenty-six feet upriver.

Local manufacturing expanded in the same years, especially in lumber, wood products, and furniture, but the biggest growth was in trade and transportation. James J. Hill, the railroad magnate who had built the Great Northern Railroad and made the fortunes of Puget Sound cities, started work on a North Bank railroad (the Spokane, Portland, and Seattle), from Pasco to Portland in 1906. Completion of the road in 1908

A deluxe bandstand, topped by flags, was erected for the Lewis and Clark Exposition in 1905. In the background is Guild Lake. The exposition celebrated the 100th anniversary of the arrival of the Lewis and Clark expedition in the Portland area. (OHS)

gave the Northern Pacific and Great Northern independent access to Portland.

Within a few years Hill was locked into one of the last great railroad-building contests, in which the adversaries vied to tap the lumber and cattle country of central Oregon. "James J. Hill spends millions to tap interior" said one headline in the *Oregonian* describing the line he built up the Deschutes River. "Harriman Road has 2600 men at work" trumpeted another article in the same issue. "Harriman" was E.H. Harriman, who controlled both the Union Pacific and Southern Pacific. After open warfare in the Deschutes Can-

yon, the two tycoons struck a deal and the rails reached Bend in 1911.

Now that the city had a link to the interior, Portland bankers financed the developing cattle, wool, and grain businesses of the Inland Empire. Portland wholesalers supplied the farmers and ranchers with tools and tobacco. Portland longshoremen loaded the ships that made the city one of the nation's leading ports for the exportation of lumber and wheat. Insurance agents, railroad hands, draymen, carpenters, lawyers, retail clerks—nearly everyone benefited from the growth of Portland's commercial empire.

Voters took steps to assure that

growth in 1910, when they approved a charter amendment creating a Commission of Public Docks. Portland's waterfront in the early twentieth century was in the tight grip of the railroads, which had a limited interest in promoting maritime trade. Every functioning dock—downtown, northwest, and east side—was privately owned. Most had been built for the coastwise trade to California and were inadequate to serve transoceanic shipping. Under the direction of Portland's business establishment, the Docks Commission opened Municipal Dock No. 1 on North Front Street in 1914. A major motivation for the annexation of the independent city of St. Johns in 1915 was to enable the Docks Commission to fund the improvement of the St. Johns city dock. Still to come in the 1920s was the Port of Portland's massive dredging project that shifted the Willamette channel from the east side of Swan Island to the west.

The boom years also opened regular

employment to thousands of Portland women, who made up only 15 percent of the city's wage earners in 1900 but 24 percent by 1920. Women dominated half a dozen job categories, ranging from servant to dressmaker to boarding-house keeper. By 1910 more than 2,000 women worked in the lower-paying professions as nurses, music teachers, musicians, and schoolteachers, and 6,000 more worked in white-collar jobs as "typewriters," stenographers, sales-people, telephone operators, and clerks.

In the early years of the century, thousands of other Portland women earned their livelihoods, in full or in part, from prostitution. In 1893, the Portland Ministerial Association found prostitution concentrated in the parlor houses and saloons of the North End and waterfront. Rich and poor alike, Portland's men could indulge in drink, gambling, and illicit sex as a single vice because, according to a report by the Ministerial Association, "saloons and

Above: *The T.J. Potter connects with a train at Megler, Washington, near the coast.*

Facing page, top: *Railroads were a major factor in the city's growth, but some were not as successful as others. The Portland, Vancouver and Yakima Railroad, seen here about 1899, was intended to cross the Cascades. However, the railroad only reached the Cascade foothills, near Chelatchie, Washington. Courtesy,* The Columbian

Facing page, bottom, far left: *James J. Hill made his reputation constructing the Great Northern Railroad across the country.*

Facing page, bottom, left: *E.H. Harriman, shown here in 1905, was a powerful figure in railroad circles in Portland, in Oregon generally, and in other parts of the West. (OHS)*

houses of ill-fame were generally combined in the same building." In 1907 and 1908, new ordinances barring women from saloons and stringent law enforcement by a reform administration forced many prostitutes out of the houses and into the roles of streetwalker and call girl. Still, the Vice Commission in 1912 found more than 400 downtown hotels, apartment buildings, and lodging houses that condoned or encouraged use by an estimated 3,000 "sporting women."

Middle-class and working-class families who wanted to keep themselves carefully separated from the seamy neighborhoods around the business district could thank the expansion of the electrified transit system that made it easy to reach outlying neighborhoods. Back room deals and Wall Street buyouts brought more than a dozen separate companies into a single streetcar monopoly in 1906. The Portland Railway Light and Power Company (PRL&P) operated 161 miles of railway and six electric power plants and carried sixteen million passengers by 1910. In that year a thousand streetcars a day rattled and clanked across the Willamette bridges, creating huge traf-

fic jams on Southwest Morrison and Washington. The volume of streetcar traffic quadrupled in the first decade of the century and Portlanders hopped on trolleys twice as often as they had a few years earlier.

The Portland streetcar system, which ran largely within the city limits, was complemented by dozens of electric interurban railroads that stimulated the growth of a suburban ring between five and fifteen miles from the center of town. At the height of the interurban system in 1915, the suburban division of PRL&P ran to Troutdale, Gresham,

Facing page, top: *This group of women turned out for a physical culture class in 1906 at Gladstone, a short distance south of Portland. The activity was part of a chautauqua. Traveling chautauquas presented popular lectures and entertainment across the nation in the early 1900s. (OHS)*

Facing page, bottom: *Beatrice Morrow Cannady, a graduate of Northwestern College of Law in 1922, was a teacher, a newspaperwoman, and the first black woman to practice law in Oregon. She established a number of chapters of the National Association for the Advancement of Colored People. (OHS)*

Left, top: *Lola Baldwin was said to be the first policewoman appointed under the U.S. Civil Service in 1905. She headed the Women's Protection Division of the Portland Police Bureau, and helped establish the Multnomah County Juvenile Court, and the Oregon Industrial School for Girls, later Hillcrest School for Girls. (OHS)*

Left, bottom: *Before historic preservation became popular, many Portland landmarks were removed without thought of the future. One of the more distinctive, now vanished, businesses of the pre-World War I period was the Lotus Buffet and Billiard Parlor on S.W. Sixth Avenue, with its fancy facade. (OHS)*

Boring, Estacada, and Oregon City. Oregon Electric, controlled by James Hill's railroad empire, ran one line to Beaverton, Hillsboro, and Forest Grove and a second through Tualatin and Wilsonville to Salem and Eugene. The Southern Pacific Red Electrics ran to Garden Home, Beaverton, and Hillsboro before swinging south to McMinnville and Corvallis.

Streetcar and interurban companies generated their own traffic by building parks and amusement centers alongside the lines. In the early 1900s, before the typical family owned their Model-T, summer weekends and holidays meant packing a picnic basket and fishing gear for an interurban excursion to Canemah Park above Willamette Falls, Estacada Recreation Park on the Clackamas River, or Dodge Park on the line to the Bull Run power plant. Closer to town were the Oaks Amusement Park, featuring concerts, vaudeville acts, skating rink, rides, and food; and Council Crest Park, whose roller coaster gave the best views in the city to riders who were brave enough to open their eyes.

Prosperity plus new streetcar lines provided the impetus for a residential real estate boom that surpassed even the subdivision mania of the late 1880s and early 1890s. The list of new developments between 1904 and 1910 includes

dozens of names familiar to Portlanders. The 1920s would see the rapid development of Council Crest, Burlingame, Arlington Heights, Willamette Heights, and other new plats in the West Hills. With relatively level land suitable for trolleys, the east side continued to monopolize residential growth in old neighborhoods and in new entries such as Overlook, Montavilla, Rose City Park, Gregory Heights, Kenton, Beaumont, and Westmoreland. The most exclusive new developments were Eastmoreland, Alameda Park, and Laurelhurst. Restrictions written into individual deeds protected residents from the intrusion of apartment buildings and nonwhites.

The Exposition boom made Portland into an "east-side" city. For a decade, virtually all the new housing was built on the east side, and the population balance between the two parts of the city tipped toward the east as early as 1906. In 1916 the telephone company estimated that there were two east-siders for every west-sider. In addition to St. Johns, other east-side neighborhoods including Mount Tabor, Montavilla, Rose City Park, Woodstock, Eastmoreland, and Mount Scott chose annexation to the city to assure good water and streetcar service.

Private developers made money from selling lots and by providing streetcar service to and from the new residents' homes. It was these new property owners, however, who footed the bill for the expanded public services needed because of rapid development. A second water pipeline from Bull Run to a second storage reservoir at Mount Tabor cost taxpayers $1,720,000 in 1911. The bill for streets and sewers came to $28,000,000 from 1905 through 1914, compared to $8,000,000 for the previous *four* decades. The development of new neighborhoods also brought the need to link their residents with downtown jobs. The replacement of three old bridges and the construction of the new Broadway Bridge in 1913 cost $4,500,000.

The Board of Park Commissioners was established in 1900, when the city decided it needed systematic management of Washington Park, Macleay Park, and smaller properties. Under the leadership of Thomas Lamb Eliot, a Unitarian minister and social reformer who was as much an environmentalist as he was a crusader, the board split the cost of hiring landscape architect John Olmsted with the Exposition Company. For a total of $10,000, Portland bought the design for the Exposition grounds and its first comprehensive park plan from the nation's premier firm of landscape planners. John Olmsted followed in the footsteps of his stepfather, Frederick Law Olmsted, who had designed New York's Central Park, and he continued the family landscape architecture and planning business. His ideas for Portland included small playgrounds and neighborhood parks as well as the improvement of large rural and suburban tracts and the development of parkways. He wanted the city to turn the wetlands along the Columbia, and at Ross Island, Guild's Lake, and Swan Island into expansive park reserves. A loop of smaller parks and parkways would rim the west hills and connect the bluffs and ridges of the east side.

Portlanders thought that Olmsted's ideas were fine but feared that the price would be too steep. A one-million-dollar bond issue was responsible for the construction of three miles of Terwilliger Boulevard, and secured public ownership of Laurelhurst, Sellwood, Mount Tabor, and Peninsula parks before the

Passengers for the Oregon Electric cars could slip into the Salem Road Cafe for food or a glass of beer. The station was at S.W. First Avenue and S.W. Jefferson Street, and the year was about 1916. (OHS)

money ran out in 1910. But voters turned thumbs down on new park spending in the 1910s. Most of the riverfront land that Olmsted had allocated for parks went to industry and airports over the following decades. Parkways seemed of less importance than roads as the automobile took over as the primary mode of transportation. The vast expanse of Forest Park is the result of public foreclosure of tax delinquent property during the Depression of the 1930s, not of systematic planning by the preceding generation.

As work lagged on the park system, a meeting of planning enthusiasts in the fall of 1909 led to the formation of a group called the Civic Improvement League, which quickly raised $20,000 from private donors to hire an outside expert to formulate a comprehensive plan for making Portland an "ideal city." The League's major contributors and executive committee comprised a "who's who" of successful Portlanders. The planner who got the job was Edward Bennett, a British-born architect who had assisted the famous Daniel Burnham in the preparation of landmark plans for Chicago and San Francisco. He received $500 a month and

Above: *Tourists were ready for a look at the sights of Portland in the open-air vehicles* Willamette *and* Multnomah. *In the years when cars were becoming common, Portland was more compact than today and could be viewed easily during a short tour. (OHS)*

Left: *Oaks Amusement Park on the Willamette River opened just before the Lewis and Clark Exposition. Concerts were frequent at the Oaks, and shortly before World War I the Oaks Park Band and Metropolitan Quartet were entertaining the crowds.*

expenses in exchange for his expertise.
Bennett presented his preliminary
sketches to the Civic Improvement
League in February 1911 and had the
final plan completed by the end of the
summer.

The plan worked outward from the
center of the city. Anticipating an even-
tual metropolitan population of two million, Bennett called for the construction
of three civic centers to anchor the business district—government offices
grouped around the City Hall for
"nobility of appearance"; a transportation center including post office and

new railway station; and a cultural center with auditorium and museum below
Washington Park. The plan suggested
radial highways, parks, and parkways
to serve the east side. New rail yards
and docks would be built downstream,
with the upper Willamette reclaimed
for parks and pleasure boats in the style
of Paris or Budapest.

Business and civic associations were
enthusiastic about the plan. Mayor Albion G. Rushlight proclaimed February
29, 1912 as Greater Portland Day. Can-
vassers fanned out through the city at
precisely 10:30 a.m. to kick off a mem-

bership campaign that eventually sold 10,000 Greater Portland Plan buttons at one dollar each. The campaign concluded with an evening parade on October 30 led by loud music and horn-tooting automobiles. The final step was to secure formal recognition of the plan by the voters, without asking them to allocate the necessary millions immediately. The vote on November 2, 1912, was two to one to approve Bennett's conception as Portland's official plan, to be followed as closely as possible so long as it proved reasonable and practical.

Within weeks, Bennett's plan took a back seat in local politics to the campaign for a commission form of city government. The narrow vote amending the city charter climaxed a decade of effort at political reform, for the clean-scrubbed face that Portland put on for tourists and businessmen at the Lewis

and Clark Exposition masked back-room politics that were as corrupt as ever. Historian Gordon Dodds, in his *Oregon: A Bicentennial History,* has described the alliance of "business interests, gamblers, and thugs" that ruled the city in the interests of licit and illicit commerce behind the figurehead mayor George H. Williams, whose term lasted from 1902 to 1905. In an era of political bossism, Portland's version of the party boss was W.F. "Jack" Matthews, who pulled the strings in the city and state Republican parties while occupying a series of patronage jobs and generally trying to keep his picture out of the papers. As muckraking journalist Burton Hendrick would write in *McClure's Magazine* in 1911, "the kind of government with which the Republican machine was identified was concretely illustrated in the municipal

Drinking water was provided for thirsty horses in front of the Commonwealth Building, on S.W. Sixth Avenue between S.W. Ankeny and W. Burnside streets. The building, dating from 1892, was typical of many ambitious, sometimes ornate, structures started before the 1890s depression. Courtesy, Fred DeWolfe

administration of Portland. Even on the Pacific Coast, Portland enjoyed a peculiar fame as a wide-open town .... the city had become a popular headquarters for all the vicious characters in the Pacific Northwest."

Then in 1904 and 1905, headline-making indictments and trials of leading politicians for involvement in schemes to obtain fraudulent title to northwest timberlands shattered the Oregon machine. President Theodore Roosevelt removed Jack Matthews from his position as U.S. Marshal, thus creating a vacuum in local politics. The mayor's office was up for grabs. The reformer who defeated Williams in 1905 was Dr. Harry Lane. A Democrat, Lane ran with the

support of progressive businessmen, the new *Oregon Journal*, and the respectable middle class. Grandson of Joseph Lane, Oregon's first territorial governor, Doc Lane was an outdoorsman of the Teddy Roosevelt mold who enjoyed making surprise visits to construction sites to find out for himself if the city was getting full value for its dollar. He was honest beyond question. When he later served in the U.S. Senate, colleagues called him "the human question mark" for his tendency to question federal spending. Lane vetoed scores of ordinances during his four years in office, but a city council that listened closely to liquor dealers and railroad executives usually overrode the vetoes on 13-2 votes. Nonetheless, Lane's record included successful cost-cutting on city contracts and an effective crackdown on saloons and bordellos. Yet he lost most of his battles to preserve the public interest against the "big boys"—Portland Railway Light and Power; the Spokane, Portland, and Seattle Railroad; the Union Pacific; and the Southern Pacific. Lane's strongest support in 1905 and in his 1907 re-election campaign came from the middle-class homeowners of the east side, who worried about the political alliance between the moguls of the Heights and the economically marginal residents of the North End.

When Tammany Hall ward boss George Washington Plunkitt told a New York reporter that "reformers are only mornin' glories," he was talking about the resiliency of political machines and the general inability of middle-class reformers to parlay single electoral victories into permanent changes. He might well have been talking about Portland

in 1909 and 1910 under the leadership of Mayor Joseph Simon. Coming to office at the end of a thirty-five year career that had taken him as far as the U.S. Senate, Simon was the smoothest of Portland's professional politicians. In public he supported such respectable causes as park acquisition and the Bennett plan, while behind the scenes he guided a well-oiled political machine.

The impetus for permanent change finally came from two objective reports. In the first, the 1912 Vice Commission appointed by new mayor Albion G. Rushlight compiled detailed documentation on the extent of prostitution, the ubiquity of venereal disease, and the complacent attitude of the police and courts. The report certainly surprised no one who had ever walked around downtown Portland with open eyes, but the Vice Commission's building-by-building inventory and its candid interviews with scores of prostitutes were difficult to ignore. So was the conclusion that law enforcement amounted to informal licensing, when fines for prostitution and for maintaining a bawdy house averaged less than a good day's take.

For many businessmen and bankers, vice may have been embarrassing but government inefficiency was intolerable—not merely an insult to public morals but an injury to every taxpayer. The second report that jolted Portland's establishment into action came in April 1913, when the New York Bureau of Municipal Research reported on an investigation of Portland's city government. Editor C.S. Jackson used his *Oregon Journal* to publicize its findings by detailing the operational problems of ten city departments. Only the water

bureau got good marks. According to the report, the police department was disorganized; city accounting and budgeting departments were in shambles; health inspections were a sham; and public works a scandal.

The impact of these reports prompted the adoption of the commission form of government, as recently developed in Galveston, Texas. The proposed charter provided for nonpartisan elections, the abolishment of the ward system in favor of citywide elections, and the replacement of the mayor and city council with a mayor and four commissioners. Meet-

ing together, the five would serve as the city's legislative body. Acting separately, each one would administer a city department and carry out the ordinances adopted as a group. The goal was to bring Portland more businesslike and less expensive government by eliminating political horsetrading and ensuring coordination among departments. In May 1913, Portland approved the charter—which has served since with minor changes—by 722 votes. Liberal Republicans, planning enthusiasts, Roosevelt Progressives, and social reformers backed the change. Old guard Republi-

cans, who were satisfied with their control of the local political machine, dug in their heels to resist the new charter. At the other end of the political spectrum, the local labor newspaper, the *Labor Press,* thought that workingmen

should wait for more significant changes. The charter represented middle-class and working-class reform, with the margin of victory coming from the east side.

Commission government meant government for homeowners, small businessmen, professionals, skilled workers, and the other members of Portland's great middle class. It also helped to set the city's tone for the next two generations. In the first years of the twentieth century, Portland had been a rambunctious town caught up in the excitement of headlong growth. There were new opportunities to try, money to be made, and new communities to build. By the 1920s and 1930s, the city would slow down and grow conservative, concerned to maintain its obvious attractions rather than risk changes. The city would continue to change, but more slowly and more cautiously, with an eye to stable neighborhoods and low taxes.

Above: *Buildings constructed on pilings extended out over the river near Portland's downtown. This view, looking toward the northwest in about 1914, shows much of the downtown, with the* Journal *tower in the distance at left. A seawall was constructed later along the waterfront.* (OHS)

Left: *C.S. Jackson took over the faltering* Journal *in 1902 and built it into a major afternoon paper, challenging the long-entrenched* Oregonian. *He previously had published* The East Oregonian *at Pendleton. At the time,* The Oregonian *was also publishing an afternoon daily, the* Telegram. (OHS)

BUILDING A CITY OF HOMES

Every newspaper and chamber of commerce likes to claim that its community is a "city of homes." The claim may be only wishful thinking in some communities, but it is fully justified in Portland. For the last three generations, the "Rose City" has had a higher percentage of homeownership than most other American cities.

The shift to homeownership in Portland dates back to the real estate boom of 1905-1912 that followed the Lewis and Clark Exposition. A few statistics tell the story: Portland in 1900 ranked 26th among large American cities in the percentage of households that owned their own homes. Just ten years later, Portland ranked fifth in the nation; 46 percent owned homes compared to 32 percent for all other large cities.

Portland has maintained its edge ever since. Most recently, nearly two-thirds of the housing units in the Portland area have been owner occupied. The comparative figure for all metropolitan areas in the United States is approximately three-fifths.

High homeownership in Portland has resulted in a population that is not only stable but conservative, exhibiting a cautious approach to public issues. A long series of journalists have found Portland's temperament "prudent and placid," to quote Freeman Tilden's words in 1931, and have remarked on its beautiful homes and conservative leaders. Local historians Tom Vaughan and Terry O'Donnell similarly have noted Portland's measured pace of life and careful approach to growth. Very recently, a team of reporters from the Chicago *Tribune* found

Portland to have a "small-scale, low-key ambiance," based on its physical beauty, tranquility, and a lack of deep social divisions.

Portland's high percentage of home ownership has also affected its physical appearance. For a century, the city has been characterized by the free-standing single-family home. Historically, residents have been opposed to apartment construction in both the city and suburbs, viewing attached or row housing as unsuitable for Portland. Thus, Portlanders have built a low-rise metropolis where residents can enjoy the advantages of both a large city and low-density neighborhoods.

It is actually possible to read the history of Portland's growth in its changing types of single-family homes. Centered in the downtown core are three "growth rings," each made up of neighborhoods built at roughly the same time and representing thirty to forty years of Portland home building. Today, all three of these rings provide sound housing and viable neighborhoods to meet the needs of area residents.

The inner ring includes the remnants of Victorian Portland, that portion of the city built before 1905. The majority of the nineteenth-century houses have been lost to time, to urban renewal, and to development. Those that remain include spacious and handsome Queen-Anne-style houses as well as smaller frame cottages with elaborate millwork on their porches and gable ends. Most of these homes can be found in a crescent-shaped area of close-in neighborhoods on the west side, including Northwest,

Goose Hollow, King's Hill, and Lair Hill. A few others are scattered in Albina and the inner southeast side, which were the centers of separate suburbs until 1891.

What survives of Victorian Portland has been preserved with the help of local government. Neighborhood plans and rezoning in Northwest, Buckman, and Corbett-Terwilliger-Lair Hill have fended off some of the pressures of land conversion and demolition. Designation of individual landmarks and creation of the Lair Hill conservation district by the Landmarks Commission and City Council have also helped.

Portlanders built a "middle ring" of housing between 1905 and 1940. This era saw the development of fine neighborhoods that spread along the crest of the West Hills. Owners of new houses in Westover, Arlington Heights, Portland Heights, and Council Crest could overlook the older Victorian city with the assurance that they had achieved economic success. Many of these homes were built in an emerging regional style that ignored "period" references in favor of natural wood and cedar shingles blending architectural design with the natural setting.

The climax of this second era was emergence of a distinct style of residential architecture defined by the work of John Yeon and Pietro Belluschi during the 1930s and 1940s. Yeon's Watzek House was based on Oregon vernacular forms, while Belluschi's Joss House spotlighted local materials with exposed trusses, unfinished cedar paneling, and spruce siding. According to historian George McMath, Belluschi's Jennings-Sutor House of 1938 had all the characteristics of contemporary design with its "concern for the setting and integration of landscaping, the open functional plan, the broad sheltering pitched roof, and the use of naturally finished native woods." By the time he moved east to head MIT's School of Architecture in 1951, Belluschi had helped to create an elegant but informal approach to housing that especially suited the needs of Portland and the Northwest.

On the east side, residential development in the first decades of the twentieth century followed the streetcar lines. Portlanders moved into dozens of new neighborhoods and subdivisions that stretched as far as six miles from downtown. The new communities ranged from Alameda to Woodstock and Woodlawn, from Sellwood to Sunnyside, Sabin and St. Johns. These areas were within a half-hour trolley ride of downtown in 1930; today, they are still only half an hour from downtown via Tri-Met. These communities are also marked by the survival of neighborhood shopping districts along the old trolley routes.

The home typical of these streetcar neighborhoods is the Portland bungalow. Only a decade ago, this Northwestern version of a California housing style seemed old-fashioned. Now we have rediscovered the appeal of wide porches, overhanging roofs, exposed rafter ends, and unboxed eaves. Today's real-estate ads show that this "Old Portland" style is popular once again. We have also discovered that the bungalow's open floor plan is as livable in the 1980s as it was seventy-five years ago. The Laurelhurst neighborhood, developed in the 1910s and 1920s, provides a particularly rich sampling of bungalow styles.

Public assistance has played an important role in maintaining the attractiveness of these middle-

A garden grows near E. Belmont Street and S.E. 54th Avenue. (OHS)

aged neighborhoods. Housing rehabilitation programs coordinated by the Portland Development Commission have made low-interest loans available for modernizing and improving more than 7,000 houses. Since 1974, Portland has used a higher percentage of its federal Housing and Community Development money for housing rehabilitation than almost any other city in the country. In a neighborhood like Irvington in Northeast Portland, the long-term impact of these efforts has been dramatic. At the same time, the city's Office of Neighborhood Associations has been available to assist community groups in improving city services and upgrading their environment.

Portland's outer ring consists of one-story neighborhoods built after 1945 and oriented to the automobile. On the east side of the Willamette, these suburbs run roughly east from 92nd Street, which marked the limit of streetcar and bus service before 1940, and south from the Multnomah-Clackamas county line. West of the river, new housing spilled down the far slope of the West Hills onto the rolling farmland of the Tualatin Valley. Annexations in Southwest Portland since 1950 have brought typical "suburban"

areas within city limits. The greatest focus for growth since 1960, however, has been Washington County.

Growth of the one-story ring has been dependent on aid from the federal government. The loan insurance and guarantee programs of the Federal Housing Administration and Veterans Administration primed the huge building boom that added more than 300,000 housing units in the metropolitan area between 1950 and 1980. Federal grants for parks, planning, and especially sewers have made it economically feasible to build the new neighborhoods that thousands of Portlanders have preferred. Without this aid, growth in Washington and Multnomah counties would have been seriously slowed after 1970.

The "city of homes" has been the product of generations of private action and investment, with a healthy assist in recent decades from local and national government programs that have helped to preserve the oldest houses, to modernize middle-aged houses, and to finance the purchase of new houses.

A new-fangled traffic sign was the focus for this scene downtown. Mayor H. Russell Albee, mayor from 1913 to 1917, surveyed the situation at the left. Cars were increasing considerably on the main streets. (OHS)

CHAPTER V
MODERN TIMES

The problems and opportunities of modern times arrived in Portland with assistance from the Great War in Europe, which turned the city's tiny shipbuilding business into a major industry. The success of Germany's U-boat campaign in 1916 and 1917 spurred Allied orders with Portland shipbuilders to replace the lost merchant vessels. After the United States entered the war in April 1917, the U.S. Emergency Fleet Corporation made itself the sole customer for scores of Portland-built steel-hulled and wooden-hulled ships. Shipyard employment climbed to 28,000 at the end of 1918. Foundries, machine shops, and sawmills that supplied materials for the shipbuilders accounted for another 5,000 jobs. Rents rose; newcomers, attracted by wartime jobs, crowded the streets; and workers on three shifts kept the city open twenty-four hours a day.

Like most other Americans, Portlanders saw the war effort not only as a chance for a better job but also as a patriotic crusade from which there could be no dissent. Suspicions against immigrants, particularly Germans, ran high. German-born residents were required to carry a registration card to work near the waterfront. The Brooklyn neighborhood showed its loyalty by renaming streets, with Frankfurt Street becoming Lafayette and Bismarck becoming Bush, but City Council members ignored the Linnton workers, who wanted Germantown Road renamed Libertytown Road.

The loudest voice for 100-percent "Americanism" belonged to George Baker, who began his sixteen-year career as mayor in 1917, a few weeks after Congress declared war. His campaign promise that "smokestacks will be as numerous as the trees in the Forest" continued the tradition of business boosterism. A last-minute revelation that his labor-backed opponent had once applied for membership in the Socialist Party successfully played to a growing wartime hysteria. Baker led Liberty Bond rallies and held breakfasts at the Civic Auditorium for each contingent of Oregonians bound for the trenches in France. Throughout the war years eighty police officers dealt with "outside activities" such as registering aliens, raiding radical organizations, patrolling railroads and docks to ward off sabotage. Baker also enlisted the police on the side of management and "Americanism" in any labor dispute.

Baker was the most colorful politician in Portland's rather bland political history. He stood over six feet tall, weighed in at more than 200 pounds, and easily earned the nomination of the *Oregon Voter* magazine as "the champion loud noise of the Pacific Northwest." Born in The Dalles in 1868, he quit school at the age of nine to shine shoes and sell newspapers on the streets of San Francisco. He came to Portland in 1889 and worked his way up from the bottom in the theater business. By the first decade of the new century, he owned downtown theaters, managed his own stock company, and joined almost every club and organization in town. He served on City Council from 1898 to 1900 and again from 1907 to 1913, representing the downtown voters and vice

kings of Ward Four.

Portland's record of intolerance showed no improvement after the Armistice. Fears of international Bolshevism and domestic radicalism intensified in 1919 and 1920. These years also brought severe inflation and high unemployment as the shipyards shut down and veterans returned home. A general strike in Seattle early in 1919 and a November shootout in Centralia, Washington, between members of the American Legion and the radical Industrial Workers of the World (Wobblies) made the Portland establishment more than nervous. Mayor Baker's response was to raid the city's IWW offices and to prohibit banners announcing strikes or workers' meetings from the streets of Portland.

Two years later, seamen in the Pacific Northwest went out on strike against a 25-percent pay cut imposed by the U.S. Shipping Board. Violence came to the Portland waterfront on June 20 when police officers appeared on the docks in plain clothes and confronted pickets. The confused melee of gunfire that ensued ended with striker Nestor Varrio dead and his union hauled into court to fight a conspiracy charge. Confrontation on the waterfront occurred again in the fall of 1922, when 1,000 longshoremen and members of the Marine Transport Workers (affiliated with the IWW) walked off the job. George Baker put the weight of city government firmly on the side of the Water-

Small businesses were plentiful downtown. Among these were confectioneries—eighteen in just five blocks of Washington Street in 1921, as listed by the city directory. One was the Foss Confectionery, above, at 753 S.W. Washington Street, offering Fatima cigarettes, Dromedary dates, and other items. (OHS)

front Employers Association. City Council appropriated $10,000 to fight the "radical revolution." A hundred special police officers descended on the picket lines, arrested all known Wobblies as vagrants, and searched trains entering and leaving Union Station. On the same day that the strike was settled to the satisfaction of the employers, the mayor took credit for averting a revolution.

By the time of the dock strikes, Portland had also heard the appeal of the "Invisible Empire" of the Ku Klux

Above: *G.M. Standifer Construction Company, with yards at North Portland, shown here in 1918, and Vancouver, was just one of a number of firms active in World War I shipbuilding. This was a forerunner of an even bigger ship construction effort in the early 1940s in the Portland-Vancouver area. (OHS)*

Left: *Increased wartime economic vitality was reflected by plants such as the Grant Smith-Porter Ship Company at St. Johns. After the Armistice in 1918, waterfronts were glutted with ships, and contract cutbacks were rapid. (OHS)*

Klan. As it spread across the South, Middle West, and West in the early 1920s, the Klan appealed to Americans who were disturbed by the rapid pace of social change. The Klan's two million members—factory workers, dentists, storeowners, clerks, and craftsmen— were united by their fear that the familiar America was disappearing. The growth of the Klan was in part a reaction against the disturbing times of high prices, scarce jobs, and labor agitation. Klansmen blamed "outsiders" and "aliens"—particularly blacks, Jews, and Roman Catholic immigrants—for these social ills, and these groups bore the brunt of the Klan's attacks.

The Klan came to Portland in the summer of 1921, finding fertile soil in a largely Protestant community that had just experienced five years of turmoil. Kleagle Luther Powell was the chief organizer. The Exalted Cyclops was Fred Gifford, an electrician who had left his union for a job with Northwest Electric Company. It is unclear whether George Baker joined the Klan, but he certainly welcomed their support. Compared to other parts of the country, Portland's Kluxers largely refrained from vigilante violence, and concentrated instead on the voting booth. In May 1922, Klan-backed candidates won two of three seats on the Multnomah County Commission and twelve of the county's thirteen seats in the state legislature. Portland supplied the victory margin in November for a statewide compulsory public school initiative, which was intended to make all private schools illegal, but the law was struck down by the U.S. Supreme Court before it went into

Above: *Many ships produced in the Portland-Vancouver area during World War I were a boon for private shipping later when they were sold by the government. One typical ship was the* West Kyska, *a steel freighter built in 1918 by Willamette Iron & Steel Works. Courtesy, Oregon State Library*

Below: *Women with large hats predominated in this milling crowd at the Baker Theater shortly after the turn of the century. George Baker, who operated the business, started the Baker Stock Company, which presented many plays before movies and radio diminished the audience for live theater. (OHS)*

effect. As in other cities and states, interest in the Klan declined when the novelty of their costumes and rhetoric wore off, and particularly when people discovered that Klan-backed politicians could be just as venal as the men they replaced.

By 1923 most Portlanders were more interested in enjoying their new automobiles and the products of postwar production than in rooting out Reds or fighting the imaginary threat of minorities. When the United States entered World War I, there was one automobile in Multnomah County for every thirteen residents. By 1925 the ratio increased to one automobile for five residents; and one for every 3.7 residents by 1929.

Automobiles were becoming a big business in Portland. At the end of the 1920s there were eighty dealers in the first "automobile rows" along North Broadway, between Tenth and Twenty-First west of downtown, and on the near east side. Portland residents spent as much on automobiles as they did on food and 8,000 depended directly on automobiles for their jobs according to the 1930 census.

As early as 1913, a hundred business and professional men formed a kind of posse of automobilists known as the "Flying Squadron," roaming town in their own cars to enforce ten- and fifteen-mile per-hour speed limits and generally trying to maintain order in the streets. The first comprehensive city code for motorists and pedestrians came in 1914. The police department set up an auto theft bureau in 1920 and a "speed squad" in 1922. Congestion downtown became a special headache as thousands of cars clogged narrow streets, fought streetcars for the right of way, and parked wherever they pleased. The twenties brought the first no-parking zones and the first automatic signals, though as late as 1931 only a quarter of downtown intersections had the two-color lights that announced their change from green to red with a clanging bell.

"Autoists" demanded wide, hard-surfaced roads and new bridges. The Interstate Bridge across the Columbia opened in 1917, connecting Portland to

Far left: *Some groups agitated for improved working conditions before World War I, as illustrated by this 1914 poster of a woman worker. Some of these groups ran into a super-patriot backlash during the war, while improved economic conditions also frustrated attempts at reform. (OHS)*

Left: *Dr. Marie Equi, physician, pacifist, and birth control advocate, served ten months in San Quentin prison for her anti-military activities at Portland in World War I. In 1913 she suffered a fractured back when she was run down by mounted strikebreakers while she supported women strikers. Critics called her "the Bolshevik Queen." (OHS)*

Below: *The waterfront presented a picturesque, if somewhat rickety, appearance in 1919 as steamboats and other craft moved in and out of docks. About a decade later, wharves and riverside buildings between N.W. Glisan and S.W. Jefferson streets were removed to make way for a seawall. Courtesy, Alex Blendl*

Vancouver over an improved Patton Street, appropriately renamed Interstate Avenue. By 1924, motorists could follow the paved Pacific Highway from downtown Portland across the Broadway and Interstate bridges all the way to Tacoma and Seattle. The city spent millions widening east and west Burnside, Sandy Boulevard, Union Avenue, 82nd, and other arterial streets. Multnomah County put millions more into reconstructing the flimsy Burnside Bridge and building the Ross Island Bridge. While the new bridges served real needs, the Sellwood Bridge, built in 1925, and St. Johns Bridge, built in 1931, were harder to justify to taxpayers in terms of traffic; but they did help to tie the two historically isolated neighborhoods, for which they were named, more closely to the rest of the city.

Left: The battleship Oregon, no longer considered necessary for the peacetime Navy of the 1920s, found a new home on the Willamette River. The ship was a reminder of Spanish-American War days, when the United States expanded its interests in the Caribbean and Pacific. Courtesy, Alex Blendl

Below: With its new seawall, the western side of the Willamette River presented a neat, uniform appearance by 1929. Warehouses and other buildings of East Portland are in the foreground. The Weatherly building, first skyscraper on the east side, was completed shortly after this photo was taken. Courtesy, The Neighborhoods Office, City of Portland

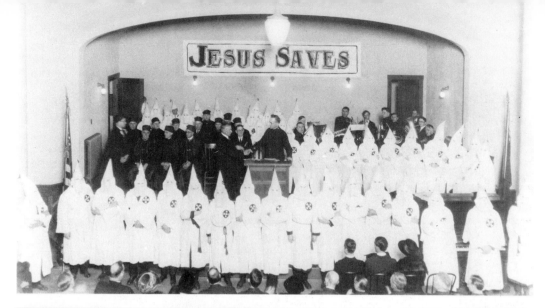

Left, top: *The Ku Klux Klan showed considerable political strength in Portland and elsewhere in Oregon in 1922. However, interest in the group soon ebbed. Nationwide, the KKK claimed five million members in the early 1920s. It opposed blacks, Jews, and other "un-American" people. (OHS)*

Left: *A Shrine group, one of many fraternal organizations in Portland, lined up in picturesque attire at the Masonic Temple. Several of the largest still-surviving downtown buildings were constructed by fraternal and social groups, including the Masonic Temple on the Park Blocks. (OHS)*

Below: *Cowboys were the inspiration for this patrol of Mooseheart Legion of the World, which won a fraternal orders drill contest at the Stock Yards at North Portland in 1929. Some of the city's social and fraternal groups demonstrated their skills in parades and drills. (OHS)*

Left: *Motorcycles were enlisted early in the auto age to chase speeding cars. City officials wrestled with speed limits, drunken driving, and other issues that had not been problems in the horse-and-buggy era.* (OHS)

Below: *Two parades, one from the east side, the other from the west, converged on the new Burnside Bridge at its opening day on May 28, 1926.* (OHS)

Automobiles and paved streets made it feasible to develop areas that had been inconvenient for streetcar riders. A building boom in the 1920s brought Portland 25,000 new houses. There was rapid development of sections of the West Hills where automobiles were almost a necessity for access. Builders and buyers also filled in vacant lots in east-side neighborhoods such as Eastmoreland, Mount Tabor, Grant Park, and Concordia, all of which were located three to six miles from the center of town. New high schools—Franklin, Roosevelt, and Grant—served the growing neighborhoods and provided a focus for community identity.

Prosperity during World War I and again in the early 1920s because of a thriving timber industry made it easier for immigrants or their children to move from core neighborhoods to new middle-class housing. Historian William Toll, for example, has traced the movement of successful Jewish shopkeepers and professionals from South Portland and older sections of Northwest Portland to Laurelhurst, Irvington, and Westover Terrace. Many German and Scandinavian families moved to newer and nicer housing within the northeast sector of the city in the post-World War I era.

These ethnic migrations opened older

parts of Albina to a gradually growing black population. Before World War I, the majority of Portland's 1,000 blacks lived between Burnside, Glisan, Northwest Fifth, and Northwest Twelfth because of the area's convenience to hotel and railroad jobs. By the end of the thirties, the census counted 2,000 black residents. Only 130 were left in Northwest. More than half lived in Albina, where inexpensive older housing allowed widespread homeownership among stable working-class families and a smattering of businessmen and professionals.

Other blacks were scattered throughout the east side. Discrimination was a matter of knee-jerk prejudice. Realtors urged each other to confine home sales to Albina, and unions ranging from hotel workers to the longshoremen barred black members. The major hospitals admitted blacks as patients but refused to accept their applications as nurses.

New neighborhoods and more automobiles also meant the expansion of commercial strips along major streets. Eighty-second Avenue changed from a country road to a string of stores and gas stations between 1920 and 1940. The new Barbur Boulevard, built on an unused Southern Pacific railroad right-of-way in the early 1930s, avoided the same fate through protective zoning. Sandy Boulevard became the shrieking symbol of an automobile city. Architect Al Staehli has described it as "a linear Disneyland of buildings which were also the symbols of their function. Stucco shoes for shoe shops, gas pumps tucked under mushroom canopies, giant milk bottles crowding a dairy, jug taverns, and the grinning black-face entrance of the Coon Chicken Inn [now mercifully vanished] provided a series of visual exclamation points."

After 1924 zoning took on the larger function of protecting residential neighborhoods against the intrusion of businesses, apartment houses, and gas stations. George Baker and his establishment allies first proposed land-use zoning in 1919 and 1920 as a response to the wartime boom and its uncontrolled growth. Voters in 1920 narrowly rejected the plan, with most working-class neighborhoods opposed, and upper-middle class areas in favor. Banker John C. Ainsworth had argued that zoning would "harmonize the property interest of owners and the health, safety and convenience of the public," but many small property holders were suspicious of any restriction on development rights.

A second try succeeded in 1924. The simple code written jointly by the Planning Commission and Realty Board divided the city into four zones—one was limited to single-family houses; another allowed apartments; a third allowed businesses; and a final industrial zone allowed virtually anything else.

With the help of the automobile Portland carried on its intense love affair with the outdoors. One of the community's most enduring accomplishments was the Columbia River Highway, opened between Troutdale and Hood River in 1915 and completed to The Dalles in 1922. Engineer Sam Lancaster designed a road that complemented and

Top: *St. Johns Bridge rises 213 feet above the Willamette and has a main span of 1,207 feet. Construction started in 1929, and the $4-million bridge was dedicated in June 1931 as part of the Portland Rose Festival. Dr. D.B. Steinman of New York designed the span. (OHS)*

Above: *This pleased cab driver opened his door circa 1930 for contralto Ernestine Schumann-Heink, known for her operatic performances, touring recitals, and radio broadcasts. (OHS)*

Left: *An amusement park was developed on Hayden Island in 1928. Courtesy, Jantzen Beach SuperCenter*

Left, below: *Before the development of shopping malls, all the major business activity was concentrated downtown. Olds, Wortman and King was a favorite of shoppers. This is an interior view of the building, later converted to The Galleria. (OHS)*

blended with the spectacular landscape of the Columbia Gorge, achieving his aim "to find the beauty spots, or those points where the most beautiful things along the line might be seen to the best advantage, and if possible to locate the road in such a way as to reach them." The highway was built jointly by Multnomah County and the state, with essential help from millionaire lumbermen Simon Benson and John Yeon. The *Portland City Directory* called the high-

way "America's newest and greatest pathway for the recreationist." Hotels, auto camps, and restaurants sprang up in the Gorge towns, and the U.S. Forest Service opened a campground at Eagle Creek and set aside its first "Recreation Reserve" of 14,000 acres. Completion of a paved road to Tillamook and Seaside and a highway loop around Mount Hood in the 1920s brought the outdoors even closer to mobile Portlanders.

Portland slid inexorably from good times to bad after 1929. The city as a whole escaped the worst ravages that the Great Depression brought to Eastern industrial cities and Southwestern farmers, but local business grew worse and worse over four very long years. The Depression cut the city's exports and banking activity by more than half. The value of new construction in 1933 and again in 1934 was scarcely over two million dollars—6 percent of the 1925 record. Business failures peaked in 1932, but the worst was still to come for retailers. Thousands of families dug up their backyards for vegetable gardens and canceled their telephone service to save a few dollars a month. Theater owners went broke for lack of

customers despite drawings and give-aways. Two of every three small businesses were behind on their property taxes by 1933.

When Franklin D. Roosevelt took office, the Portland Public Employment Bureau listed 24,000 unemployed householders. Welfare payments, though inadequate, helped to support 9,100 families. From May 1932 through the end of the year, the City of Portland sold $845,000 in bonds to fund work relief projects. Eighteen thousand men signed up for jobs and 4,000 actually went to work on park and street improvements. In March 1933, when the money ran out, the city continued the program by paying the workers with scrip—formal IOU's which 2,500 merchants agreed to accept as cash, with the promise that the city would later redeem the scrip at full value.

Beyond the public jobs programs, the 1930s were a time when communities helped themselves out of necessity. The Catholic Women's League found temporary jobs for 500 women and girls in 1932 and gave short-term assistance to 500 others. The members of the Council of Jewish Women opened a bake shop to give supplemental employment to poorer residents of South Portland. The city's most prestigious families rallied around the Portland Symphony Society with contributions and memberships to keep the symphony playing in the 1931-

1932 season.

The citywide Council of Social Agencies organized ten neighborhood councils in 1934 to coordinate services for children and fight juvenile delinquency. By the late 1930s many of the councils had expanded their concern to the larger issue of neighborhood livability and to problems such as housing, health, and city services. These groups were the predecessors for Portland's neighborhood associations that have developed in the last twenty years.

Portlanders who went unassisted by public and private relief agencies often ended up in one of the city's "Hoovervilles"—shantytowns for the homeless. The biggest of these stretched along the slopes of Sullivan's Gulch from the Union and Grand avenue overpasses to 21st Street. Hundreds of men lived in self-built shacks made with scrounged lumber, scraps from construction sites, and liberated tarpaper. Much like a frontier mining camp, the settlement had its own rules and its own informal leadership. There were other squatter settlements at Ross Island and on the filled site of Guild's Lake.

The Depression polarized Portland politics. A wide spectrum of views and bitter arguments replaced the unventuresome "hail-fellow-well-met" City Council of the 1920s. On one extreme was the Red-baiting councilman J.E. Bennett, described even by the conservative *Oregon Voter* as contentious and obnoxious. At the other extreme was Councilman Ralph Clyde, a strong and persistent advocate for municipal ownership of electric utilities. Joseph Carson, mayor from 1933 to 1940, was a states' rights Democrat who worked hard to keep the New Deal out of Portland. He was a special friend of the private utilities and an enemy of organized labor. Proposals for new government programs such as public housing often lost three votes to two, with future mayor Earl

Left: Simon Benson purchased and donated land that included Multnomah Falls and Wahkeena Falls as part of the Columbia River highway project. Benson was not only a wealthy lumberman, hotel builder (The Benson and Columbia Gorge Hotel), and temperance advocate, but he also donated Benson Polytechnic School to Portland. (OHS)

Below: Open-air touring cars carried passengers past scenic landmarks such as Shepherd's Dell on the Columbia River Highway. Courtesy, Cross and Dimmitt

Above: *The Oriental Theater, which opened January 5, 1928, at 148 N.E. Grand Avenue, could seat 2,040 people, second in size only to the Paramount. Sculptor Adrien Voisin provided designs in East Indian and Angkor Wat motifs. The showplace, shown here circa 1935, was torn down in 1970. (OHS)*

Left: *As payrolls dropped and unemployment soared, many men found themselves with a lot of idle time. The Men's Resort at Fourth Avenue and W. Burnside Street was full of jobless individuals in 1931. (OHS)*

Riley joining Carson and Bennett in opposition. The liberal Ralph Clyde was joined in the minority by architect Ormond Bean, who would serve on City Council from 1933 to 1939 and again from 1948 to 1966.

Not just the City Council but the entire community was divided over the Longshore strike of 1934, one of the most bitter labor-management battles in Portland's history. Since the strike of 1922, in which the workers lost, Portland's docks had been run by waterfront employers. In the fall of 1933, in response to deteriorating working conditions and wage cuts, the International Longshoremen's Association (ILA) organized a single local for the entire Pacific Coast. A coastwide strike started on May 9, 1934, and closed down the

port of Portland. Before it was over, 82 days later, the strike had directly involved 3,000 waterfront workers and idled another 15,000 Portlanders in trade-dependent jobs. The central issue was the balance of power on the docks, with the strikers demanding employer recognition of the ILA and union control of hiring halls.

The Portland police were in a pivotal position between the antagonists. In the first weeks of the strike, they allowed pickets to run strike-breakers off the docks and attack the shipping company security forces. Strikers raided one ship—the *Admiral Evans*—and cut it loose to drift against the Broadway Bridge. By early summer, Mayor Carson gave in to demands from the business community and enlisted the city on the side of waterfront employers. July 5, 1934, became known as "Bloody Thursday," when a concerted effort to break the strike in all the Pacific ports led to several deaths in other cities and a number of arrests in Portland. Senator Robert Wagner of New York arrived on the 12th as a special representative of President Roosevelt, who was scheduled to visit the site of Bonneville Dam in August. Wagner's mission was to settle the strike before Roosevelt steamed into Portland harbor in the *U.S.S. Houston*. Company guards shot at his car when he tried to visit Terminal 4, perhaps without knowing who he was. Fortu-

Above: *Income was scarce in the Depression. In Oregon City, Clackamas County relief workers ended a 1935 protest parade by abandoning an empty coffin. They were seeking parity with Multnomah County allotments. Workers such as these were employed on public projects.* (OHS)

Left: *Many young men joined the federal government's Civilian Conservation Corps projects during the Depression, and were employed in forests. Some are shown on trail construction in 1935 in Gifford Pinchot National Forest north of the Columbia River.* (OHS)

provided paychecks for 5,000 workers and held out the possibility of transforming Portland into what FDR described as "a vast city of whirling machinery."

New Deal liberals in Oregon hoped for an independent Columbia Valley Authority that would distribute the new power at equal rates throughout the Northeast. But the Portland Chamber of Commerce, Mayor Carson, and a procession of businessmen argued that Bonneville's electricity should be available at lower rates within a fifty-mile radius of the turbines. A Congressional compromise created the Bonneville Power Administration to market electricity

Left: One of the Northwest's largest art projects was completed in the Depression. The Reverend Bernard F. Geiser, a priest-artist, worked on murals at St. Mark's Episcopal Church for seven years, starting in 1931. Courtesy, Oregon Journal, (OHS)

Below: Despite poor economic times, the Rose Festival continued, helping unite and entertain the community. Decorated floats pass the Oregon Journal Building in 1931. (OHS)

nately, the only injury was to the reputation of Portland. This incident, plus the threat of holding up Bonneville, gave Wagner leverage to force employers to agree to arbitration. Portland's establishment worked out the painful details in a secret meeting at the Arlington Club, tacitly recognizing the union by agreeing to submit the dispute to arbitration. The victorious longshoremen went back to work on July 31.

As Portland's business community well knew, the best chance for a new Portland during the troubled years of the Depression was the development of cheap hydroelectric power. From Franklin D. Roosevelt's visit to dedicate the site in August 1934 to official completion in September 1937, Portlanders on weekend excursions could watch the great bulk of Bonneville Dam rise across the channel of the Columbia forty miles east of the city. Construction

from Grand Coulee Dam as well as Bonneville over a grid connecting Portland, Spokane, and Seattle-Tacoma.

The key decisions involving Bonneville came in 1940. First, voters in the May primary turned down the creation of a public utility district which would have been empowered to buy out Northwest Electric (now PP&L) and Portland Electric Power (now PGE). As a result, private utilities remained the intermediaries that brought hydro power from BPA and retailed it to consumers. Second, the Bonneville Power Administration offered to sell cheap energy directly to major industries to encourage economic development. In January Alcoa Aluminum signed the first direct contract for its new aluminum reduction plant in Vancouver. By the following year, Bonneville electricity was also powering federally owned aluminum operations at Troutdale and at Longview, Washington. Within a decade, the dam

had made electro-chemical and electro-metallurgical industries the leading manufacturing sector in the greater Portland region.

The practicalities of power policy (and politics) defined one direction for a post-Depression Oregon. Portlanders who wanted other choices could listen to Lewis Mumford, the nation's leading writer on urban planning who visited in the summer of 1938. In a speech to the City Club and in a pamphlet called *Regional Planning in the Northwest*, Mumford called for active yet careful regional planning. He advised Portland to stabilize its population to allow time

Above: *Mayor Joseph Carson conferred with Fiorello LaGuardia, New York City's reform mayor, during a LaGuardia visit in 1940. (OHS)*

Above, left: *The mayor's job includes many ceremonial duties, along with weightier chores. Portland mayor Earl Riley was chosen to place crowns on two winners at the Redhead Roundup at Delake, a coastal community. Delake was later absorbed into Lincoln City. (OHS)*

Above: *A public market was a long-time downtown feature at S.W. Fifth Avenue and S.W. Yamhill Street. About 1930 William C. Hoffman's floral stand provided a colorful display at the market. In 1984 a new Yamhill Market was completed two blocks east.* (OHS)

Left: *President Franklin D. Roosevelt, with Mrs. Roosevelt and Governor Charles E. Martin of Oregon, visited Bonneville Dam for its dedication on September 28, 1937. Roosevelt pushed a button to start the first power unit. On the same day, he also dedicated Timberline Lodge. Courtesy,* Oregon Journal

Left: *The partially completed Bonneville Dam loomed impressively at the rugged Cascades of the Columbia in 1936. Since the arrival of the first settlers travelers had been forced to bypass these rough waters. Completion of the dam resulted in the flooding of the Cascades. (OHS)*

Below: *Motor vehicles proved useful in a variety of ways. Multnomah County Library began using trucks to bring books to patrons. J.J. Phillips was the driver of this truck, and page Esther Hawkes was seated at the table in this 1932 scene. (OHS)*

to clean up thousands of unfit houses, overcrowded apartments, and slum hotels. He also suggested decentralizing new industry into satellite towns whose carefully chosen locations and reliance on electricity would protect the natural environment.

Mumford set his suggestions within an even broader challenge to Portland's abiding conservatism:

I have seen nothing so tempting as a home for man as this Oregon country . . . and I am going to ask you a question which you may not like. Are you good enough to have this country in your possession? Have you got enough intelligence, imagination, and cooperation among you to make best use of these opportunities? . . . In providing for new developments you have an opportunity here to do a job of city planning like nowhere else in the world.

In fact, it took another thirty years of boom, bust, and business as usual before Portland and Oregon came to agreement on an agenda for the future. Not until the administration of Governor Tom McCall in the early 1970s would the sort of regional planning that Mumford called for attract the necessary combination of political leadership and popular support.

Wartime shortages of gas and tires forced many shipyard workers to ride the bus. This shift-change scene is at Oregon Shipbuilding Corporation near the mouth of the Willamette River about 1943. (OHS)

CHAPTER VI
THE WAR AND AFTER

World War II brought more excitement to Portland than anything since the great Exposition. In the language of city officials who worried about problems of the home front, the Portland metropolis was a "congested war production area." But in terms of the pace of daily life, it was a boom town—another Leadville or Dawson City with defense contracts in place of gold and silver mines.

Portland's new boom came from a single industry— shipbuilding. The first federal orders for new ships went to the Commercial Iron Company, the Albina Shipyard, and Albina Iron and Steel in 1940 and 1941. Industrialist Henry Kaiser of California, fresh from the construction of Boulder and Grand Coulee dams, also opened the huge Oregon Shipbuilding Company north of St. Johns in 1941. His Swan Island and Vancouver yards went into production two months after Pearl Harbor.

At the peak of wartime production in 1943 and 1944, metropolitan Portland counted 140,000 defense workers. Federal contracts totaled $2.4 billion for more than 1,000 oceangoing ships. The record-breaker for construction time was a Liberty ship launched on September 23, 1942, less than eleven days after workers laid down its keel.

The boom brought thousands of new faces to Portland. The Kaiser yards placed help-wanted ads in eleven states. The response almost emptied the rest of Oregon, and drew the unemployed from small towns in Idaho and Montana. Workers were brought in by chartered trains from the East Coast. Portland's population grew from 501,000 to 661,000 between 1940 and 1944. One could safely assume, in the war years, that every third person standing in line for the bus or a double feature was a newcomer to the city.

This phenomenal growth brought unprecedented problems for local governments. The job explosion on the north side of the city strained public transportation in an era of gasoline and tire rationing. Two hundred new buses, 150 trucks, and ferry service across the Willamette to Swan Island were scarcely enough to keep up with the demand. The tens of thousands of shipyard workers, many of whom were unmarried or without their families, also had money for liquor, gambling, and prostitution. While the circulation of books from the public library dropped, the pari-mutuel handle at the dog tracks skyrocketed. A clean-up drive in 1942 swept out the red-light district north of Burnside. Gamblers, however, simply moved their shops to the side streets. Protection of public safety was especially difficult since the military services took about half of the city's police officers and fire-fighters.

With a seemingly endless demand for workers, the Portland and Vancouver shipyards provided high-paying jobs for tens of thousands of Portland women. By the end of 1943, the 20,500 women employed at the Kaiser yards made up nearly a quarter of their total work force. One out of three of these women filled the sorts of office jobs that were already open to women, but hundreds of others who had recently graduated from training classes at Benson High filled

jobs as electricians, painters, machinists, and pipefitters. More than 5,000 earned what was then an impressive $1.20 per hour as welders. Welder Ree Adkins later remembered that "in all this kind of work, the women and men were paid the same . . . there didn't seem to be a speck of jealousy. The men did the same things that we did." Other women at Swan Island, Kaiser-Vancouver, Commercial Ironworks, Willamette Iron and Steel, and smaller firms were tool checkers, ship fitters, warehouse clerks, and shipwright helpers. Newly employed mothers relied on an instantly devised childcare system made possible by federal subsidies to the schools, to nonprofit agencies, and to employers. Kaiser's special Women's Services Department operated childcare centers on round-the-clock shifts synchronized with those of the shipyards and provided

Special publications were issued for shipyard workers in World Wars I and II, telling of production activity and promoting good work habits. The best known in the Portland area in the 1940s was the Bos'n's Whistle, a Kaiser publication, which printed this cartoon. Courtesy, Bos'n's Whistle

"Here comes Mom with her home work!"

take-out meals that could be ordered ahead of time and picked up by busy wives on their way home.

The influx of new residents affected the availability of housing as early as the spring of 1941. Newcomers fought for shelter in a city where only one out of every two hundred houses and apartments was for rent. Rented rooms and decent family apartments were at a premium.

By the time the United States entered the war, few observers thought Portland would be able to cope with its growth. Long-time residents regarded their new neighbors with mixed emotions—puzzlement, hostility, and often jealousy of their relatively high wages. "The people of Portland make it clear that an Arkie or Okie is the most undesirable person on earth," complained one refugee from the dust bowl. A writer for *Fortune* magazine summed it up: "Portland neither likes nor knows how to accommodate its Virginia City atmosphere."

Portland's actual record included a mixture of accomplishments and missed opportunities. On the positive side, it met the immediate emergency and managed to house 150,000 extra people. But at the same time, the city emerged from the war with a legacy of problems, and its leaders often took the easy route and treated only the short-range symptoms.

Portland's response to the housing emergency represented both aspects of its wartime experience. As industry began to mobilize during 1941, the City Planning Commission tried to meet housing needs with Columbia Villa, Portland's first public housing project, which offered newcomers 400 apartments near the shipyards on north Woolsey Avenue. Although its low-rise design and wide lawns pleased architects, the elaborate process of selecting among competing sites seemed excessively cumbersome.

The focus shifted from permanent to temporary housing when the City Council created the Housing Authority of Portland as an emergency measure.

Days after the attack on Pearl Harbor, the council picked a realtor, a banker, an apartment owner, and a union leader to serve on the new agency. Their goal was not to use public housing to shape a more efficient or pleasant city, but to build the minimum number of necessary units, which could be torn down after the war.

The housing crisis peaked in the summer of 1942, when federal officials projected the need for 30,000 additional rooms and apartments. Edgar Kaiser, managing his father's enterprises in Portland, took direct action. At a closed-door meeting in August, he signed a contract with the United States Maritime Commission for an immense 6,000-unit housing development (soon increased to 10,000 units). To the astonishment of city officials, Kaiser broke ground soon after Labor Day. Nearly 5,000 construction workers descended on one square mile of Columbia River floodplain outside the Portland city limits—the present site of Delta Park—to begin construction of 700 identical buildings. Less than six months later, on December 12, 1942, the first tenants moved into the instant city of Vanport.

Vanport paid a price for its hasty development. Though the "miracle city" had been built from a single blueprint, Housing Authority director Harry Freeman vehemently denied that it was a "planned city." Recognizing the antipathy of Portland's business leaders to anything that reminded them of government planning through New Deal programs, Freeman insisted that Vanport "grew on paper and on the ground as many other American cities have grown." With a population that exceeded 40,000 by 1944, Vanport was the nation's largest housing project and was billed as the second largest "city" in Oregon. No amount of promotion, however, could conceal the reality of its dull

gray buildings awash in a sea of winter mud.

It was the responsibility of the Housing Authority to maintain public safety in Vanport and to provide the minimum of social services such as schools and recreation. The former city manager of Oregon City took on the job of community manager. Although members of the social work staff tried to build community cohesion through tenant councils, the Authority ignored them more often than not. It was equally cautious about a proposal for a community newspaper. The result of this general disinterest was that nothing in either the development's community life or its crackerbox design could convince residents that Vanport was anything more than a huge tourist camp.

Vanport also contributed toward establishing racial segregation as a fact of Portland life. The city's black population had increased from 2,100 to 15,000 during the war and presented Portlanders with a new challenge that they largely failed to meet. During 1943, when the black migration had reached significant proportions, the weekly *People's Observer* chronicled racial incidents on the city buses, harassment by the police, and conflict with the segregated Boilermakers Union. Plans to set up a segregated USO in Northeast Portland were an additional slap in the face to many blacks.

Housing lay at the heart of the racial tensions. In 1942, white workers complained about sharing shipyard dormitories with blacks. For both single black men and black families, little private housing was available outside the Albina neighborhood in near northeast Portland. Neighborhood groups raised loud protests at every rumor of new black residents moving into their areas. Former City Commissioner J.E. Bennett even went so far as to suggest that Kaiser stop hiring black workers. Mayor

Earl Riley agreed in private that the racial migration threatened Portland's "regular way of life."

During the course of the war, the black population of Albina rose from 2,000 to 3,000, but most of the newcomers found homes in Portland and Vancouver defense housing projects where they were effectively segregated from the majority of Portlanders. The Housing Authority blandly denied a policy of discrimination, but it carefully steered the thousands of blacks at the Vanport and Guild's Lake projects into certain sections and buildings. Vanport blacks sent their children to integrated schools but there was a segregated hospital. The Multnomah County sheriff's office triggered a series of nasty confrontations when it tried to enforce segregated use of recreation centers.

By V-J Day, Vanport housed a largely segregated population of 6,000 blacks in addition to thousands of white veterans and their families, who occupied temporary quarters while the civilian housing market hurried to meet their needs. Until the Columbia River flood of May 30, 1948, which wiped out the "instant city" and forced its black residents to crowd into Albina, Vanport provided Portland a convenient district where blacks could be isolated from the rest of the city.

Vanport's postwar record had been mixed. Many established Portlanders shuddered at its undeserved reputation for crime and were quietly relieved when the brown floodwaters tore its buildings from their foundations and swirled them into a logjam of broken memories. But for many demobilized veterans, the college-level courses offered at the Vanport Extension Center by the Oregon State Board of Higher Education opened the door of new opportunity. When the classes were relocated to the old Lincoln High School building in downtown Portland in 1952, after a stopover at the old Oregon Shipyards, the city was well on its way to gaining its own public university. The legislature recognized it as Portland State College in 1955.

Portlanders greeted the end of the war with an immense sigh of relief. The

Albina, once a separate community, became home for many of the blacks moving into Portland. Businesses serving the residents occupied old Victorian buildings along N. Williams Avenue, shown above at N.E. Russell Street in 1962. (OHS)

Left: *Shipyard jobs were terminated soon after the end of hostilities, but many employees who had come from other states decided to stay. A large number of blacks found homes in North Portland. Young North Portlanders are shown here in 1949 at a neighborhood dance. Courtesy,* Oregon Journal, *(OHS)*

Below: *Stunned residents were able to move some vehicles to safety after the Columbia River inundated Vanport, but many were swept away by the rising waters. At the right is the N. Denver Avenue ramp, part of a dike system that was supposed to have protected the community. (OHS)*

Oregonian noted in 1945 that a few younger entrepreneurs were working diligently at industrial development, but that older and established businessmen were shrugging off their aggressive promotional efforts with the argument that Portland and its hinterland lacked the customers to attract manufacturing. Writing two years later in the *Saturday Evening Post*, journalist Richard Neuberger argued that "most Portlanders, if polled by Doctor Gallup, would probably say they want their city to go on being the sort of place it has always been. This means a slow and easygoing trading center, with lumber its principal shipment and scenery the great nonexportable resource." Having experienced the fever of the shipbuilding boom, residents were grateful that the economic and social temperature of their city was dropping back down to normal. Neuberger—a liberal Democrat later to be

elected to the United States Senate—made the observation that everything in Portland was slowing down, from the speed of its traffic to its search for new industries to replace wartime ship-building.

In the first decade after the war, Portland voters consistently turned down spending measures that would have improved the quality of life. Voters did approve $24 million in bonds in May 1944, to fund highway, sewer, dock, and school projects called for by city planner Robert Moses in a special report titled *Portland Improvement.* But they later followed by rejecting tax increases or bond measures for a civic center, a war memorial, sewer improvements, urban redevelopment, and general city expenditures. Voters also turned down a forty-hour work week and pay increases for city employees. They rejected an ordinance to make racial discrimination a misdemeanor; a proposal to establish low-income housing in 1950; and bond issues for the zoo and symphony in 1952. Portlanders carefully filled their school board positions with realtors who could be trusted to keep property taxes low. A climax of sorts came to this conservative era in the spring of 1958, when Portlanders handed a stinging defeat to proposals for public transit funding and for a ten-year capital improvements program.

The city did flirt briefly with political change in 1948. Even during his wartime vice crackdown, Mayor Earl Riley had complained that it made more sense to regulate illegitimate businesses than to try to legislate human nature. It became apparent to concerned citizens soon after the war that many law enforcement officials were living well beyond their salaries. Riley's new police chief was Lee Jenkins, an old friend who had served sixteen years in the same position for George Baker and who was unlikely to reform the department. In January 1948, the nationally respected criminal justice expert August Vollmer, whom Riley had hired as consultant under pressure, found the Portland police to be demoralized and mismanaged. A month later, the City

Above: *Writer Richard Neuberger and his wife Maurine from Portland were the first husband-wife team in the Oregon State Legislature. (OHS)*

Left: *Locomotives headed for the Soviet Union under the Lend-Lease program were photographed at the Guild Lake yards about 1945. (OHS)*

Facing page, top: *Farmers, peddlers, and wholesale and retail buyers gathered at the Eastside Farmers' Market in 1949. Courtesy, James Rayner, (OHS)*

Facing page, bottom: *Lambert Gardens survived for a while into the postwar era. (OHS)*

Club counted eleven brothels and ten gambling dens that operated openly in the old red-light district north of Burnside.

Finance Commissioner Dorothy McCullough Lee stepped forward to challenge Riley in the May 1948 primary election when it looked as if the downtown establishment was willing to go along with business as usual. After her victory and inauguration as mayor in 1949, Lee reinvigorated the vice squad and took on the issue of basic reform in Portland's governmental structure. Asserting that rapid growth required a more efficient municipal administration, she appointed businessmen and civic leaders to a Committee on Municipal Reorganization. However, the city council balked at placing a city manager charter, recommended by the

mayor's committee, on the ballot, as individual commissioners defended their independent domains. Lacking the support of the daily papers, which argued that Portland enjoyed quite adequate, if somewhat unwieldly government, the city manager advocates failed to gather enough signatures for their petitions to place the proposal on the ballot.

After Portlanders refused Dorothy Lee a second term in 1952, city politics moved on two levels for the next decade and a half. Day-to-day decisions were dominated by three men who became local institutions. Public Works Commissioner William Bowes (1939-1969) modeled himself on Robert Moses and snorted at what he considered the disastrous notions of Lee and other reformers. Finance Commissioner Ormond Bean (1948-1966) was a curious combination of liberal and pragmatist who liked to bombard other members of City Council with pedantic memos. Mayor Terry Schrunk (1956-1971) walked the line between fiscal caution and the implementation of city projects. Whether his leadership seemed temperate or plodding depended on one's own point of view.

During the same years, citizens who had been disappointed by the failure of the city manager movement in 1950 could take heart from the continuation of what the *Oregonian* called "a line of municipal reform that had been bubbling for a decade or more." An impressive array of reports by legislative study commissions, the City Club, and the Public Administration Service all pointed to shortcomings in city government. A Committee for Effective City Government revived the city manager idea in 1957-1958 with support from the League of Women Voters, Junior Chamber of Commerce, Young Democrats, the *Oregonian,* and the *Oregon Journal.* Determined opposition from Bowes, Schrunk, and labor unions con-

Left: *Dorothy McCullough Lee, mayor from 1948 to 1953, tossed out a baseball to start a Portland game. Lee served in the Oregon House of Representatives and Senate and was a city commissioner before her election as mayor on an anti-gambling platform.* (OHS)

Facing page, top: *Ice hockey players, shown here in 1945, competed with baseball for fans' interest. The hockey teams went through several name changes, becoming Winter Hawks by the early 1980s. In the 1970s professional basketball began to dominate the local headlines for sports fans.* (OHS)

Facing page, bottom: *A public accustomed to American aerial feats in World War II began riding airplanes in greatly increasing numbers after the war. Air controllers, shown here in 1948, were needed to control the Portland traffic. They were, from left, William Palmer, Bernard Basford, and Ralph Bateman.* (OHS)

vinced Portlanders to turn down the proposal by a margin of 7,000 votes. The same groups backed a proposal for a strong mayor charter in 1966, but that also went down to defeat. Portlanders were at the least consistent in their opposition to a strong executive for their city government.

It was fear of failure that aroused Portland from its hibernation. As early as 1953, the *Oregon Journal* had posed the question: "Big league city or sad sack town?" The recession of 1958-1959 had a painful impact on real estate development and underscored the weakness of downtown businesses. Retailers in the central core bounded by Burn-

Left: *Announcer Red Dunning welcomed a horse and rider at Television Station KOIN. Television was the major new innovation in communications in the postwar era, bringing entertainment and news and providing competition for movie theaters and newspapers. (OHS)*

Left, below: *Portland listeners enjoyed live music on the radio in the early years. Roy H. Jackson's Northwesterners performed on KEX, one of the earlier Portland stations. Some Big Band music was aired by radio from the Golden Canopy ballroom at Jantzen Beach. Courtesy, 1190 KEX*

Facing page, bottom right: *The Fox Theater ticket box recalled an era of opulence in theater attendance, when uniformed ushers aided patrons in finding seats. In the 1960s the ticket box looked out on a street clogged with teenagers' cars, "cruising" on weekend nights. Courtesy, Ted Van Arsdol*

side, Jefferson, and Twelfth did less business in 1960 than they had immediately after the war. The number of people coming downtown for movies, doctor's appointments, and shopping had dropped by a third. The census of 1960 brought another disappointment when it recorded a small loss of population within the city limits (373,628 to 372,676). Population for the entire metropolitan area was up only 16 percent for the decade—just half the growth rate of booming Seattle.

With its relatively slow growth overall, no one would have described postwar Portland as an "exploding metropolis" like San Jose or Los Angeles. In the sedate Portland style, however, more and more residents chose to load their station wagons and head for a house in the suburbs. Clackamas County added 26,000 residents in the 1950s. Washington County added 31,000. Eastern

Left: *Jane Powell was a former Portland resident whose career was followed closely by the Rose City populace. Television had started making inroads into family attendance at films when this 1955 musical, "Hit the Deck," was released, but times were still good for downtown theaters. Courtesy,* The Columbian

Below: *Multnomah County Fair was crowded with fun-seekers in August 1961 at Gresham, a community that experienced rapid post-war growth. The fair later was moved to Multnomah County Exposition Center, in Delta Park, sharing a multi-purpose area with other events. (OHS)*

Multnomah County from the city line to the Sandy River was the most popular destination with a gain of 50,000. The under-engineered lanes of the Banfield Freeway gave "east county" the area's first limited access freeway as it crept inward from the town of Fairview to Union Avenue and helped to attract families to new subdivisions in Parkrose, Powellhurst, Rockwood, and Gresham. The first generation of shopping centers along 82nd Street and 102nd Street and the commercial ribbons along the arterial roads served the needs of auto-oriented suburbanites and set a direct challenge to downtown businesses. The total suburban population in the three counties surpassed that of the City of Portland in 1962.

An intangible factor that prodded Portland into action was a change in the population mix. Portland was an aging city at mid-twentieth century. Despite the influx of young workers during the war years Portland had far more than its share of retirement-age residents. The median age in the city in 1950 was over 35, compared to 30 for the United States as a whole. By the early sixties, however, a steady decline in the number of elderly voters reduced the power of the group most likely to vote against tax increases. In their place came the most rapidly increasing group of Portlanders, men and women in the ambitious years from the late teens into the early thirties, who were likely to see the benefits of an active local government.

The key step in Portland's revitalization was the use of the federal urban renewal program to remake the southern edge of downtown. Portland planners had toyed with urban renewal in the early 1950s but found little support in the unadventurous political climate. In 1956, however, members of the Planning Commission and City Council took the plunge and designated fifty-four square blocks of the South Portland neighborhood as an urban renewal district. Their intention was to clear the land for a planned coliseum. The federal government awarded a grant in May 1956.

Portland's politicians had long neglected the public. East-side Portlanders

Unemployed men have long loitered on Skid Road around Burnside Street. In recent years the territory available to them on the west side of the Willamette has shrunk because of the construction of new buildings. Courtesy, Fred DeWolfe

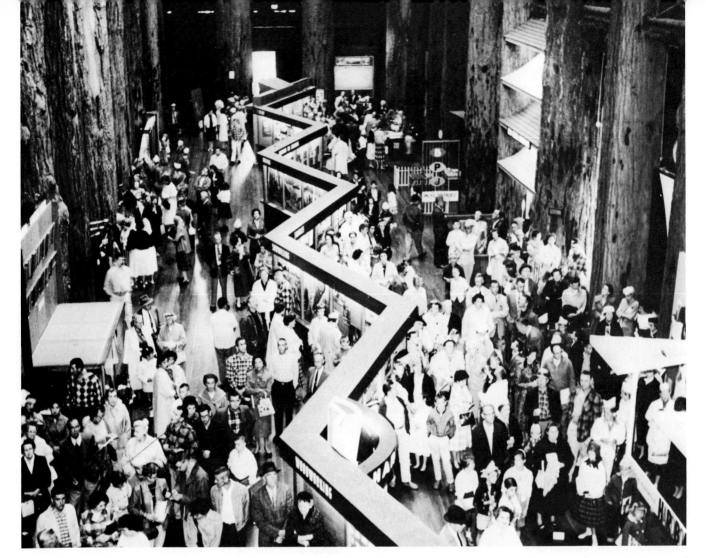

had complained for decades that city buildings were always located on the wrong side of the Willamette for the majority of citizens. The old feud heated up in 1956 when an east-side businessman led a petition drive to put the location of the coliseum to a vote. In May and again in November, voters defied the advice of downtown businessmen, politicians, and newspapers and voted for construction east of the river. But federal administrators, who had been persuaded by the city's plaintive portrait of South Portland as a hopeless slum in need of clearance, refused to transfer their grant to the east side. When the new Development Commission was organized in 1958, it had an urban renewal site but no idea what to do with it. Not until 1960, when the Oregon Highway Department decided to swing the loop of Interstate 405 *south* of the renewal area, was it clear that the south end could successfully be considered part of the downtown.

There is no doubt that South Portland was simultaneously an eyesore and a real neighborhood. The eighty-four acres inside the project boundaries were a jumble of junkyards, marginal businesses, and abandoned storefronts that had lost their usefulness with the disappearance of streetcar and interurban service. Most of the area's buildings were survivors from the nineteenth century, and 60 percent were officially substandard. Rundown apartments and narrow streets were an annoyance to commuters and housewives heading downtown from the southwest hills. At the same time, many residents remembered the days when South Portland had been the first stop for Italian and Jewish immigrants, with the shops and social organizations that eased the transition to American life. The Development Commission evacuated 2,300 people before the bulldozers arrived. A third were over sixty years old; two-thirds lived alone or as couples without

A crowd milled inside the giant Forestry Building to view an exhibit following the building's rededication in 1952. The log building was a relic of the Lewis and Clark Exposition of 1905. It was destroyed by fire in 1964. (OHS)

THE RIVERS AND THE PORT

Like other river cities, Portland is a working city built around a working river.

On a typical Portland day, half a dozen ships load at the docks and terminals that line the Willamette from the city center to its confluence with the Columbia River. Auto carriers or container ships cast off from new terminals on the Columbia itself. The ships carry such cargoes as grain, wood chips, lumber and logs, scrap metal, and merchandise that has arrived on barge tows down the Columbia-Snake river system, or on freight trains and trucks from Oregon's farms, forests, and orchards.

From the city's bridges and bluffs, Portlanders can see a waterfront lined with grain elevators and flour mills, chemical tank farms, cement plants, shipyards, factories, and warehouses. With more workers in wholesaling, finance, trade, and transportation than many cities of its size, Portland is a regional commercial metropolis. Sales agents, shipping clerks, and insurance brokers who handle the paperwork for this riverfront enterprise overlook the river from downtown offices. Although not all employment is directly tied to the river trade, 70 percent of the jobs in the city of Portland and 50 percent in the metropolitan areas are located within a mile of either the Willamette or Columbia.

Besides serving as a center of Portland's industries, the Willamette also enhances the city's visual ambiance. The river flows high in the winter and spring, carrying a runoff that is twice as great as that of the entire Colorado River basin. By summer's end, when the snow has melted from the Cascades, the river has slowed enough for fishing and canoeing. Whether high or calm, the Willamette cuts an open space through Portland's center that sets off views in both directions. Looking down from the hills west of downtown, the river appears as a seam which joins the two halves of the city together.

Like other river cities, Portland is conservative in both social values and politics. It is a city content to have its pace set by the flow of its rivers and the cycle of their seasons.

Facing page: *The crew of the* Hassalo *poses circa 1900.* (OHS)

Top, left: *The* La Rochefoucauld *docks at the Pacific Coal Company.* (OHS)

Top, right: *A steamboat passes under the Steel Bridge in 1912 while it was under construction.* (OHS)

Above: *The small fleet of the Shaver Transportation Company was arrayed near the foot of Washington Street in 1897.* (OHS)

Left: *A tugboat tows a log raft past oceangoing vessels in this early 1960s view.* (OHS)

Left: *Crowds turned out for a Portland Air Terminal airshow in 1958. The airport east of the site of the city of Vanport had been developed on low, flat land near the Columbia that had been a special favorite of golf course developers. (OHS)*

Left, below: *Nurses were an attentive audience at an observation clinic at the University of Oregon Medical School. A major medical complex was developed on Marquam Hill, comprising Veterans Administration and Oregon Health Sciences University facilities. (OHS)*

Facing page: *Even before Vietnam demonstrations, protests were part of the Portland scene. In October 1962 "Women for Peace" joined students in protesting the U.S. blockade of Cuba. (OHS)*

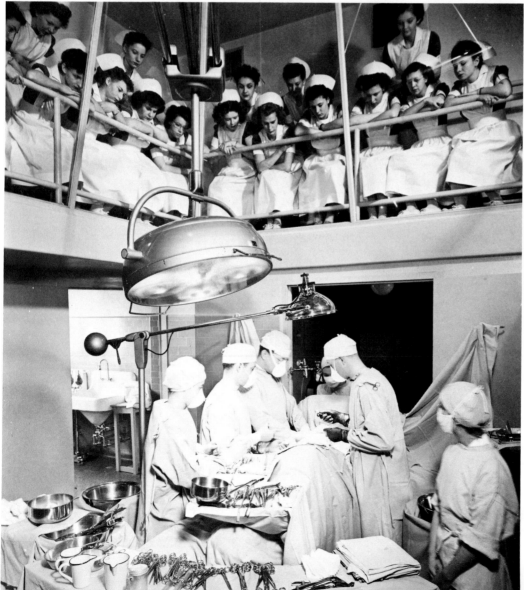

Above: *Whites and blacks joined in a 1963 "march of mourning" on N. Williams Avenue following the killing of civil rights leader Medgar Evers in Mississippi. (OHS)*

Left: *Members of the Albina Neighborhood Improvement Association broke ground in 1964 during a tree-planting drive. (OHS)*

children. Nearly all depended on cheap rents in crumbling hotels and apartments and found companionship in informal neighborhood networks.

The successful start of the "South Auditorium" renewal project made it easy for City Council to extend the boundaries north to Market Street in 1966 and to designate another forty-eight-acre renewal zone to assist the expansion of Portland State College. Compared to the architecturally bombastic Aztec temples and concrete launching pads built in urban renewal areas all over the United States, the plan for South Portland, prepared by the firm of Skidmore, Owings and Merrill, warrants at least a B-plus for handsome urban design. The plan follows the hillside contours with small parks, gardens, and walkways that preserve pedestrian scale. The new office towers and high-rise apartments work with the site rather than overwhelm it. The Lovejoy and Forecourt fountains flow, in a seemingly natural pattern, across the sloping site. The Portland State campus uses the South Park Blocks to link the urban university to its city.

The east side of the Willamette also witnessed a spectacular change in the early 1960s. In a warm morning drizzle on August 1, 1960, Mayor Terry Schrunk snipped a 100-foot ribbon to open the Lloyd Center shopping mall. Governor Mark Hatfield watched 700 homing pigeons explode from their cages to carry news of the opening to twenty-nine northwest cities. Lloyd Center was the climax of a dream by California oil millionaire Ralph Lloyd, who had begun to buy up Portland east-side real estate in the 1920s with the vision of building an alternate downtown close to the concentration of population. Despite suspicion from downtown businesses and banks, Lloyd opened a Sears store and dug the foundation for a hotel before the Great Depression put his

plans on hold. But he continued to acquire land until he owned nearly 100 blocks in northeast Portland at his death in 1953.

Over the next three years the Lloyd Corporation unfolded plans for a massive shopping center only five minutes from the center of Portland. Downtown merchants watched the announcements with dismay and tried to agree on ways to ease their parking problems. Their reactions were mixed with worry about downtown decline and anger over the east-side vote on the coliseum. Financing for the shopping mall came not from local banks but from the Prudential Insurance Company. The Lloyd Corporation broke ground in April 1958, and opened the mall twenty-seven months later. *Business Week* in 1960 noted that Lloyd Center's 1.2 million square feet of rentable space and its eighty-plus stores gave Portland the nation's largest urban shopping center, a distinction that, of course, lasted only a few years. *Time* called it a "consumer's cornucopia" for the 595,000 people within a twenty-minute drive.

For the better part of a generation, Portland was a city that could not quite make up its mind between east side and west side, between growth and stagnation. City Commissioner Bill Bowes summed up the problem in 1943 when he remarked, "I hear people say that they long for the day when Portland can return to what it was before our present industrial progress." Bowes for one had no interest in looking backward: "We are standing at the doorway of a new Portland and a great opportunity." Other Portlanders took fifteen or twenty years to reach the same conclusion. The *Oregonian* announced the start of a Portland building boom in 1958, but the real importance of the Lloyd Center, the Coliseum, and Portland Center towers was to show that the sober city on the Willamette was again ready for change.

The Fremont Bridge, newest of the spans crossing the Willamette River, broke with tradition in its soaring style. Traffic congestion through Portland was eased considerably by the bridge. This 1973 view is toward the east and Mt. Hood. (OHS)

CHAPTER VII
THE MOST LIVABLE CITY

Portland is not one of the nation's most livable cities by accident. During the past two decades, city leaders and residents have replanned and rebuilt the older parts of the city for another generation of use, while constructing a new suburban environment for a quarter of a million new residents.

Much of the city's success has been due to its willingness to experiment. In the last two decades government has taken a leading role in Portland's revitalization. Between 1968 and 1972, for example, local politicians and business leaders cooperated with the Oregon legislature to establish a new set of public agencies to tackle the problems that faced the entire metropolitan area. The results were the Tri-County Metropolitan Transportation District (or Tri-Met), the Metropolitan Service District (Metro), and an expanded Port of Portland that absorbed the old Portland Docks Commission.

Within the city, citizen groups and downtown businesses cooperated on formulating a downtown plan that introduced sophisticated concepts for the functions and future of the city's core. At the same time, active and often angry neighborhood associations shifted much of the initiative in local planning to the neighborhoods themselves. Citizen planners were less interested in comprehensive development schemes than in preserving the advantages and values of individual districts.

Portlanders chose a new generation of leaders to implement the ideas about planning and development. As a County Commissioner and then County Executive, Don Clark led the way in adapting traditional Multnomah County government for modern times. Lloyd Anderson, Connie McCready, Neil Goldschmidt, Charles Jordan, and Mildred Schwab brought new ideas to Portland City Council. As city commissioner (1971-1972) and mayor (1973-1979), Goldschmidt, in particular, capitalized positively on the surge of citizen activism and used it as a foundation to implement a range of new programs. Under his administration Portland gained a national reputation as a city pioneering new directions in public policy.

Portland's new vitality was rooted in its ever evolving resources. New people, new politicians, new industries, and new customers for established businesses gave new life to a maturing city.

Americans tend to assume that livable cities are small cities, and many Portlanders like to be told that they live in an overgrown town. In fact, a city is truly livable only if it is *big enough.* To give all its residents the opportunity to realize and utilize their abilities, a city must offer an adequate base of public and private resources. Residents benefit by the opportunity to interact with others of different backgrounds and cultures. A city needs to be a certain size to be able to provide support for higher education and the arts. It also needs to be large enough to offer a variety of jobs and to develop the sophisticated business services that promote economic innovation and spinoff industries.

The threshold population for a truly

Far Left: *Neil Goldschmidt took office in January 1973 as the youngest mayor of any major U.S. city. He left the Portland post in 1979 for a job as U.S. transportation secretary, but returned to the area in 1981 as an executive of Nike and served as governor of Oregon 1987-1990. Courtesy, U.S. Department of Transportation*

Left: *Charles Jordan arrived in Portland in 1970 to head the Model Cities program, and in 1974 was picked as the first black on the City Commision. He was elected to later terms, and left in 1984 to become parks and recreation director of Austin, Texas, later returning to the same position in Portland. Courtesy, City of Portland*

Left, below: *After serving as an airport and later as a World War II shipyard, Swan Island became a major part of the Port of Portland. This 1960s scene shows a new shipyard repair and dry dock at lower left, and other facilities. Courtesy, Pacific Power & Light Company*

livable metropolitan area is a million or two—the size range of Denver, San Diego, Seattle, Minneapolis, or Vancouver, British Columbia. Portland passed the million mark in population in late 1969. The four-county metropolitan area had 822,000 residents in 1960, 1,007,000 in 1970, and 1,240,000 in 1980. Subdivision sprawl and rush-hour traffic tie-ups are the obvious signs of this 50-percent increase in population. Just as significant is a new sophistication about everything from music and theater to city planning and politics.

One key to the boom of the later 1960s and 1970s was the revitalization of Portland's role as a river city. The port lost business to Seattle in the 1960s when the Docks Commission failed to modernize shipping facilities and ignored the growing market for containerized cargo. Under the persistant prodding of Governor Tom McCall, city leaders agreed to merge the Docks Commission into the Port of Portland in 1970 as an economic development measure. In 1973, the legislature expanded the port to serve Washington and Clackamas counties as well as Multnomah.

These decisions helped Portland in the last fifteen years to regain ground lost to its West Coast rivals of Seattle, Tacoma, and Oakland. Terminal 6 is now a major container dock. Japanese imports such as Hondas and Toyotas make Portland the largest auto port on the West Coast. Dry dock No. 4, opened in 1978 to serve Alaska oil tankers, is the largest on the coast and the third largest in the world.

The energetic Port Authority has helped the city to benefit from the growing importance of American trade with the Pacific Rim. United States commerce with foreign nations out of West Coast ports increased from 17 percent of the national total in 1970 to 24 percent by 1983. Every month ships

Left: *Dredges were essential in deepening the Columbia and Willamette rivers so that larger ships could reach Portland. This picture shows the cutting edge of a dredge, lifted out of the Columbia about 1965. The Army Corps of Engineers has had charge of river clearing. Courtesy, The Columbian*

Left, below: *This aerial of the Willamette River before construction of the Fremont Bridge shows the trainyards at lower left and right center. Swan Island, site of a Kaiser shipyard during World War II, is at upper right. Courtesy, Portland District, U.S. Army Corps of Engineers*

leave Portland for Melbourne and Singapore, Kobe and Yokohama, Penang and Pusan, Hong Kong and Taiwan, Callao, Valparaiso, and Panama. They arrive in Portland carrying steel, petroleum, palm oil, autos, and general merchandise. They depart with wheat, lumber, wood chips, and even frozen french fries for McDonald's restaurants in Tokyo. The real value of Portland trade in constant dollars tripled between 1966 and 1983.

A remarkable expansion in local electronics industries has also contributed to the Portland boom. Companies like Tektronix and Electro-Scientific Instruments originated in empty storefronts and warehouses in southeast Portland in the early 1950s. Symbolizing the transition from one industrial era to another, Electro-Scientific operated for several years out of the facility that was once the knitting mill for the company that evolved into Jantzen sportswear. As business grew, electronics companies migrated to vacant land in Washington County. Spinoff companies like Floating Point Systems and local plants of other national and international electronics

firms such as Intel and Wacker Siltronics came to Portland in the 1970s. By the early 1980s, the Portland area's "silicon forest" on the west side of the Willamette employed an estimated 25,000 assembly line workers, electronic engineers, and software writers.

The city can look forward to further growth in high technology. A recent study published by the U.S. Department of Labor showed that high-tech jobs accounted for 10 percent of *all* of Ore-

Above: Freeways circle downtown Portland in this 1974 photo by photographer Lewis Clark Cook, looking north. Willamette River bridges pictured, starting in the foreground, are Marquam, Hawthorne, Morrison, Burnside, the Steel Bridge, Broadway, and Fremont. (OHS)

Left: Portland State University is at left, and Broadway curves in the foreground looking north from near the edge of Portland Heights in 1975. Some of the results of the urban renewal effort started in the 1960s are visible at the right and center. Courtesy, Portland Chamber of Commerce

gon's nonagricultural job growth from 1975 to 1982, ranking it sixth among all fifty states in relative growth of the high-tech sector.

Portland's role as the economic capital of western Oregon and the Inland Empire is as important now as it was at the turn of the century. Today, it is a city of diversified industries and services—bankers, freight forwarders, insurance agents, wholesalers, and major law firms. Medical and architectural professionals draw patients and clients from hundreds of miles away. Portlanders working with such major corporations as Louisiana Pacific and Tektronix or with the Bonneville Power Administration make decisions that affect the future of the entire Northwest. Under pressure from the national recession of the early 1980s, Mayor Frank Ivancie tried to build on the city's strengths with economic development as the central theme of his administration.

Like many cities, Portland's growth as a regional metropolis has brought a boom in downtown building, but it has been a boom with a difference. Portland serves as a remarkable example of how

Above: *Indians from several tribes are among minorities residing in the Portland area. Some of the descendants of the native Americans practiced traditional dance steps at their encampment at a park near the Willamette River in 1979, against a downtown backdrop. Courtesy, Ted Van Arsdol*

Left: *Waterfront Park, renamed in 1984 in honor of former Oregon governor Tom McCall, has been the setting each year for celebrations and the Fun Center of the Portland Rose Festival. Portlanders played along the Willamette River at this 1982 Fun Center. Courtesy, Ted Van Arsdol*

to plan for new development without turning a downtown area into a highrise ghost town that comes alive only from eight to five. Some officials believe that the downtown plan adopted by City Council in December 1972 was the result of a lucky convergence of circumstances. By the late 1960s the ugliness of the waterfront, the shortage of downtown parking, the decline in bus service, the competition of suburban shopping centers, and the shortage of municipal office space were long-standing problems. What was new, however, was the willingness of business and political leaders to consider new ideas and to think creatively about ways that a solution to one problem might also help with others.

Government, business, and citizens worked together to organize a downtown plan during 1970, 1971, and 1972. The initial impetus came from a business group known as the Portland Improvement Corporation, which represented major local corporations, utilities, and downtown investors. Governor Tom McCall and Portland City Commissioners Lloyd Anderson, Frank Ivancie, and Neil Goldschmidt made key decisions that contributed to downtown revitalization. At the grass roots level a Citizen's Advisory Committee gathered ideas from more than a thousand Portlanders through public meetings, questionnaires, and neighborhood groups. It was the Advisory Committee that made variety, activity, and people the interlocking foundations of the plan. Portland's goal was to design a downtown that was everybody's neighborhood—a district that would offer something for workers, shoppers, pedestrians, bus riders, the young, the elderly, commuters, and permanent residents.

The transformation of the Willamette riverfront is the most obvious change from the Portland of 1965. The old *Oregon Journal* building was razed in 1968. The two-block building situated east of Front Street between the Morrison and Hawthorne bridges had been a white elephant from the day it opened in the early 1930s as a public market. Demolition opened up views of the river and raised hopes for a riverside park. When the Fremont Bridge completed a new freeway loop around downtown in 1973, Portland was able to close the old Harbor Drive expressway and rip up the six lanes of concrete that had divided downtown from the river. The replacement has been Waterfront Park, renamed in 1984 to honor Governor Tom McCall, who had initiated the movement to dispense with Harbor Drive. The South Downtown Waterfront redevelopment project south of the Hawthorne Bridge is an extension of Waterfront Park. With a marina, esplanade, and more than 500 units of new housing, it will add to the life and vitality of Portland's rediscovered riverfront.

The Transit Mall is a Portland innovation that has encouraged development of a high-density office corridor running north and south along Fifth, Sixth, and Broadway. The mall evolved from a suggestion for single bus lanes during an early downtown planning session in 1971. Today, buses are the dominant transportation on two of the most important downtown streets. The Transit Mall has cut air pollution, speeded bus service, and simplified bus transfers. Since the mall opened in 1977, it has served as a model for similar plans in cities from Denver to Ottawa.

Portland's downtown office spine is crossed by a retail axis along Stark, Alder, Morrison, and Yamhill. Mayor Goldschmidt himself made a number of trips to Seattle in the mid-seventies to convince Nordstrom's, a major retail chain, to open a new downtown store covering a full block. Businessmen Bill and Sam Naito, who played a key role

Above: *East of Portland, Women's Forum Park commands this dramatic view of Crown Point and the Columbia River. Courtesy, Frank M. Redmond*

Left: *The south side of snow-clad Mt. Hood towers over Highway 26. Courtesy, Gregory Lawler*

Above: *Mt. Hood rises above vivid autumn colors on Larch Mountain. Courtesy, Frank M. Redmond*

Left: *The forest emerges from fog in Columbia Gorge. Possible ways of conserving the gorge have been frequently discussed. Courtesy, Frank M. Redmond*

Above: *Stretches of the Willamette River are tranquil and untouched. Courtesy, Frank M. Redmond*

Left: *Balch Canyon in Forest Park is a lush remnant of Northwest wilderness. Courtesy, Frank M. Redmond*

Facing page: *Tanner Creek Falls rushes along boulders in Columbia Gorge. Courtesy, Frank M. Redmond*

Left: *The sun sets on the Willamette River in Champoeg State Park. Courtesy, Frank M. Redmond*

Below: *The Columbia River moves placidly at dusk. Near Portland, the river is used extensively by boaters and other recreationists. Courtesy, Frank M. Redmond*

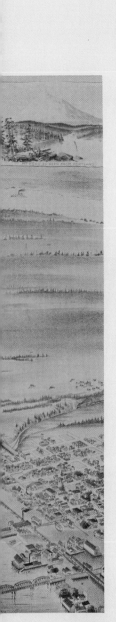

Facing page, top: *The long neck of land at the junction of the Willamette and Columbia rivers has been known for a long time as the Peninsula. Portland occupies the lower center, East Portland is at right, and Vancouver is in the distance, at upper center, in this 1890 sketch. (OHS)*

Left: *Construction of railroads helped spur a boom in public and commercial buildings. The impressive new Chamber of Commerce building was started shortly before the depression of the 1890s. Its ornate tower is shown in this 1891 sketch. (OHS)*

Facing page, bottom: *Residential streets with palatial homes extended below Portland Heights, west of the downtown area in the 1880s. This semi-parklike scene from West Shore magazine looks east toward the Willamette River, with Mt. Hood in the distance. (OHS)*

Below: *Henry Villard started construction on Hotel Portland, but the job of completion was left for George Markle, Jr. (OHS)*

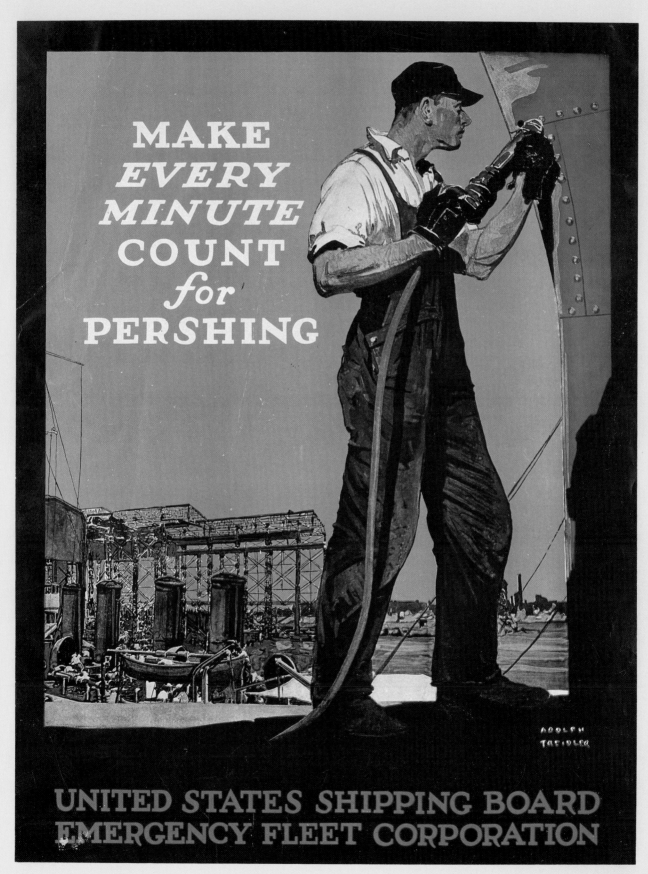

Facing page: *World War I brought prosperous times to the Portland area as jobs increased, but most yards in the lower Columbia area closed after the war. (OHS)*

Left: *Searchlights probed night skies and more than 7,000 sailors swarmed ashore to visit Portland during Fleet Week in 1936. A special pass was issued for Portland Traction Company riders. (OHS)*

Below: *New shipyards were built during World War I and existing yards were expanded to meet the need for "a bridge of ships" across the Atlantic. Posters and slogans were displayed to encourage workers to greater efforts. (OHS)*

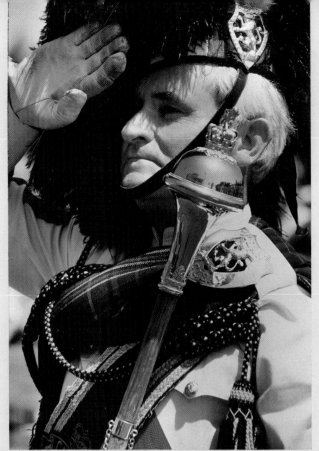

Facing page: *Native American traditions are preserved at gatherings such as the Delta Park Indian Pow-Wow in 1978. Courtesy, Frank M. Redmond*

Left: *Tribes of a different sort gather at the Annual Highland Games and Clan Gathering in Portland. Courtesy, Frank M. Redmond*

Below: *The Clackamas County Fair in nearby Canby draws bronco riders from all over. St. Paul and Molalla also host popular rodeos. Courtesy, Frank M. Redmond*

Facing page, top, far left: *Strollers enjoy the Japanese Gardens in Washington Park. Courtesy, Barbara Gundle*

Facing page, top left: *Portlanders choose the perfect jack-o'-lantern on Sauvie Island. Courtesy, Frank M. Redmond*

Facing page, bottom: *Lake Oswego has the look of the Northwest. Courtesy, Frank M. Redmond*

Left: *A hiker reaches the 8,000-foot level of majestic Mt. Hood. Courtesy, Frank M. Redmond*

Below: *A hiker rests in the Mt. Hood Wilderness. Courtesy, Frank M. Redmond*

Facing page, top: *A couple share a sunny afternoon in the Shakespeare Garden at Washington Park. Courtesy, Frank M. Redmond*

Facing page, bottom, far left: *Autumn leaves carpet the walkway in the Park Blocks. Courtesy, Gregory Lawler*

Facing page, bottom left: *Nearby Columbia Gorge is the site of spectacular views such as this one. Courtesy, Barbara Gundle*

Left: *Spring is a riot of color in the Crystal Springs Rhododendron Garden. Courtesy, Gregory Lawler*

Below: *Crystal Springs Lake comes to life with blooms. Courtesy, Frank M. Redmond*

Above: *Sauvie Island features rural alternatives to city living, such as this houseboat community. Sauvie Island's farms, wildlife sanctuary, and popular recreations are just thirty minutes from downtown. Courtesy, Barbara Gundle*

Left: *Visitors enjoy the spectacular International Rose Test Gardens. Courtesy, Frank M. Redmond*

in revitalizing historic Old Town as a shopping area during the 1970s, turned an abandoned department store into the Galleria, a vertical downtown shopping mall. Pioneer Courthouse Square opened in the spring of 1984 on the block occupied previously by the grand Portland Hotel. Pioneer Square provides Portland with a central public plaza in the heart of the retail district. The Morrison Street project between Third, Fifth, Morrison, and Taylor will add shopping, office space, and a hotel and extend the retail core to the Yamhill Historic District and the river. The Banfield light rail line, to be opened from downtown Portland to Gresham in 1986, is designed to tie this whole retail district together with streetcars that loop along Morrison and Yamhill streets.

The near east side—also to be served by light rail—is as much a part of Portland's central area as the old downtown. From the industries around the Southern Pacific rail lines to the south, through the Produce Row warehouse district and the Coliseum-Lloyd Center area, to the Union Pacific yards and Swan Island, the east-side corridor provides jobs for about 65,000 Portlanders. The stores, hotels, and office towers in and around Lloyd Center constitute a substantial downtown area in their own right.

Downtown Portland in the 1980s is bigger, brighter, and more businesslike than it was twenty years ago. Its white collar workers occupy millions of square feet of new office space and downtown employment totals more than 80,000— up from 50,000 in 1960. At the same time, the city has taken major steps toward its goal of establishing an active and varied downtown that reaches out to the rest of the city. The high-rise boom has destroyed a vital community that housed the elderly in the Lownsdale district and now threatens to displace Skid Road residents north of Burnside, but it has complemented other revitalization plans. Office work-

A wide-angle lens took in the fountain in front of the Civic Auditorium in 1971, before trees and shrubs had grown. The auditorium is at left and St. Mary's Academy at the right, in the distance. Courtesy, The Oregonian

161

As shown here in 1971, the Ira Keller Fountain in the Civic Auditorium Forecourt had an almost pastoral feeling shortly after its completion. In the background is old St. Mary's Academy. The area has been almost completely transformed by urban renewal since the fountain was dedicated in 1970. Courtesy, Fred DeWolfe

Freeways crowded out residences and other development in some parts of the city as highway officials sought to keep pace with traffic needs. This recent view from Burnside Bridge shows roadways east of the Willamette, and the high rises of the Lloyd Center area. Courtesy, Ted Van Arsdol

ers on their lunch hours utilize new parks and patronize new restaurants and established retailers. The increased numbers of business visitors justify new hotel construction. More jobs and more after-hours attractions are gradually making downtown sites attractive for new middle-income housing.

Downtown development has complemented the increasing volume of business in the suburbs. Taken together, suburban Washington, Clackamas, and eastern Multnomah counties surpassed the city of Portland in total population in the mid-1950s and in retail sales in 1972. The number of jobs located in the suburbs matched the number inside Portland's city limits in the early 1980s. Projections for the next decade indicate that the largest number of new jobs will be created in a west-side crescent from Wilsonville through Tigard and Beaverton to Hillsboro. Northern Clackamas County along I-205 and both shores of the Columbia, from Rivergate to Troutdale on the south and Vancouver to Camas on the north, also offer land suitable for industrial development.

Portland preserved and "recycled" its older neighborhoods as its ring of suburbs grew. Despite rapid growth in Multnomah and Washington counties after World War II, a substantial 60 percent of the population within the city limits of Portland in 1970 lived in houses built before the war. By the mid-1960s, residents showed an increasing interest in neighborhood rehabilitation. Government assistance spurred neighborhood improvements. A city code compliance program targeted Irvington and University Park, with their blocks of bungalows dating to the beginning of the century. Another program was the Albina Neighborhood Improvement Project, aimed at refurbishing housing in a section of Portland's black community.

As previously noted, a minor revolution in neighborhood planning came about because of a score of largely self-defined community organizations that began to fight vigorously for change in the late 1960s. Many of these organizations were started to resist freeway construction or plans for urban renewal. By the early 1970s, active neighborhood associations and planning committees had

begun to define their own agendas and force recognition from politicians and planners. On the east side, neighborhood mobilization began in 1967 and 1968 with efforts to provide local input for planning federally assisted programs. Northeast Portland neighborhoods helped to plan and implement a Model Cities program that forced many public agencies to rethink the racial bias in their programs and policies. Portland Action Committees Together (PACT) helped to organize half a dozen neighborhoods in southeast Portland to participate in anti-poverty programs. Southeast Uplift was a locally organized equivalent of Model Cities serving the entire group of southeast neighborhoods that had developed in the first half of the century, including several low-income communities.

The neighborhood movement gained its most articulate spokespersons among middle-class "colonists" of the physically deteriorated neighborhoods of the west side, who united to fend off urban renewal bulldozers. The Northwest District Association was formed in 1969 to deal with the proposed expansion of Good Samaritan Hospital which would have intruded into residential blocks. The group worked with the city's Planning Bureau from 1970 to 1972 to develop an alternative plan that would preserve Northwest as a high-density residential neighborhood of Victorian houses and vintage apartment buildings of the 1920s. Today, Northwest is Portland's most cosmopolitan neighborhood, with a mix of the elderly, students, second-generation immigrants, and young professionals.

The Hill Park Association was organized in 1970 to fight the possible obliteration of the Lair Hill neighborhood, whose location just south of the downtown urban renewal zone made it an attractive target for land clearance and apartment development. After the Johns

Landing development, converting abandoned industrial land along the Willamette 1.5 miles south of downtown into offices, trendy shops, and riverbank condos, was unveiled in 1971, the Corbett, Terwilliger, and Lair Hill neighborhoods joined in the development of their own district plan to preserve old working-class neighborhoods for a new generation.

The cooperative effort between the Planning Commission and the Northwest District Association was the catalyst for giving neighborhood groups an officially recognized role in city decision-making. City Council established the Office of Neighborhood Associations in 1974 to provide support services for local organizations through central and district offices. Neighborhood associations must be open in membership and record minority as well as majority opinions. In return, city officials have learned to listen carefully to neighborhood opinion. The Planning Bureau notifies neighborhood associations of zoning change requests and has worked with individual communities on district plans and rezoning proposals to preserve residential environments. Activists in Lair Hill and Ladd's Addition persuaded the city to designate their neighborhoods as Historic Conservation Districts. Other community groups have been increasingly involved in local economic development and self-help efforts aimed at establishing affordable housing and local jobs.

The vitality of Portland's community business districts has complemented the preservation of many of its residential neighborhoods. The Sellwood and Hawthorne districts have become successful specialty shopping areas. The Hollywood and Northwest districts are serving new generations of local residents. In the face of competition from new shopping malls, the North Portland Citizens Committee secured a grant from

Facing page, top: *Mt. Hood is a dominating backdrop for downtown. Portland Hilton is at the left, the tower of the old First Congregational Church is in the center, and the forty-story First National Bank building is at the right in this 1970s view looking east. Courtesy, Oregon State Highway Travel Section*

Facing page, bottom: *Northwest Portland, near W. Burnside Street, has remained largely residential. The Elliston Apartments is one Victorian survival in the neighborhood, at 425 N.W. 18th Avenue. A horse-and-buggy ride was a quick way to town when the building was constructed. Courtesy, Ted Van Arsdol*

Left: *Visitors in 1978 gazed out at Burnside Bridge and passing boats from a vista at Tom McCall Waterfront Park. The Rose Festival Fun Center and Neighborfair are just a few of the many events staged annually at the park on the Willamette River. Courtesy, Ted Van Arsdol*

Facing page, top: *Dancers perform at an autumn celebration in 1977 in Old Town, a neighborhood in northwest Portland revived in the 1970s with arts and crafts shops, restaurants, and other businesses. The area was formerly a Skid Road. Courtesy, Ted Van Arsdol*

Facing page, bottom: *Hawthorne Bridge provided the background for a troupe staging Middle Eastern dances at a Neighborfair celebration in the late 1970s. Contributions of diverse cultures have been emphasized in the annual Neighborfair, which has drawn huge crowds to Waterfront Park. Courtesy, Ted Van Arsdol*

the federal Neighborhood Reinvestment Corporation for revitalizing the St. Johns neighborhood business district. By 1982, the success of the pilot project in St. Johns had helped to persuade federal officials to make neighborhood commercial revitalization a national priority.

The neighborhood revitalization movement also played an important part in one of Portland's major political upsets. When tavern-owner and businessman J. E. Clark decided to challenge incumbent mayor Frank Ivancie in the May 1984 primary, few experts gave hin a chance to win. Clark's last elective office, after all, had been as treasurer of the senior class at Portland's Lincoln High in the late 1940s. In fact, years of activity in Portland neighborhood associations and community service programs had given Clark both name recognition and access to a network of volunteer political workers. While Ivancie misjudged his own

campaign strategy and failed to shake an image as ally of the downtown business establishment, Clark made quiet gains to emerge with a stunning victory in which he carried 235 out of 291 precincts. Clark's combination of fiscal conservatism and political populism appealed both to an older generation of neighborhood businesspeople and the new generation of neighborhood activists.

Portland's natural landscape puts its own unmistakable stamp on the city's character. Since the late 1960s, Oregon has pioneered in the conservation of the natural environment. In 1983, the Conservation Foundation reported that Oregon ranked fifth among all the states in its commitment to environmental protection. The state's system of land-use goals adopted in 1974 has guided local planners toward decisions to meet social and environmental goals. Traveling journalists give Portland high marks as one of America's cleanest and most en-

vironmentally conscious cities.

For the typical Portland resident, a protected environment has meant a usable recreational network of parks, rivers, and mountains. Within a 90-minute drive, Portlanders are able to enjoy the beaches and headlands of the Pacific shore, the steelhead streams of the Coast Range, the trails of the Cascades and Columbia Gorge, and the ski slopes of Mount Hood—including the country's only late-summer skiing, at Timberline Lodge. Closer to home, Portlanders canoe on the Willamette, sail on the Columbia, jog through the city's fine park system, and generally make use of the area's outdoor opportunities. It seems appropriate that the Jantzen, White Stag, and Nike sportswear companies are based in the Portland area.

When not exercising, many Portlanders are afflicted by a sports mania known as "Blazeritis." The National Basketball Association's Trailblazers are the city's only major-league sports franchise, making the team indispensible to the civic ego, for it is a symbol that Portland is itself a "major-league city." The Blazers have sold out their home *seasons* for more than a decade. Their high point was the 1976-1977 season, when Bill Walton led the unheralded Blazers to a sweep of the powerful L.A. Lakers in the playoffs and a hard-fought victory over the Philadelphia 76ers in the championship series.

Portland's recent decades of increasing livability have also seen the development of institutions for education and the arts. With 700,000 visitors annually, the Washington Park Zoo is gaining a national reputation for Northwest American exhibits and specialized research and the breeding of elephants, primates, and penguins. The Portland

Housing projects sprouted in many parts of the outlying areas near Portland in the postwar era. This scene is in a section of Beaverton, a suburb where pressure for more schools and other civic facilities accompanied the residential expansion. (OHS)

Art Museum and the Northwest Film Study Center are important cultural resources. Conductors Lawrence Smith and James DePriest have helped the Oregon Symphony mature into a major regional ensemble. Since its first season in 1971, Chamber Music Northwest, held on the Reed College campus every June and July, has become a leading national music festival. The Portland Performing Arts Center, partially opened in the fall of 1984, was developed through a combination of tax money and private contributions. It will feature new 450-seat and 900-seat theaters and a refurbished movie palace with 2,750 seats that was originally in the 1920s. The center is complemented by downtown movie houses, the Oregon Historical Society, the Art Museum, and Portland State University, creating a cultural focal point for the city on the southwest edge of downtown.

The arts have flourished in part as a result of the expansion of higher education in the Portland community. Among private colleges in the area, Reed College was recently ranked one of the top ten liberal arts colleges in the country in a poll conducted by *U.S. News* magazine; Lewis and Clark College ranked fourth among regional liberal arts colleges. Portland State University is one of Oregon's three major universities. It plays a vital role in the fields of engineering, business, international studies, and urban and public affairs.

More than 140 years have passed since Lovejoy and Pettygrove tossed their penny into the air to give a name to the new settlement on the Willamette. Over those decades, Portlanders have made their share of mistakes, but they have also managed to build one of the country's most attractive and livable cities. The challenge for the future is to do as well.

Portlanders care about their city. They worry about their neighborhoods,

about access to the Willamette, about the preservation of parks and views, and about the impact of new development. They may disagree about specific political issues, but they participate actively in political campaigns and elections. Citizens who invest their time and energy can make their voices heard, whether they've lived in Portland for just a few years or a lifetime. The inscription on the Skidmore Fountain at First and Ankeny tells us that "good citizens are the riches of a city." Portland's greatest strength is that its residents take the message seriously.

An elk statue was presented to the city in 1900 by D.P. Thompson. The unusual Portland Building, designed by Michael Graves, is now a background for the statue and fountain. "The Coming of the White Man," another statue provided by Thompson, is at Washington Park. Courtesy, Ted Van Arsdol

PORTLAND'S DOWNTOWNS

Portland has already outgrown two downtowns in the course of its history. And a third has been under construction since the 1960s. Each of the city's downtowns has been bigger, and taller, than the last, as the city's commercial and professional activities demanded more and more space.

The first downtown, started in the 1850s, was built in a long strip parallel to the Willamette River by early merchants and real-estate speculators. After 1871, horsecar lines made First Street between Davis and Salmon the main business thoroughfare. From the mid-1860s through the 1880s, as the city's growing economy demanded more business space, downtown property owners replaced flimsy wood buildings with an elegant city of cast iron. The typical mercantile building was a three- or four-story masonry shell with an elaborate facade of cast iron. Detailed pillars and pilasters, capitals, cornices, and medallions imitated carved stone and turned ordinary buildings into "commercial palaces."

By the end of the 1880s, nearly 200 cast-iron fronts were attached to Portland's downtown structures. The twenty that still remain have survived nineteenth-century floods and fires and twentieth-century neglect. Most are now protected within the Skidmore-Old Town and Yamhill historic districts, designated by City Council in 1975 and recognized on the National Register of Historic Places. Restored buildings in both districts now house fashionable shops, restaurants, and offices. The heart of this first downtown (and of Portland's

Left: *Even the great flood of 1894 couldn't douse the enthusiasm of Meier & Frank's loyal clientele. Courtesy, Meier & Frank Company*

Below: *Streetcar tracks and bricked pavement were widespread in the earlier business district. The view is on S.W. First Avenue between S.W. Alder and S.W. Morrison streets, looking north. Courtesy, Fred DeWolfe*

Facing page: *A passerby takes note as pedestrians stop in 1913 at one of the drinking fountains donated by wealthy lumberman Simon Benson. He thought they would help keep people from going into saloons for drinks. Courtesy, Fred DeWolfe*

present historic districts) was the corner of First and Ankeny streets. The New Market Theatre, built for Captain Alexander Ankeny in 1872 according to the design of W.W. Piper, was the hub of Portland in the 1870s and early 1880s. A drive-through market was on the first floor; a theatre lit by a hundred gas jets and a cafe were on the second. A few steps away was the Skidmore Fountain, built with a bequest from pioneer Stephen Skidmore for the refreshment of "horses, men, and dogs." Within a short walk were the Board of Trade, the telegraph office, and the docks of the Oregon Steam Navigation Company. Since the mid-1970s, the crafts fair of the Portland Saturday Market along Ankeny Street has brought thousands of residents back to the very center of Portland's first downtown to admire the fountain, the New Market Theatre (restored in 1983), and the other buildings that recall the nineteenth century.

The second downtown began to develop uphill from the Willamette after the great flood of May 1894, which made Third and Fourth streets look like safer sites for investment than First. New electric trolley and interurban lines also used Third Street and generated such traffic jams that the city's first traffic officer was stationed at the corner of Third and Washington in 1901. A scattering of dark stone office buildings in the ponderous style of the Romanesque revival stand along Second and Third streets as reminders of Portland's taste at the end of the century. Some of the better examples include the Hazeltine Building (1893) at Second

and Pine and the Dekum Building (1892) at Third and Washington.

While the first downtown covered only about fifteen acres, the second downtown covered 120 acres by 1930 and provided four times as much office space as had been available at the start of the century. The Lewis and Clark Fair triggered this downtown expansion. A new generation of architects pillaged European architectural design to create classical banks, a French baroque hotel, an English Renaissance library, and office structures vaguely resembling Italian palazzi. The favorite new material was white or tan glazed terra cotta. Both technically and aesthetically, it was an excellent choice for facing Portland's new steel-frame skyscrapers and department stores. It was economical, fireproof, light in weight, and light in color. As downtown soared into the air with sixteen buildings of ten stories or more at the end of World War I and another eight by the end of the 1920s, terra cotta surfaces helped to re-

Above: *Horse-drawn wagons still competed for business downtown, and movie admission was only five and ten cents about the time World War I broke out. The Oregonian clock tower was still a notable feature, seen here at right center. Courtesy, Webfooters Postcard Club*

Left: *A "big-eared kid" named Clark Gable worked in the necktie department of Meier & Frank's store in 1922 before he began acting in the Astoria Stock Players Company and eventually found fame in Hollywood. Courtesy, Meier & Frank Company*

Facing page: *Some buildings shown in this scene looking west on S.W. Oak Street are still in use today. The section is north of the urban renewal which transformed a considerable part of Portland starting in the 1960s. An ice wagon is parked at right center of photo. Courtesy, Fred DeWolfe*

flect light onto the city's narrow streets.

Streetcar systems replaced the horsecar lines of the first downtown and established the center of the enlarged business district. Trolleys entered downtown from the east along Morrison Street and from the west along Washington. The core of Portland's retail district lay between Morrison, Washington, Third, and Tenth streets. Merchants built new department stores within this trolley loop, especially Meier and Frank; Olds, Wortman and King; and Lipman, Wolfe and Company. Besides the retail core, the larger

downtown—bounded by the railroad depot, the civic auditorium, and Twelfth Street—housed half of Portland's business firms in the 1920s, as well as distinct entertainment, finance, and government centers.

Downtown changed little during the Depression or the two decades after. It was not until the 1960s that a third downtown of steel and glass broke the boundaries of the pre-war business district. The Portland Center Renewal Project marked the beginning of the new construction boom, which pushed the border eight blocks south. Dozens of

mid-rise and high-rise buildings were built during the 1970s and early 1980s to accommodate more than 80,000 downtown workers. Most of the new offices line the southern end of the Transit Mall and portions of the waterfront. By the end of the 1980s, this third downtown will have the focus Portland has lacked for decades. The city's public center, Pioneer Courthouse Square, which covers the block where the grand Portland Hotel stood from 1890 to 1951, is an American version of the European town plaza. The Morrison Street project, covering three of the four blocks between

Above: *The Masonic Temple constructed in the 1900s is among prominent downtown landmarks. Many public events are held in the building. Courtesy, Ted Van Arsdol*

Left: *Many special events and the regularly scheduled Saturday Market help draw crowds downtown. Arts and crafts and food vendors set up shop at the Saturday Market on weekends. Entertainers are also on hand, such as the musician shown here serenading two young girls in 1974. Courtesy, Ted Van Arsdol*

Facing page: *Arcs of lights once spanned S.W. Third Avenue. This view is from S.W. Morrison Street looking north, with Owl Drug Company at right and a newsstand at lower left. Corner drugstores and newspaper stands are among downtown features that have disappeared over the years. (OHS)*

Above: *Pioneer Courthouse Square was cited by* Time *magazine as one of the ten "most notable design achievements of 1984." Courtesy, Ted Van Arsdol*

Left: *Development of a Transit Mall helped segregate buses from car traffic. Courtesy, Ted Van Arsdol*

Fifth, Third, Morrison, and Taylor, will further reinforce the retail center.

Today's downtown Portland is an eclectic mixture of nineteenth-century buildings and modern high-rises. Architects are now bringing more color into downtown structures, with surfaces of black and pink glass, red brick, and glittering aluminum in addition to tan concrete. The most spectacular is the controversial city-county office building by post-modern architect Michael Graves, who used its surface as a paint store sampler. Overall, the strength of downtown lies in its variety, which allows it to serve the needs of different groups within the city—high-powered business-people and elderly shoppers, joggers in Waterfront Park and pensioners in residential hotels, patrons of stylish restaurants and students at Portland State. Downtown is the one part of Portland that is everybody's neighborhood.

Far left: *Mt. Hood provides an imposing backdrop for this sailboat on the Columbia River. Courtesy, Frank M. Redmond*

Left: *The Soldiers Monument on Lownsdale Square is silhouetted against the setting sun. Courtesy, Frank M. Redmond*

Below: *Balloonists work to get aloft during the Folkfest at the annual Neighborfair in Waterfront Park. Courtesy, Frank M. Redmond*

Facing page, top: *The sternwheeler* Columbia Gorge *is a reminder of the days when such craft were predominant on the Columbia and Willamette rivers. The excursion vessel, built for the Port of Cascade Locks, is moored at Portland during the winter. Courtesy, Ted Van Arsdol*

Facing page, bottom: *This dulcimer player and his audience braved uncertain weather at Artquake in 1983. Artquake, a celebration of the visual and performing arts, opened on the Transit Mall but later moved its booths, exhibits, and shows to the Park Blocks. Courtesy, Barbara Gundle*

Left: *A flower wagon was a mobile business at Pioneer Courthouse Square shortly after its completion in 1984. Events scheduled at the square help make it a major focus of interest and activity in the downtown. Courtesy, Ted Van Arsdol*

Left, below: *Portland's Old Town features distinctive shops and restaurants, and brick courtyards for lingering. Courtesy, Frank M. Redmond*

179

Left: *Picturesque old monuments mark River-view Cemetery and frame Mt. Hood. Courtesy, Frank M. Redmond*

Facing page, top: *Rooster Rock State Park in Columbia Gorge is a wonderful place from which to watch the sun set over the Columbia River. Parks and scenic viewpoints are important facets of the Columbia Gorge. Courtesy, Frank M. Redmond*

Facing page, bottom: *A notable reminder of Albina's past is a residence at 4314 N. Mississippi Avenue. It was restored as part of the trend toward refurbishing inner city homes. Courtesy, Ted Van Arsdol*

181

Above: *Modern sculpture provides a dynamic focal point for the Portland Transit Mall downtown. Courtesy, Frank M. Redmond*

Above left: *The skywalk at the Willamette Center becomes a dramatic urban space. Yamhill Market and Waterfront Park are neighboring attractions. Courtesy, Frank M. Redmond*

Left: *Mt. St. Helens rises beyond the east bank of the Willamette River. The peak in neighboring Washington began erupting in 1980, scattering ash through the Portland area. Courtesy, Barbara Gundle*

Facing page, top: *Port-land's 1983 skyline frames Mt. Hood. Courtesy, Gregory Lawler*

Facing page, bottom, far left: *Pioneer Courthouse Square provides a variety of interesting views. Courtesy, Ted Van Arsdol*

Facing page, bottom, left: *The Rose Festival fleet arrives in 1982. Courtesy, Frank M. Redmond*

Right: *The Bank of California tower forms part of Portland's sleek new down-town skyline. Courtesy, Frank M. Redmond*

Below: *People throng the lively Fun Center at Wa-terfront Park during the 1982 Rose Festival. Cour-tesy, Gregory Lawler*

Above, left: *New housing has been built along the river downtown at McCormick Pier. Courtesy, Barbara Gundle*

Above: *The distinctive Portland Building adds a lively aspect to the downtown skyline. Courtesy, Barbara Gundle*

Left: *A barge pulls a timber raft down the Willamette River in 1984. Courtesy, Gregory Lawler*

Facing page, top, right: *The battleship* Oregon *was a floating museum at Portland, and the marine park was named for the famous Navy vessel. Courtesy, Frank M. Redmond*

Facing page, top, far right: *Portland's skyline glows in the sunrise. The skyline has been greatly altered by urban renewal dating back to the 1960s. Courtesy, Gregory Lawler*

Facing page, bottom: *High rises tower against the sky near Portland State University, as seen from the Stadium Freeway looking northwest. Urban renewal started in this area and has moved north in the downtown section. Courtesy, Frank M. Redmond*

Left: *The south Park Blocks and Portland State University are ablaze in fall colors. In the distance are the West Hills. Courtesy, Frank M. Redmond*

Below: *Rain never dampens a parade-goer's enthusiasm in Portland, but it makes a high window the best vantage point from which to watch. Courtesy, Gregory Lawler*

Left: *Canadian destroyers dock at the seawall during the Rose Festival in 1982. Courtesy, Frank M. Redmond*

Below: *Flowers are used to cover Rose Festival floats. The festival dates back to 1907, but rose show tradition dates back even further, to 1889. "For you a rose in Portland grows," was a long-time booster slogan for the City of Roses. Courtesy, Gregory Lawler*

Above: *Activists staged a protest sit-in at the Trojan nuclear plant at St. Helens in 1977. Courtesy, Barbara Gundle*

Right: *A bike rider flips high in the air at a demonstration in Pioneer Courthouse Square. Courtesy, Ted Van Arsdol*

Far right: *This view across the Willamette River shows the construction of Portland's new downtown in the early 1980s. Courtesy, Don Eastman/Earth Images*

Portlandia, 37 feet high in crouched position, has occupied a perch on the Portland Building since 1985. Raymond Kaskey completed the artwork, said to be the largest copper-hammered sculpture outside of the Statue of Liberty. Courtesy, Ted Van Arsdol

CHAPTER VIII
BUILDING FOR THE FUTURE

Portlanders enthusiastically adopted two civic icons in the mid-1980s.

In 1985, the city installed "Portlandia" in her niche over the entrance to the Portland Building. This huge copper statue of a kneeling woman clutching a trident in one hand and reaching out to pedestrians on the Fifth Avenue Transit Mall with the other, was based on the figure of "Lady Commerce" on the city seal. On the drizzly autumn morning of October 6, the completed statue was barged up the Willamette from its assembly point in the Northwest Industrial District like a red-orange Cleopatra. Thousands of Portlanders turned out in a spontaneous civic celebration. They lined the waterfront, joined Mayor Bud Clark in canoes and boats, or crowded downtown to watch it hoisted into place. Parents lifted their children to touch the outstretched finger as it passed in the street.

Although reviews of the Michael Graves' Portland Building continue to be mixed, sculptor Raymond Kaskey's creation inspires nearly universal affection. It weighs 6.5 tons and stretches nearly 37 feet high (it would be 50 feet if Portlandia were to stand up). Kaskey spent three years hammering copper sheeting the thickness of a dime around complex steel frames. The result is the largest work of its kind short of that other copper goddess, New York's Statue of Liberty.

A year later, Portland turned to a very different but complementary symbol in designating the great blue heron as one of the official symbols of the city. Bud Clark, who enjoyed canoeing on the Willamette before the start of a day in City Hall, made frequent references to herons in a welcoming speech to a convention of wildlife managers. Mike Houck, of the Portland Audubon Society, picked up on Clark's

interest and suggested official status. Everyone on the city council was enthusiastic and the formal proclamation came in December 1986.

If Portlandia represents the strength of the city center and civic involvement, the blue heron reflects the deep affection that Portlanders hold for their natural surroundings. A bird of rivers and marshes, the blue heron connects contemporary Portland to its origins as a straggling riverfront settlement. It also speaks to the ongoing commitment to build a thriving metropolitan region without destroying its natural setting.

In the mid-1990s, urban experts in other parts of the United States thought that Portlanders were carrying through on their commitment. Indeed, the city's press clippings could sometimes be so glowing that residents might wonder if they could measure up to their reputation.

To many observers, Portland is one of the few large metropolitan areas "where it works," to quote a 1990 headline in *The Economist*. Over the past twenty years, it has frequently appeared near the top of urban livability rankings aimed at groups as different as working women and bicycling enthusiasts. An informal poll of planning experts in 1988 rated Portland's efforts to deal with urban design issues among the best in the United States. The City of Portland makes regular appearances as well on lists of the nation's best managed cities.

Overall, many experts believe that the Portland area is among the nation's most successful in balancing economic growth and environmental protection. Inspection junkets have become a steady contributor to the Portland tourist economy as journalists try to discover "how Portland does it" and civic delegations make the rounds

Left: *The RiverPlace development, with marina, is shown in this 1988 view, looking toward the northwest from the Willamette River. Pyramidal-type roofs distinguish the Riverplace Hotel, right center, with the Marriott Hotel in the background. Courtesy, Portland Development Commission*

Below: *Visitors strolled along the Esplanade of the RiverPlace about 1987. Work started in 1985 on this waterfront area, which is comprised of businesses, condominiums and a marina, along the Willamette River. Courtesy, Ted Van Arsdol*

of Portland's leaders in search of lessons for their own cities. Their common question is how a city can prosper without destroying its natural setting through sprawl. The most frequent answer, as summarized in a federal government report on "America's New Economy and the Challenge of the Cities" (1996), is that metropolitan Portland prospers *because* it is compact and efficient. As HUD Secretary Henry Cisneros noted, "Communities that emphasize cooperation over competition within their region have succeeded in expanding economic prosperity and creating jobs in the New Economy."

At the heart of modern Portland is a strong and vibrant downtown. Visitors to the city nearly always start at the center. *Time* and the *Atlantic Monthly*, *Architecture* and *Landscape Architecture* magazines have all reported to their readers on the strength of downtown, the careful conservation of a sense of place, and the enhancement of the center with public art. *The New Yorker* in 1985 pointed to "closely controlled new building, the carefully monitored rehabilitation of worthy old buildings, [and] the vigorous

creation of open space" as key factors creating a city of "individuality and distinction." Downtown design earned a City Livability Award from the U.S. Conference of Mayors in 1988 and an Award for Urban Excellence from the Bruner Foundation in 1989.

The central business district continued to prosper in the 1990s, with employment hitting 105,000, up from 63,000 in 1970. Two-thirds of the metropolitan area's "class A" office space (the newest and best

Two azure blue, glass towers, 250 feet high, loom over the Oregon Convention Center on the east side of the Willamette River. The center opened in September 1990 adjacent to the MAX light rail line and a short distance from The Rose Garden, home of Portland professional basketball. Courtesy, Portland Development Commission

equipped buildings) could be found downtown in the early 1990s, far above the national average and second only to the Pittsburgh, Pennsylvania region. Some companies moved routine office workers to suburban locations, but downtown remained the place to be for most corporate executives. At the close of the 1990s, a tight market and low office vacancies meant that downtown was poised for another wave of high rise construction.

Downtown Portland has gone upscale as it has prospered. The last five-and-dime store shut down in the mid-1990s, but five luxury hotels have opened since 1985. J. C. Penney closed its doors but Saks opened a block away. When the Pioneer Place retail mall opened in the heart of downtown in 1990, it climaxed a twelve-year effort at retail revitalization; it also replaced a deli and a candy store with Banana Republic. The supply of expensive downtown apartments and condos has not kept up with demand, but there are fewer affordable apartments and rooms for janitors and espresso-makers.

The popularity of downtown triggered new housing to the north and south of the historic core. The Riverplace project on the south waterfront added several hundred apartments, a retail esplanade, and marina

in 1985 and expanded in the 1990s. The old warehouse district north of Burnside Street experienced a makeover into the "Pearl District." Art galleries, artists' lofts, and new apartments blossomed nearly overnight. Plans for a massive River District development on outmoded railroad yards north of Union Station were proceeding in 1997, aiming at a mixed use community of 5500 new housing units and 1.8 million square feet of commercial space on 100 acres.

After decades of separation, the 1990s also made the east side of the Willamette River part of the central business core. The Central City Plan (1988) called for the historic downtown to grow outward rather than upward, spreading north and south along the river and across the river to the east side. The Oregon Museum of Science and Industry recycled an old power plant for a beautiful new facility on the southeast river front; since opening in 1992, attendance has far exceeded that in the old site in Washington Park. The Lloyd District sported new office towers, the Oregon Convention Center opened in 1990, and the Rose Garden sports arena complex hosted its first games in 1995. Built largely by software billionaire Paul Allen, owner of the Portland Trail Blazers, the Rose

Left: The New Theatre Building, opened in 1987 on Broadway, houses the Intermediate and Dolores Winningstad theaters. Many events also are staged in Portland Civic Auditorium and the Arlene Schnitzer Concert Hall (the renovated Paramount Theater). Courtesy, Portland Performing Arts Center

Below left: James DePriest, music director of the Oregon Symphony since 1980, has become one of Portland's best-known personalities. He also was music director of the Quebec Symphony from 1976 to 1983, and has been music director of the Monte Carlo Philharmonic in Monaco since 1994. Courtesy, Oregon Symphony

Below: New construction forced the removal in 1991 of this landmark "peacock" sign and the theater it advertised on Broadway. The tall new building at the site provides offices and parking, along with four underground theaters. Courtesy, Ted Van Arsdol

Garden gave Portland a state-of-the-art arena for sports, concerts, and meetings.

As many of these examples suggest, the Portland core remained the preferred site for the region's most important institutions of culture and higher education. The four theaters of the downtown Performing Arts Center (1987) host music, theater, and lectures. The central library reoccupied its beautifully renovated downtown building in 1997. Oregon Health Sciences University and related hospitals on "pill hill" overlooking downtown continued to grow as a center for medical research and education. Portland State University defined an evolving mission as an urban university, linking classrooms and community through innovative course offerings. With the leadership of President Judith Ramaley (1990-1997), Portland State gained a national reputation as a pioneer in public education. Closely linked were plans for the development of the University District in which the intermixture of new classroom buildings, housing, and business space would tie the university even more closely to its community.

Interspersed with the new offices and entertainment complexes are strong factory and warehouse districts. Portland lacks the "dead zone" of derelict industrial districts and abandoned neighborhoods that surrounds the high rise core of many cities. Portland decision-makers have recognized that a seaport and regional trade center needs to push both payloads as well as paper. An innovative industrial sanctuary policy protects the Central Eastside and Northwest industrial districts. Altogether, major employment centers within two miles of downtown house roughly 100,000 jobs in addition to those in the central business district.

Behind these strong employment totals, the story of Portland's economy since 1985 is its slow recovery from severe recession in the early 1980s turning into headlong economic boom in the 1990s. Between 1981 and 1985, the Portland metropolitan area actually lost more residents than it gained through immigration as people looked for opportunities elsewhere. The picture was startlingly different a few years later. In 1993, *Fortune* found

Above: *Heavy motor vehicle traffic relies on a series of bridges linking the two sides of the Willamette River at Portland. The nearest pictured here is the Hawthorne, said to be the world's oldest lift bridge, built in 1910, and the most distant is the Fremont, with curved span, opened in 1973. Courtesy, Portland Development Commission.*

Left: *Construction of a span alongside the present Interstate Bridge was proposed in the mid-1990s to carry light rail between Portland and the Vancouver area, to alleviate growing traffic congestion. The average daily traffic count on the bridge had reached 112,000 in 1995. Courtesy, Ted Van Arsdol*

Portland one of the "best cities for knowledge workers." By 1995, *Forbes* magazine could write that "a good quality of life, high immigration levels, and computer smarts helped make this rainy town a winner . . . a town that's far better than most for a young company to be in." Two years later *Time* put Portland on its cover as one of the nation's economic hotspots.

The key to the boom was new vitality in the electronics industry, helping to complete Portland's transition from traditional resource-based manufacturing to high technology manufacturing and information industries. Several homegrown electronics firms, such as Tektronix and Floating Point, struggled in the rapidly changing marketplace in the 1980s, but the wealth of talent and affordable land made Portland attractive to outside firms in the late 1980s and 1990s. Led by Intel, seven major electronics manufacturers announced plans to locate or expand in Portland in 1994-95. The programmed investment totaled more than $10 billion. A significant software industry with specializations in business and engineering applications developed to accompany the chip plants and research-and-development facilities.

The electronic industry touched all corners of the metro area, with major new plants in Gresham and Clark County, but the epicenter was Washington County. The county's employment roughly quadrupled from 1970 to 1996. The Washington County cities of Beaverton, Hillsboro, Tigard, and Tualatin emerged as important centers of employment, retailing, and services. Increasingly, business interests in Washington County's "Silicon Forest" chafed at what they saw as Portland-oriented regional policies.

Apart from the high tech excitement, Portland's gateway role remained strong. It continued as a major port and service center for much of Oregon, Idaho, and eastern Washington and the largest wheat export center in the nation. The french fries that McDonald's serves up in Tokyo move

through Portland. So have many of the Toyotas and Hondas that populate American roads. The leading overseas trading partners were Japan, Korea, Taiwan, China, and the Philippines. Air traffic also boomed through the repeated expansion at Portland International Airport.

The Portland area economy as a whole outperformed the United States every year from 1985 to 1996. Jobs grew at nearly twice the national pace. After the recession, unemployment rates dropped below the national figure and stayed there. The core industries of the new Portland economy were electronics, communications, transportation and trade, medical products and services, business and professional services. A telling statistic was the news that the value of Oregon's manufacturing exports exceeded the value of farm and forest exports for the first time ever in the early 1990s.

Along with the overall strong economy, it is also noteworthy that the Portland area offers unusual opportunities for women. The metropolitan area and state have a high proportion of woman-owned business (Oregon is eighth in the nation) and women in managerial and professional jobs (Oregon is tenth). The pay gap between the average earnings of men and women is also narrower than in the nation as a whole. In addition, Portland and Oregon voters frequently choose women for political leadership as mayors, county commissioners, and state legislators.

Strong economies attract new people, and Portland in the 1990s has been no exception to the rule. As was true in previous eras of rapid growth—such as the early 1900s, the 1940s, and the 1970s—Portland in the 1990s was a community of new faces.

Overall population growth was impressive. The three county core grew from 1,050,000 residents in 1980 to 1,174,000 in 1990 and 1,326,000 in 1996. By the early 1990s, the Census Bureau defined the metropolitan area to include a total of six

counties (Multnomah, Clackamas, Washington, Columbia, and Yamhill in Oregon and Clark in Washington) with a population of 1,747,000. The total ranked Portland as larger than Salt Lake City, smaller than Denver, and nearly equal to Sacramento and Kansas City.

Many Portlanders tended to call all newcomers "Californians." There was truth to the generalization, for the Golden State supplied by far the largest single group of out-of-state migrants. Some were attracted by the surging electronics industry; others were looking for a new start as the California economy sputtered with defense spending cutbacks. Until Portland real estate prices began to skyrocket in 1994 and 1995, the affordability of Oregon land and houses also enticed them north.

Far more important to the character of Portland was its evolving ethnic mix. Between 1980 and 1990, federally identified minority groups grew from 7.8 percent to 11.4 percent of the population in the three core counties of Multnomah, Washington,

At O'Bryant Square, a fountain, foliage and benches lure workers on a lunch break, and others with time to relax. The square also is multipurpose—housing a parking garage in its large basement. Courtesy, Portland Development Commission

The Taiwanese government, Portland Development Commission and numerous other donors joined to fund the Chinatown gateway, which is nearly 40 feet high. This arch at Fourth Avenue and Burnside Street was dedicated in November 1986, under sponsorship of the Chinese Consolidated Benevolent Association. Courtesy, Ted Van Arsdol

Since early Portland days, residents have enjoyed downtown fountains. Water is recycled through this fountain at S.W. Fifth Avenue and Ankeny Street, unofficially called "The Carwash." Courtesy, Ted Van Arsdol

and Clackamas. In 1960 the Portland phone book listed only six people named Gonzales and none named Nguyen. By 1992 there were 338 Nguyens and 172 phones in the name of a Gonzales or Gonzalez.

Although minority communities are small in comparison with most other American cities, the increases have had a major impact on the Portland area. Since 1980 the fastest growing ethnic categories have been Latinos (88 percent increase in the 1980s) and Asians (110 percent increase). The Native American and African American populations grew more slowly at 42 percent and 21 percent. Multnomah County retains the largest minority population overall, but the suburban counties are rapidly diversifying.

As was true of European immigrants three generations ago, many of the new immigrants cluster in specific neighborhoods or districts. A substantial Korean community has settled in the Beaverton and Aloha areas of Washington County. Latinos are especially prominent in the Hillsboro-Forest Grove region of western Washington County. Vietnamese-Americans concentrate on the east side of Portland. Immigrants from former Communist nations, especially Russians and Rumanians, cluster in southeast Portland; the Woodstock branch library has developed special book collections to serve these new neighbors.

North and Northeast Portland remained the core of the residential community for African Americans. However, their degree of isolation was far below the norm in other cities. Only six Portland neighborhoods in 1990 were more than 50 percent African American, meaning that people of all races mingle in every part of the metropolitan area. The 1980s and 1990s brought a gradual opening of suburban neighborhoods to black residents. Professional life was also open at the top. African Americans in prominent positions included City Commissioners Charles Jordan (1974-84) and Dick Bogle (1985-92), Multnomah County Commissioner and Commission Chair Gladys McCoy (1979-93); Portland school superintendent Matthew Prophet (1981-92); Oregon Symphony conductor James DePriest (1980-); and Portland police chief Charles Moose (1993-).

Immigration and racial change have created problems as well as success stories. While some Portlanders have welcomed ethnic diversity, others have struggled to cope with the changes. Political leaders in the late 1980s sometimes underestimated the impact of the newcomers, ignoring the rise of black and Asian street gangs until they were well established. White supremacists made Portland a center of activity and recruiting in the late 1980s before meeting a wave of community revulsion.

Nevertheless, the 1990s also brought improvements to old North and Northeast Portland neighborhoods, where Union Avenue became Martin Luther King, Jr. Boulevard. The crack epidemic slowed and community policing began to make gains in neighborhood safety. As some African Americans began to take advantage of opportunities to move to other neighborhoods, white households began to find the area's diversity an attraction—one more example of the willingness of Portlanders to recycle older neighborhoods for successive generations of families.

Left: Portland lost one of its top community leaders with the death of Bill Naito in 1996 at age 70. Naito developed a former department store building into the Galleria and revitalized other historical buildings for new uses, in addition to promoting worthwhile community projects. His long-time business partner was brother Sam. Courtesy, Micki Naito

Below: J.E. (Bud) Clark, wearing designer overalls, lifted a glass of port at his Goose Hollow Inn tavern in 1996. Clark stunned many Portlanders with a victory over veteran politician Frank Ivancie in 1984 and served two four-year terms as mayor. He frequently rode a bicycle to work. Courtesy, Fred De Wolfe

A powerful symbol of Portland's past and future hope for racial relations is the Japanese-American Historical Plaza in Waterfront Park. Conceived by business and civic leader Bill Naito, designed by Bob Murase, and completed in 1990, the Plaza is a miniature landscape of bronze sculpture and granite boulders engraved with haiku. It commemorates the forced removal of Japanese Americans from Portland during World War II *and* their reintegration into Portland and American society.

The acceleration of growth in the last decade has created political tensions as Portland area residents try to envision a changing future. At the same time, the city and region have preserved a strong sense that politics is public service.

The dominant political figure in the late 1980s was Portland Mayor J. E. "Bud" Clark (1985-1992). A big and friendly man who usually wore a Portland rose on his lapel, Clark made citizens feel at home in City Hall. He was also a strong and careful manager who scrutinized city budgets and left Portland with a financial reserve. Bud Clark's accomplishments included the new Oregon Convention Center, important steps for improving services for the homeless, and the initiation of community-based policing.

The 1990s brought an entirely new set of faces to City Council. Gretchen Kafoury took office in 1991 and Charles Hales in 1993. Vera Katz, previously Speaker of the Oregon House of Representatives, followed Bud Clark as mayor in 1993. Then in 1997, Eric Sten and James Francesconi replaced longtime council members Earl Blumenauer and Mike Lindberg.

The Katz administration extended many of Clark's initiatives, such as community policing. The rate of reported crime began to fall in 1996. The city and Multnomah County worked together to disperse services and shelters for homeless people and those in need of transitional housing. The city also gave renewed attention to

Vera Katz, the second woman to be elected Portland mayor, served from 1993 to 1996, then won a new term. Earlier, she represented her district in the Oregon House of Representatives, and was the first woman speaker of that legislative body. Courtesy, City of Portland

promoting new housing at all income levels. The rapid rise of housing prices in the mid-1990s, including the middle class "discovery" of many old working class neighborhoods east of the Willamette, made the affordable housing initiative especially urgent.

Portland residents told opinion pollsters in 1996 that overall they were satisfied with the quality and availability of public services. But satisfaction declined with distance from City Hall. Neighborhoods in outer Southeast and Northeast, many of them annexed to Portland since the 1980s, worried that they were yet to receive equal services.

Public reaction to region-wide services was also mixed. Voters approved a Home Rule Charter for Metro in 1992. This marked the third time that voters had affirmed support for the regional service agency. The new charter freed the agency of direct state control. It consolidated the twelve Metro Council districts into seven— with the result that Metro Council elections began for the first time to attract substantial attention and campaign contributions. The charter maintained a separately elected

Would-be passengers rushed to board a MAX (Metropolitan Area Express) train after it started operating between Portland and Gresham in 1986. Tri-Met started work on a light rail extension to Hillsboro in 1993. Most Tri-Met passengers are transported in numerous buses. Courtesy, Ted Van Arsdol

executive (Mike Burton in the mid-1990s) and an advisory council of mayors and county commissioners as checks and balances.

One of Metro's more popular initiatives was the acquisition of open space. Fearing that private development would overrun the region's remaining hills and stream valleys, voters in May 1995 approved spending $126 million to purchase open space in the tri-county region.

There was greater turmoil over public transit. A fifteen mile light rail line from downtown Portland to Gresham opened in 1986. MAX (for Metropolitan Area Express) carried 27,000 passengers per day in 1996. It helped to leverage $1.2 billion in new investment, including a makeover of downtown Gresham into a thriving community center and redevelopment in the Lloyd District. Combined with one of the nation's better bus systems, it has also supported jobs and entertainment in the core. Thirty-six percent of all work

trips into downtown in 1990 used public transit (three times the proportion in San Diego).

Voters okayed the extension of MAX with an eighteen-mile westside line to Hillsboro at the start if the 1990s. Portlanders watched with fascination as Tri-Met punched a long tunnel through the West Hills with a deep elevator to serve the zoo stop. After it opens in 1998, the westside line is expected to prevent further clogging of the Sunset Highway and focus development in Washington County along the Sunset corridor.

At the same time that the west side line was beginning construction, residents and business interests in Washington County battled over a proposal for a new highway to directly connect the Tualatin-Tigard and Hillsboro areas. The Westside Bypass met many business needs but aroused fierce opposition because it was planned to run outside the Urban Growth Boundary. State officials finally killed the proposal in 1994.

A third stage in the area's light rail system ran into trouble in the mid-1990s. Plans called for a long north-south line from Vancouver, Washington through downtown Portland and south to Clackamas County. Tri-county voters approved a local contribution in 1994, but Clark County said "no" to the segment north of the Columbia River in 1995. Then in November 1996, voters statewide rejected a state contribution to the north-south line. It is unclear whether the vote represents the first fracture in the city-suburb coalition, general anti-spending sentiment, downstate response to environmentally oriented ballot measures that could be read as anti-rural—or all of the above. With support still substantial in the tri-counties, Tri-Met officials in 1997 were back at the drawing board looking at a smaller line.

Light rail is part of a regional effort to plan for a compact city. Nearly all opinion leaders—environmentalists, homebuilders, utility executives, politicians—claim a commitment to some degree of compact growth. Portlanders want their metropolis to be clean and green. The result has been a potent political alliance between the friends of urban values and the friends of trees.

In pursuit of this goal, Portlanders through the 1990s have engaged in a prolonged and intelligent debate about metropolitan growth and form. Metro, as the regional government with responsibility for regional planning, has been the lead agency for responding to expected population growth through its "Region 2040" plan for accommodating up to a million more residents in the four core counties. The process is remarkable for the breadth of participation, including homebuilders and commercial real estate interest as well as growth management advocates. It was also remarkable for actually changing ideas, starting with as an effort to figure out how far the Portland area should grow and ending with a debate over how best to limit outward expansion.

A giant ape dominated the Portland building in a promotion for the first sale of Oregon Lottery tickets in April 1985. The lottery, created by the initiative process, has helped finance the state's schools and other activities. Courtesy, Ted Van Arsdol

The Metro Council adopted the "Region 2040 Growth Concept" in December 1994 and more detailed measures to implement the plan in late 1996. The broad goals of the 2040 plan for the next half century are to focus new jobs and housing on downtown Portland, urban and suburban centers, and transportation corridors. It identifies rural reserves to remain permanently undeveloped. Between them, Gresham, Milwaukie, Hillsboro and Beaverton anticipate 50,000 new housing units, while Portland anticipates 70,000.

In February 1996, widespread flooding on the Willamette and some other rivers caused considerable damage. The rampaging waters even flooded out Willamette Falls, south of Portland. The curvature of the rim of the falls can be seen at center and left. Courtesy, Bill Johnson, U.S. Army Corps of Engineers

Despite the rapid growth of the metro-politan area, Portlanders often prefer the small scale and the comfortable. Portland is still a city of proper manners and sensible shoes that is still learning how to boogie. Old families bank their dividend checks and comport themselves with quiet good taste in the wooded dells of the West Hills. In various city rankings, Portland wins honors not only for economic vitality but for politeness. Portlanders go to bed promptly in the rainy nights of winter and get to work at 8 a.m. When they venture onto their freeways, natives drive too slowly, not too fast, leaving the display of horsepower to California immigrants.

Portlanders pass their idle hours in the outdoors, curled up with a good book, or sipping beer from the city's dozens of microbreweries. On weekends they leave town to climb mountains, ride bikes, catch fish, shoot at deer and elk, and stare at waves crashing endlessly on Oregon's rocky coast. They are strong supporters of public libraries, bookstores, small theater companies, and poetry readings.

Even more basic is the way in which Portlanders value and identify with their neighborhoods and work hard to protect the quality of neighborhood life. Millions of Americans who have grown up or raised children over the past forty years have already encountered Portland neighbor-hoods in Beverly Cleary's children's books about Henry Huggins and Ramona Quimby. Their sort of ordinary middle class neighborhood, with square white houses, parks, movie theaters, and corner stores is alive and well throughout much of Portland—although many corner drugstores have given way to latte and cappuccino shops.

The vitality of old shopping districts is one of the best indicators that Portland is different from other cities. Portland area consumers are familiar with fashionable 23rd Street, trendy Hawthorne and North-east Broadway and Sellwood, all of which came on strong in the late 1980s and 1990s. Just as important are everyday

Left: In 1988, Paul G. Allen arrived on the Portland sports scene as a new owner of the Trail Blazers professional basketball team. Allen was a co-founder of Microsoft Corporation with Bill Gates, and owns and invests in a number of multimedia digital communications companies. Courtesy, Richard Brown Photography

shopping strips from Hillsdale in South-west Portland to St. Johns in North Port-land. Family movie theaters survive in North, Northeast, Southeast, and North-west, still holding their own against the new multiplex competition.

At the same time that it is adamantly low-keyed and middle American, Portland continues to grow more diverse and sophisticated. The first direct flights to Asia left Portland International Airport in 1987. In 1970, the Yellow Pages listed 55 non-European ethnic restaurants inside the Portland city limits (nearly all Mexican and Chinese). By the mid-1990s, the total was more than 300, with cuisines from Morocco to Mongolia.

After the economic slowdown of the early 1980s, the last twelve years have seen continued change. Growth is likely to slow by the end of the decade, but Portland has been irreversibly changed. Future historians are likely to look at the 1990s like the 1940s—an era that irrevocably changed the metropolitan area.

Portland's economy is still regional, but becoming increasingly dependent on corporate headquarters in California or Texas or Korea and on international markets. The metropolitan area is still comfortable, but once quiet streets carry far more traffic. The challenge is to enjoy the benefits of diversity and prosperity without losing Portland's sense of place and its sense of community—without losing the things that make Portland special.

Facing page, left: Most participants in the Starlight parade of the Portland Rose Festival turn out in costume,— "they are wild and crazy," said a festival official. This is separate from the festival's Grand Floral parade, which always is scheduled on a Saturday. Courtesy Vern Uyetake, Portland Rose Festival

Left: *More than 10,000 youngsters take part in the annual Junior Parade, said to be the largest children's parade in the United States. The youngster here participated in the 1996 parade through the Rose City and Hollywood districts. Courtesy Gayle Aman, Portland Rose Festival*

Far left: *High school musicians displayed their talents in the 1995 Rose Festival's Jazz Band classic. Large crowds flock to the city during the annual festival, and U. S. Navy ships tie up at the Willamette River waterfront, near the Fun Center, a huge carnival-like attraction. Courtesy, Vern Uyetake, Portland Rose Festival*

Middle photo: *Volunteers spend many hours decorating floats for entry in the Grand Floral parade in early June, and hope to win top awards. This float was among many in the 1996 Rose Festival. Courtesy Paul Schroeder, Portland Rose Festival*

Right, below: *Occasionally huge numbers of flowers are brought in for display at Pioneer Courthouse Square, pictured here in 1996. Music concerts and other events also are staged frequently at the square. Courtesy Paul Schroeder, Portland Rose Festival*

The arch is the one time entry to old Portland Hotel, now the site of Pioneer Square. Courtesy Fred DeWolfe

CHAPTER IX
CHRONICLES OF LEADERSHIP

"Heads!" Portland's name may have been decided by the flip of a coin in 1845, but subsequent decisions and the growth of Portland have depended on much more business acumen than the random turn of a penny. From horse-drawn "Stumptown" to jet age "PDX," Portland entrepreneurs and institutions have been an integral force behind making the Rose City what it is today, one of the most livable cities in the nation.

Other towns aspired to be the metropolis of the Willamette, but this young village of Portland attracted men such as Captain John Couch who, in the 1840s, declared Portland was the Willamette River's true head of ocean-going navigation, promoted this fact to other sea captains, and settled here to help the harbor grow. A second advantage came in the early 1850s, when Stumptown's leaders and merchants banded together to form the Portland and Valley Plank Road Company to construct what became Canyon Road, tapping the fertile Tualatin Valley, and linking Twality farms with Portland docks and oceangoing commerce.

The town grew steadily, attracting a diverse group of merchants, hucksters, and dreamers. Gold discovered in California in 1848 translated into a swelling, eager neighboring market for previously isolated Webfoot merchants who soon discovered mining the mines was far more lucrative than sifting through the gravels of icy High Sierra streams. In the 1860s gold was found in eastern Oregon and Idaho, making Portland "the town that gravity built," as lumber and foodstuffs drifted down the Willamette and gold poured down the Columbia.

As Portland became the financial and trade center of the region, railroad baron Henry Villard took note. In 1883 Portland became the terminus of "the most stupendous scheme yet undertaken on the American continent," Villard's Northern Pacific Railroad, the Pacific Northwest's first transcontinental rail link.

Though the struggles of the city may be familiar, we tend to overlook those "Empire Builders" who struggled with it. These civic leaders made their way to Oregon by hitching a yoke of oxen to a covered wagon or buying a steerage ticket for America in Europe. They crossed the continent on some of the West's earliest railroads and sailed around the Horn. Later immigrants packed their worldly belongings in a pickup truck bound for Oregon or flew in by jet. Some were born here. The streets weren't paved with gold, but those who persevered gave Portland some impressive credentials.

The organizations whose stories are detailed on the following pages have chosen to support this important literary and civic project. They illustrate the variety of ways in which individuals and their businesses have contributed to the city's growth and development. The civic involvement of Portland's businesses, institutions of learning, and local government, in cooperation with its citizens, has made the community an excellent place in which to live and work.

PORTLAND STATE UNIVERSITY

Portland State University is a dynamic institution with a distinctive mission. With its roots planted deeply in the commitment to widely accessible higher education, the institution has matured over the past 50 years into a nationally recognized urban university distinguished by its close partnership with the community. PSU has worked to nurture its relationship with the community through academic, research, and service programs that reflect regional issues and priorities and, at the same time, provide students with the kind of education they need for success. These commitments have won PSU both admiration and national awards.

Portland State grew out of a small extension center cobbled together in 1946 as a temporary measure to meet the needs of thousands of veterans returning from World War II. The

"GI Bill" had enabled them to pursue college educations. In what is now Delta Park, the temporary city of Vanport had been built in the early 1940s to house shipyard workers. It was there that the Vanport Extension Center opened its doors.

Two years later the Extension Center disappeared in a massive flood that destroyed Vanport, forcing the school into another temporary location at the Oregon Shipyards. In 1952 the Center moved to a permanent home downtown, the old Lincoln High School, thanks to pressure from students, faculty, and the community. From that cornerstone building—now called Lincoln Hall—Portland State began to grow. By 1955 it was a four-year, degree-granting college. Graduate programs were added in 1961, and in 1969 university status was granted.

Nearly 15,000 students attend Portland State, and they reflect a variety of ages and ethnic origins. About 80 percent work to help finance their education.

Today nearly 15,000 students are enrolled in day and evening classes. They can choose from 61 bachelor's degree programs, 56 master's programs, and seven doctoral programs. PSU grants one-quarter of the state's graduate degrees. In addition, 25,000 students are served through the University's School of Extended Studies.

From the single building that housed the entire campus in the early 1950s, the campus has expanded to cover 49 acres and 41 buildings. Located in the tree-lined South Park Blocks district of downtown Portland, PSU is within easy reach of half of Oregon's population. Most recently, PSU and the city of Portland have established the University District, a 52-block area that will provide a "gateway" to campus. A bricked plaza on SW Montgomery Street between SW Fifth and Sixth avenues will feature a new Urban Center Building, which will be home to the College of Urban and Public Affairs and include a distance-learning center, retail shops, and underground parking.

The transformation from small extension center to major urban university is rooted in the strong influence of Portland State's faculty, staff, and students, and the aspirations

When Portland State moved downtown in 1952, the entire campus was this building, now called Lincoln Hall. Today the campus has 41 buildings and covers 49 acres.

Students can access more than 1 million volumes in the Branford Price Millar Library, as well as a growing number of CD-ROM and on-line computer databases.

and involvement of the metropolitan area. The task has been filled with challenges. Consistently, the community and University have joined together to turn adversity to advantage. In recent years, PSU has overcome difficult fiscal and organizational tests through creativity, new levels of accomplishment, and an atmosphere that has fostered academic entrepreneurship.

Perhaps the most striking result is Portland State's new general education program. Called University Studies, it is an interdisciplinary, team-oriented curriculum for all undergraduates, regardless of academic major. The program consists of four sequential components, all of them emphasizing four competencies: communication; inquiry and critical thinking; diversity and multiculturalism; and ethical issues and social responsibility. One of the most important aspects of Univer-

sity Studies is the "senior capstone" project. Led by a faculty adviser, student teams conduct a community-based project, applying what they have learned as undergraduates to address a "real-life" problem.

University Studies has garnered extraordinary recognition for Portland State. In 1996, the Kellogg Foundation selected PSU as one of four institutions to receive a $1 million grant for support of institutional transformation. That same year the University was one of three institutions selected by the Pew Charitable Trusts to receive the Pew Leadership Award for the Renewal of Undergraduate Education.

The senior capstone is perhaps the most talked-about of Portland State's community-based programs, and the extent of PSU's effort is truly remarkable. It reflects the University's commitment to employ its resources in collaboration with the community, developing the community's capacity to address priority issues and concerns. The efforts certainly benefit the community and the University's students, but they also are helping to fuel a national reform movement in higher education.

Among recent initiatives:

• Portland State has been designated as the headquarters for the "Invisible College," a national clearinghouse for service learning, which

PSU faculty created University Studies, a new general education program for undergraduates. The program has won national recognition for Portland State.

provides a means for educators to exchange ideas, experiences, and assessments of curricular designs that link community service with academic study. PSU also is national headquarters for the Society for Values in Higher Education.

• The School of Business Administration has established two "Business Outreach Centers" in inner northeast and southeast Portland to help new small businesses with planning, market research, accounting, human resource management, inventory control, and training.

• PSU and the state of Oregon have developed the Childhood Care and Education Career Development System, providing education and career development to persons teaching and caring for children.

• PSU's Institute for Metropolitan Studies acts as a catalyst for change by connecting academic and research resources with efforts to address current and future community issues in the six-county metropolitan area.

• The University is home to the Institute for Nonprofit Management to help develop leadership in nonprofits, and has established the Center for Community Research to assist community organizations with research on vital issues.

The values surrounding the establishment of Portland State 50 years ago are reflected today in the University's innovative academic and research programs that respond to the needs of the state and region; its partnerships with the community; its commitment to broad access to higher education throughout a lifetime; and the mutual growth of the institution and community when both work cooperatively.

Portland State University is a national model for the urban university. The values that led to that recognition will serve as a foundation for Portland State's growth for many years to come.

OREGON HISTORICAL SOCIETY

For more than 120 years, the Oregon Historical Society (OHS) has provided a place for history—a home for our heritage, our beginnings and our future. Since its inception as the Oregon Pioneer Society on October 18, 1873, the organization's major goal was to preserve the state. In 1898 the Society was incorporated by Oregon's state legislature as a private, non-profit organization chartered to "collect, preserve, exhibit and publish materials relative to the history of the Oregon Country and the United States."

Theodore Roosevelt recognized the value of the Oregon Historical Society's endeavors in 1904, when he wrote to its first director, George H. Himes, "God speed in the work you are doing...You lay the foundations upon which the mighty historic master of the future must build."

Today, the Oregon Historical Society has expanded far beyond its original mission into an organization with over 70 staff members, more than 300 volunteers and an operating budget of over $3.5 million. Membership has grown to nearly 8,000, and an affiliate program—established in 1930 —now includes more than 100 local historical societies throughout Oregon. In addition, OHS has been accredited by the American Association of Museums since 1974.

Since its creation, OHS has been located in Portland, the largest urban center in Oregon. In 1965-66, OHS constructed and occupied a six-story building located on the historic Park

*The **PORTLAND!** exhibit offers visitors a chance to explore the history and development of some of Portland's neighborhoods with an interactive computer program, "Neighborhood Windows."*

Blocks in downtown Portland. An additional 10,000 square feet of space was completed in 1989. This OHS facility—the Oregon History Center—houses over 16,000 square feet of museum exhibition space, a research library, a photographic archive, the OHS press, and is home to the Oregon Folklife Program and a wide variety of educational outreach services. In addition, OHS has a 160,000 square-foot warehouse located in Northwest Portland, and operates the historic 1858 James F. Bybee House on Sauvie Island.

OHS is proud of its collections which include more than 85,000 artifacts, ranging from a 12,000 year-old Fort Rock sandal and sixteenth-century maps, to Deja Shoe's popular contemporary footwear made of recycled materials. The Research Library holdings include more than 2.5 million photographs, 20,000 maps, manuscript materials dating from the eighteenth century, an extensive film archive, and over 5,000 hours of oral histories. The collections reflect and document the broad history of human cultures in the Oregon Country— present day Oregon, Washington, British Columbia, Idaho, and Western Montana. Highlights

*Women drink out of a Benson Bubbler in the 1950s. Named for lumber baron Simon Benson who donated $10,000 in 1912 for 20 drinking fountains, one of the bubblers is on display in the Oregon Historical Society's **PORTLAND!** exhibit.*

from the museum collections are now easily accessible on the OHS Web Site at http://www.ohs.org. Tour the photo gallery with stunning historical images that document the growth and development of Oregon and the Pacific Northwest or browse through selected museum artifacts, maps and manuscripts.

The Oregon Historical Society Press is the most prolific publisher of books on the Pacific Northwest and the history of the Oregon Country. In addition, since 1900, OHS has published the *Oregon Historical Quarterly*, today one of the oldest continuously published historical journals in the United States.

Finally, OHS views itself as an organization whose strengths lie not only in the breadth and depth of its collections, but in the ability of its staff to integrate exhibitions, programs, and publications. It is through the integration of these elements that the Society's role as a historical interpretive center for the citizens of Oregon can best be performed.

AON RISK SERVICES, INC. OF OREGON

Aon Risk Services, Inc. of Oregon began as a local company in 1936. Richard M. Cole opened a one-man agency that he operated out of the law office of his father, where he shared a secretary and kept his own books. In 1940, Maurie Clark joined Cole and added his second-hand desk and his used Chevy as the company vehicle. William Cunningham joined the pair in the Fall of 1941, but within weeks America went to war and the threesome joined the Navy, Army and Coast Guard. Cole hired Marshall "Duke" Brown to keep the business running during their absences.

After the war Cole, Clark and Cunningham regrouped, opened a new office and began offering attractive industrial packages to companies burdened with several different types of insurance needs. The package offered included liability, property damage, fire, workman's compensation as well as group life, accident and health, all handled by a single agent.

Cole and Clark are both Portland natives who had worked in the lumber business and were familiar with Oregon's forest products industry. They developed a package program that was specific for the forest industry and offered it to the then Willamette Valley Lumber–known today as Willamette Industries–an account that to this date still maintains a strong client relationship with Aon Risk Services.

The firm expanded in the 1950s into a wide spectrum of Oregon's traditional economy (i.e. canneries, fruit growers, heavy manufacturing, transportation and shipping) establishing a strong presence in the business community and developing a reputation for excellence in the local insurance industry.

In addition to the package insurance coverage program, Cole, Clark & Cunningham also developed what they called "protectioneering" insurance: protection through the application of engineering industrial insurance problems. By hiring personnel with experience in safety, engineering, and boiler and machinery, the company was able to help their clients buy, build and protect property and reduce the hazards of fire and accident by assisting in safety inspections.

In 1971 Cole, Clark & Cunningham merged with Rollins Burdick Hunter (RBH), an international company that was part of the Chicago-based Aon Corporation. The merger elevated the Oregon company to the next level of service with access to a network of expertise and insurance programs.

RBH moved its office in 1984 to the company's present location in the Pacwest Center in downtown Portland. Since 1992 the company has changed is name twice. The first change to

Richard M. Cole. Photo circa 1950

Maurie Clark. Photo circa 1950

Rollins Hudig Hall reflected the merger of Rollins Burdick Hunter with Hudig-Langeveldt and Frank B. Hall & Co. and in 1996 the name became Aon Risk Services. The last change gave all the subsidiary companies of Aon Corporation the world-wide name recognition and clout of the parent company's strength. Aon Risk Services is part of the Aon Group which is a fast-growing international insurance brokerage and consulting services organization that offers clients a broad range of insurance services, including retail brokerage, reinsurance and wholesale brokerage, alternative risk solutions, risk management consulting and employee benefits and human resources consulting, through its directly owned global distribution networks.

Early in 1997 Aon Corporation completed the acquisition of Alexander & Alexander (A&A) a large international brokerage firm. A&A had an office in Portland which merged into the locally managed Aon Risk Services' office. Aon Risk Services, Inc. of Oregon now has a staff of over 95 insurance professionals who are committed to providing the company's philosophy of *Signature Service* to all its clients. Presently the Portland office represents several Oregon-based Fortune 500 companies, about 30% of the state's top 100 private companies and hundreds of fine local businesses.

Aon Risk Services, Inc. of Oregon was built on a strong foundation of client service. The reputation for excellence in risk management will continue to grow through the strong support provided by Aon Corporation and the superior relationships with our many valued clients.

BURNS BROS., INC.

It was a cold and wet March 3, 1947, when Jack and Bob Burns opened the newest hub of the northwest trucking industry with nine employees, including themselves. Fresh out of the Navy in 1946, Art Mosley and Jack and Bob selected a block across the river from the downtown area on old Highway 99E for their southeast Portland business location. The Burns Bros. Truck Stop became the first station in the Pacific Northwest when its nine employees began pumping gas and maintaining eighteen-wheelers in 1947.

In 1969 Burns Bros. opened one of the largest truck plazas in the United States on I-5 freeway at Wilsonville, Oregon, to offer road-weary truckers and auto travelers an oasis of creature comforts. Today the firm operates

Below: Convenience store, deli, and fast food for the traveler.

Above: A typical Burns Bros. Travel Stop: Troutdale, Oregon.

travel stops in nine western states and has over 1500 employees.

Standard amenities at Burns Bros. Travel Stops include well-stocked convenience stores with great food and beverages; telephones; fax services; an array of truck accessories; video games; large, private showers for both men and women; clean public restrooms; and, at most locations, a 24-hour restaurant and deli. Some travel stops also include quick service restaurants such as Subway, Taco Bell Express, and TCBY.

Food Service and Lodging

Burns Bros. 24-hour Mrs. B's Homestyle Restaurants, Burns West and Super 8 Motels, and their Quick Service Restaurants serve several million satisfied customers every year.

TABB

Truckstops of America (TA) and Burns Bros. Travel Stops (BB) have joined forces for a nationwide fuel network: TABB. With this combined strength and service, the company now reaches coast to coast.

Wholesale Fuel and Transportation

Burns Wholesale Fuel, founded in 1994, has quickly become one of the premier petroleum marketing companies in the Northwest. Burns Bros. Transportation was founded in 1978 to supply petroleum products and business supplies to its 19 travel stops in nine western and mid western states.

Lumilite

Founded in 1981, Lumilite has grown into one of the largest flashlight and lantern companies in the world.

Above: Lumilite's broad array of flashlights and lanterns.

Left: Security Chain Co.—a world leader in traction devices.

They now offer the widest range of battery-operated lighting products in the industry. Lumilite Special Markets, which is an operating arm of Lumilite Products., Co., is located in Minneapolis, Minnesota, and services the premium incentive markets and the advertising specialties trade.

Security Chain Co.

SCC, known for innovation, in 1989 designed a totally new concept in winter traction products: The Z-Chain. This new product is very easy to install and extremely durable with improved traction and handling qualities. The new Z-Chain, with its Z-shaped footprint and patented spring traction design, sets the standard of quality and dependability for winter traction products. The Z-Chain has undergone grueling tests by testing agencies around the world. Today, many of our nation's police forces, ambulance services, and mass transit bus systems are using the Z-Chain for winter traction and safety.

COAST CUTLERY CO.

Coast Cutlery Co. was founded in 1919 by Henry W. Brands, the first of three generations of the Brands' family who would eventually operate this Portland manufacturer and distributor of cutlery. Mr. Brands had worked for several years as a sales manager for a large wholesale hardware company in the Midwest. In this position he discovered the Northwest as a land of opportunity and managed to transfer to Portland in 1915. Traveling the large and small towns of the Northwest, he sold hardware products, including cutlery, to the local merchants. He was continually asked for special types of knives including fillet knives for Northwest salmon fishermen and working knives for loggers. The demand for these specialty knives was the birth of one of today's oldest cutlery companies in the U.S.

Three generations of the Brands family have operated COAST continuously since 1919; Henry W. Brands Sr. (left), Henry W. Brands Jr. (right) and David C. Brands (below).

In 1919 Henry Brands Sr. founded Coast Cutlery Co. two blocks from the Willamette River in downtown Portland. Today Coast sells their products all over the World from their headquarters less than 3 miles from their original location.

Coast's original product line included fillet knives, traditional multi-bladed pocket knives, hunting knives and butcher knives. Mr. Brands served as designer, production manager, sales manager and bookkeeper.

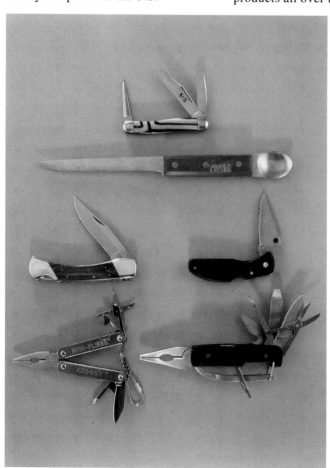

The selection of COAST products includes two of their earliest models (top) as well as four of their current production models.

Much of his selling consisted of filling his car with products and calling on local merchants, returning home only when all his products had been sold.

Coast continued as a small specialty manufacturer through the 1920s, the depression years of the 1930s and into World War II. During World War II materials were hard to obtain, as almost all of the steel was being used in the war effort.

Shortly after the war Henry Brands Sr. was joined in the business by his twin sons Henry and Dwane. This increase in manpower allowed Coast to expand their production and sales efforts. During the late 1940s and 1950s, Coast's product lines expanded greatly and for the first time included products made in Germany, Switzerland and Japan, in addition to their U.S. made products.

With Henry Brands Jr. now handling most of the operations, Coast's business expanded throughout the Western U.S. and included such prominent customers as Fred Meyer, Payless Drug, Meier and Frank and Northern Wholesale Hardware. During this time period Coast achieved wide acclaim in the cutlery business for their high quality products and their innovative merchandising displays. These displays were literally pieces of fine crafted furniture used to display Coast's products in their customers' stores. At one time in the 1960s Meier and Frank displayed over 200 Coast Cutlery products in their sporting goods department.

In the late 1970s Henry Brands Jr. was joined in the business by his youngest child, David. During the

1980s the company expanded its' distribution nation-wide and dramatically increased production capabilities. New production techniques included the use of high density plastics for knife handles, new, easier to sharpen stainless steel blades and the use of aluminum alloys in knife linings and bolsters.

Coast was also a pioneer in the Multi-Tool business. Borrowing ideas from products his grandfather sold as a wholesale hardware salesman, David Brands designed and developed a line of multi-function pocket tools that include: pliers, scissors, screwdrivers, wrenches, saw blades and files, all in small, compact, easy to carry units. Coast is now one of the world's largest manufactures of Multi-Tools under the names POCKET MECHANIC, SPORT MECHANIC, POCKET PLIERS, PLIERS PLUS, POCKET WRENCH and MINI-PLIERS.

Coast products are known by consumers throughout the world for their high quality, durability and lifetime guarantee started by Henry

Brands Sr. way back in 1919. Coast products have been selected for use by the U.S. Olympic Team, the U.S. Navy Blue Angels, the U.S. Air Force Thunderbirds flight teams and the National Football League.

The Coast brand name can be seen as a sponsor of the Coast Multi-Tool NASCAR Race Team and the Coast POCKET MECHANIC Hydroplane Team.

In 1995 Coast expanded its' product line of Multi-function products to include a patented "Liteknife" with an infra-red flashlight built into the handle, another industry first.

Coast has a distribution network of over 10,000 retail outlets in the U.S. and in 30 foreign countries. What started as a desire to provide specialty knives to fishermen and loggers of the Pacific Northwest has developed into a world leader in the production and distribution of cutlery products.

COAST CUTLERY'S modern day marketing includes NASCAR and HYDROPLANE sponsorships.

COLLINS PINE COMPANY

On July 8, 1855 the Collins lumber story began when 24-year-old Truman Doud (Teddy) Collins and four others bought 1,600 acres of virgin White Pine in Northwestern Pennsylvania and a steam sawmill for $600 down per man with a $17,000 mortgage. By 1860 Teddy had bought out his partners. And today, Collins has grown to become the second largest private landowner in Pennsylvania with over 125,000 acres.

But the eastern story soon became the western story as the family came to Oregon, Washington, and California. In 1887, Everell Stanton Collins, Teddy and Mary Stanton Collins' only son, began the journey by coming to the West Coast to explore business opportunities and live out-of-doors while recovering from an illness. That same year, the Root family, also from Pennsylvania, purchased a portion of timberland from the Ostrander brothers that was located on the Cowlitz River in Washington. Teddy and Mary met Everell in Portland in 1888, visited Ostrander, and invested in the Root holdings. Two years later when the Roots had management problems, Everell returned and took over. By building Washington's first long timber mill, he tripled the production.

In addition, Everell built one of the first railroads in Washington–The Ostrander Railway & Timber Company. He also started a successful logging operation at Silver Lake, Washington, represented Cowlitz County in the state legislature, and finally made his move into Oregon by purchasing 100,000 acres of timberland near Molalla. He was also married in 1899 to Mary Laffey, and by 1902 they had three children, Alton, Grace, and Truman. While Everell was concentrating on expanding in Washington and Oregon, Teddy and his partners, Curtis and Holbrook bought 67,800 acres in the Almanor basin of Northern California.

In 1914, Teddy died and Everell and his family returned to Pennsylvania to

Founder of Collins Pine Company (1855), T.D. Collins.

settle the estate and manage the timberland and mills. But the excitement and opportunities in the West were not to be denied, and in 1918 Everell returned–only this time to establish corporate headquarters in Portland, in the Pittock Block. He chose Portland to be close to the Molalla logging operation. In 1927-28, the headquarters moved to the new terminal Sales Building where they stayed until 1989, when they moved to their current Riviera Plaza location.

Everell brought to Oregon a Collins tradition of community participation and served as a trustee of Willamette University and the Portland YMCA, as well as on the board of U.S. National Bank and St. Helens Pulp & Paper Company.

When Everell died December 18, 1940 the Collins timber business turned to the third generation, Truman W. Collins. Even before Everell died, Truman was involved in the family business and had begun considering how to implement a philosophy and set of values that envisioned long-term stewardship of sustained yield forests.

The California timberland had never been logged, so in the late 1930s Truman hired the nation's leading forestry and biology experts to help create a management plan that would ensure the health of "the total forest ecosystem" in perpetuity.

That plan became the basis and backbone of Collins Pine Company's Almanor Forest, a forest that today contains as much wood as it did then, with trees ranging from one year-old to 300 years-old. It is a forest that has never known a clear cut, remaining a biodiverse, multilayered, canopied forest that celebrates and protects its bald eagles, black bears, rubber boas, and blue herons along with its meadows, springs, creeks, and lakes.

Truman followed in his father's footsteps, not only as a thoughtful forester but as an integral part of this community. He graduated from Lincoln High School in Portland, earned a BA degree from Willamette University in 1922, and an MBA from Harvard in 1924. He studied engineering at the Oregon Institute of Technology during 1925-26 while working as a chemist for Oregon Pulp and Paper.

Everell Stanton Collins, second generation, son of Teddy Collins.

His community involvement was extensive. In 1947 Truman and other members of the family of Everell Collins created the Collins Foundation–an independent private foundation to improve, enrich, and give greater expression to the religious, educational, cultural, and scientific endeavors in the state of Oregon and to assist in improving the quality of life in the state. The Portland Board of Realtors named him its first Citizen of the Year in 1962. Truman served as President of the Board of Trustees of Willamette University (where the law school was named in his honor) and on the board of directors of Crown Zellerbach Corporation, Standard Insurance Company, the U.S. National Bank, and the National Board of Missions of the

Collins Pine Company at the turn of the Century in the Northwest.

Truman Wesley Collins, third generation, son of Everill Collins.

Methodist Church. He married Maribeth Wilson, daughter of Clarence and Maude Wilson and they became the parents of four children.

In addition to his commitment to forestry, family, and community, Truman formed Ostrander Construction Company. Along with his college friend, George Atkinson, of the Guy F.

Atkinson Construction Company, they built the McNary and Rock Island Dams on the Columbia River, the Trinity Dam in California, and the 2-mile long Mangla Dam in West Pakistan–at the time the world's largest earthen dam.

When Truman died in 1964, his wife, Maribeth carried on the Collins tradition and became Chair of the Board of Collins Pine Company, a position she holds to this day. James E. Quinn is

Maribeth W. Collins, wife of Truman W. Collins, Chair of the Board.

currently president. Past presidents have included Elmer Goudy, husband of Grace Collins Goudy, Alan Goudy, and Robert Lastofka, all of whom perpetuated the family's values and philosophy.

In 1993 Collins Pine Company's steadfast commitment and dedication to sustained-yield forest management resulted in its 94,000 acre Collins Almanor Forest in Chester, California being the first privately-owned forest in the United States to be comprehensively evaluated and independently certified by Scientific Certification Systems in accordance with the rules of the Forest Stewardship Council. The Collins Pennsylvania Forest/Kane Hardwood also became certified in 1994. These achievements were honored in 1996 with the Presidential Award for Sustainable Development. Continuing in this spirit, Collins Products, L.L.C. in Klamath Falls, brought certified plywood to consumers in North America in 1997.

The Collins family and management is committed to carrying these traditions of stewardship and leadership into the 21st century.

COLUMBIA STEEL CASTING CO., INC.

The city of Portland and Columbia Steel Casting Co., Inc., have seen many changes during the years between 1901 and today.

Columbia Steel Corporation was organized in the West by Central California industrial leaders who saw a need for heavy machinery that would be required for forest-products industries and metals mining. Logging and gold mining were active businesses during the 1920s and 1930s. Columbia products included sawmill loghauls, carriages, and buckets for gold-mining dredges. Prior to this, hydraulic water rams, early water-driven pumps, also were popular for irrigation on remote homesteads.

Manganese steel dredging buckets were made by the Columbia Steel Corporation for service in the Federated Malay States, south of China in the 1920s.

Around 1931 Columbia's Portland foundry was sold to A.M. Clark, an eastern industrial manager. Columbia Steel Corporation (CSC) decided it was not essential for the Portland foundry to supply parts to it when they could obtain castings from one of its other locations. Both the Torrance, California, and Portland foundries had supplied castings to the parent company with an identifying mark of a diamond T or a diamond P for later recognition of the supplier. Portland did not abandon this mark until 1952.

Hobart Bird, Sr., was an imaginative employee of the company in the years around the turn of the century.

The firm's early facility was this 2.5-acre site, located at Northwest Tenth and Johnson streets.

He was moved into leading roles in CSC's independent status, providing growth in the foundry's gold-mining markets in the western United States and Alaska. Bird acquired ownership of the company and was its president through the late 1930s.

During this time CSC's capacities were committed solely to making castings for the maritime industries, which during the World War II years employed over 100,000 people in shipbuilding and related industries. CSC made hawse pipes, stern frames, stern tubes, propellers, and rudder stocks for the shipbuilding programs in the area.

After the war, Bird returned to guiding CSC in restoring markets lost during the disruptive war years. His work was cut short by his death in 1946. Following the loss, his son, Hobart Bird, Jr., left the Coast Guard, where he had served as first officer on a patrol vessel during the war. He assumed the assignment of CSC president and reorganized the market pursuits and operations to take a significant place in manufacturing wear-replacement parts for the primary metals, construction, and heavy-equipment manufacturing industries.

Today the company's main offices and plant are in north Portland, situated on about 100 acres of land. It is a far cry from the old Northwest Tenth and Johnson location where the plant had been located until 1962. The main foundry bay building is 1,000 feet long. The pattern storage building alone spans more than an acre. The products are designed, proof-cast of specifed material, and machine-finished in Columbia Steel Casting Co.'s complete "one-place" facility.

Workmen in the "outdoors" 10th street ramp annex in 1949.

The company continues to discover and serve markets that are key industries in U.S. manufacturing, construction, energy producers and building of the nation's infrastructure.

In 1996 Columbia Steel celebrated it's 95th year of continuous business. The Columbia Steel product logo has become recognized as representing product integrity and value in their technically enhanced products nationwide and internationally.

This confidence has been sustained by the same proof of value that carried the day in the '30s with the postcard mail-out to the mining industry. Talk about getting your money's worth in advertising!

Prior to relocating and expansion of facilities at their present North Portland Oregon location they were practically in Downtown Portland, Oregon.

The workers shown grinding castings in this picture (opposite page) did the job under the N.W. 10th street ramp which was rented from the City of Portland, for $40.00 per month during W.W.II. The original total area site was 2.41 acres compared to the 92 acre industrial center at the present time.

The old historic location at N.W. 9th & Johnson is now the location of a 199 unit housing complex, completed in fall 1997.

The firm's growth, especially during the past 35 years, has been accomplished recognizing community and good neighbor goals of

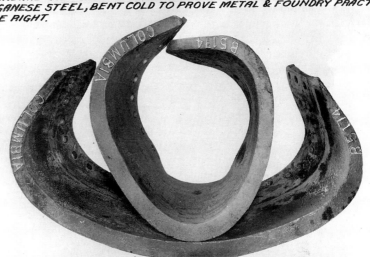

One "historic" post card sales mail out showing the remarkably ductile properties of the products offered in 1938.

North Portland and its residents.

The company's progress in manufacturing and achievements in growth, especially during the past 35 years have been accomplished without compromising environmental goals.

Today's modern manufacturing facility is located on nearly 100 acres in north Portland.

DAN HANNA CAR WASH

When you hear the words: 'car wash', the first name that comes to mind is Dan Hanna. For more than forty years, Dan Hanna has been washing cars, manufacturing car wash equipment and perfecting the car wash process.

Oregon native Dan Hanna is an entrepreneur who has been called the Henry Ford of the car wash industry. Dan Hanna has more than 100 car wash component patents to his name. Personal attention and long hours has been always been Hanna's style. The Hanna commitment to a safe and effective washing is reflected in every car that exits his car wash.

Dan Hanna started constructing his first car wash in 1953. Since the beginning Hanna Car Wash was a family business. It was his mother who helped him get started by mortgaging the family home. For many years, Mrs. Hanna spent each day at the Oak Grove location on McLoughlin Boulevard as cashier. Today, long time customers still remark on how she was always there to greet them.

In 1955 the first Hanna Car Wash opened and by 1963 Hanna had expanded to nine locations. Also in 1963 came the birth of Hanna's manufacturing operation. It was in this year that Hanna was approached by the Malsbary Company, the maker of hot water heaters. Malsbary officials asked him to design and manufacture a more automated car wash system. He worked directly with Malasbary and they were soon marketing his car wash system along with their hot water heaters.

In 1967 Malsbary was purchased by the Carlisle Company. Carlisle had no interest in car wash equipment. It was then that Hanna decided to manufacture under his own name and took over the marketing of his state-of-the-art car wash equipment. Innately gifted in engineering, the founder spent long hours developing equipment and concepts. With product in hand, he soon proved to have a gift for marketing as well. A Lear Jet became a business partner and by the end of the 1960s, Hanna Car Wash had taken an instant leap into the global market place.

During the economic slump of the 1970s, Hanna Car Wash flourished. The Portland area was home to 32 of the over 50 Hanna Car Washes located on the West Coast. Over 90 percent of the parts and components in Hanna Car Washes were manufactured in Portland. In all, Hanna made over 400 different parts used in car washes. In the early 1970s, Dan Hanna was appointed Commissioner of Mass Transportation for the State of Oregon.

This growth continued into the 1980s. A former race car driver himself, Hanna was a sponsor of world champion Mario Andretti. He also provided support to Olympic Gold Medal Skier, Bill Johnson. Hanna Car Wash became the leading car wash firm in the world. Hanna manufactured, sold and serviced equipment for car washes in more than 60 different countries, on all six of the world's inhabited continents. Hanna was the first car wash to penetrate the Iron Curtain and enter Russia.

In 1990, Dan Hanna suffered a setback. A combination of high interest rates, massive expenses to clean up soil contamination and the loss of financing due to a bank leaving Portland, resulted in Hanna being forced to cease operations.

As the years have passed, Hanna continues to perfect the equipment, cleaning solutions and operations that have made him famous. His car washes are easy to use, energy and water efficient, environmentally safe, and known in the industry as "almost bullet-proof." The 1990 setback has proven to be temporary. Today, Dan Hanna has begun the process of rebuilding his car wash organization. He has introduced his Dan Hanna CAREFUL WASH Franchise and Dan Hanna NEW GLOSS Concept. The idea of failing does not enter his mind. Ever progressive, Hanna has established a website at www.hannacar wash.com, for those wanting information about franchise opportunities.

You can still find Dan Hanna at his original existing location on McLoughlin Boulevard in Oak Grove. From early morning to late at night, Hanna is inspecting cars, adjusting equipment or experimenting with new cleaning solutions. All the while, trying to build an even better car wash process.

Original location on McLoughlin Blvd. in Oak Grove.

GENERAL TOOL & SUPPLY CO.

If you owned a socket wrench in the early 1920s, it was made of carbon steel: a metal prone to break under stress. Ned Boyd observed this. He also observed that the automobile industry had developed a chrome-vanadium steel for manufacturing axles. Using this new material, he developed a way to manufacture hand tools from discarded axles. He shared this innovation with John Peterson and Charlie Carlberg, who as "P&C Tool Company" started manufacturing wrenches and sockets, while Boyd concentrated on selling them.

Meanwhile, a friend of Boyd's, John Derville, Sr., was working as a Morse telegraph operator for the Associated Press. Suddenly, the teletype machine made his position obsolete, and Derville was out of a job. Boyd suggested he join him at P&C, and the two men developed a thriving business, operating out of a store at 388 West Burnside. When Boyd decided to move to California, Derville sold his house for $3,500 and used the money to buy him out. The relationship with Peterson and Carlberg ended in 1929, and the distribution side of the business became The General Tool Company, eventually located at 325 NW 15th Avenue.

General Tool's first customers were automotive garages and hardware stores, but when World War II came, the company entered industrial distribution by supplying tools to shipyards.

Left to right: Ron Brady-office manager, Byron Forbes- sales manager, John Derville Jr.-general manager and John Derville Sr.-president. Circa 1950.

General Tool's building at 325 N W 15th Avenue, 1948.

After the war, John's son, John Derville, Jr., returned to Portland from the Army Air Corps and joined the company. Although half of General Tool's business was selling tools directly to manufacturing companies, the other half was still in wholesale hardware. In 1959 the city's largest industrial distributor closed its doors. John Jr. heard opportunity knocking, and decided to discontinue the whole-sale-hardware operation and concentrate on the industrial market. He hired the defunct distributor's sales people and approached the tool manufacturers with a proposal to become become their local representative. It was a bold move—but one which enabled General Tool to grow into the Northwest's largest industrial distributor.

John Jr. became president in 1962. By that time, the state had built the I-405 freeway through General Tool's location, and the company had moved again—this time to 407 NW 17th Avenue. The name was changed to General Tool & Supply Co. to reflect its wide range of products.

John Jr.'s son Bill joined the company in 1972, and ten years later became the third generation to head the company. Never forgetting the lesson that in change lies opportunity, Bill Derville has led the company in new directions.

General Tool was one of the first industrial distributors to offer partnering arrangements to key customers, not only to supply tools, but also to provide inventory-management services and a commitment to reducing overall costs.

In 1983, in response to the development of the "Silicon Forest," General Tool became a distributor of specialized tools and equipment for high-tech industries—a move which is still regarded as innovative among general-line distributors.

The company added a Seattle branch in 1984, and in 1992 moved its Portland operation to the present location at 2705 NW Nicolai. In 1995, General Tool restructured its organization into self-directed business units focused around specific customers, and in 1996 it was named by *Oregon Business* magazine as one of the 100 Best Companies to Work For in Oregon.

E C COMPANY

E C Company's progenitor, Marine Electric, was founded on Portland's waterfront in 1927 by Damon Trout to repair ships. Along the way the company moved to Northwest Third Street and made old time generators.

When World War II started, the move was made to the present location at 21st and Thurman where they made parts for ships. The company played a vital role in the war effort, helping to build Liberty Ships under construction at the Kaiser Shipyards. Working twenty-four hours a day seven days a week, they manufactured generators from scratch, first laminating the steel core from raw steel then winding it with copper wire.

In 1946 Damon Trout advanced money to one of his workers, Stan Adams, Sr., to start Electrical Construction Co. It was a separate company, under Stan's direction, and housed in the same building.

Marine Electric moved the ship repair part of the marine business to Swan Island in 1952. Electrical Construction took over the whole building at Thurman Street, including the motor rewinding facilities. In 1958 E C Company entered into an agreement with a major supplier of generator sets to sell and service their products. This was the beginning of the distribution and service arm of E C Company.

In the early 1960s, Northwest Marine Iron Works, which stayed at its separate location on N. W. 29th Street, became the parent company of both Marine Electric and Electrical Construction Co. when Damon Trout sold the firm to George and Joe Griebe. As marine work lessened while more and more electrical construction work was performed, the Marine Electric name faded and the Electrical Construction Co. name gained wider and wider recognition.

The present owners, purchased Electrical Construction Co. from Northwest Marine Iron Works in 1985.

Electrical Construction Co.,Thurman Street location. (Photo circa 1938.)

The E C Company name was adopted at that time.

Today E C Company has become a diversified, multi-division organization employing a field and office staff exceeding 1,200 employees. As one of the country's largest electrical contracting and power systems distribution firms, the company's steady growth since 1946 reached revenues of $14 million in 1986, $120 million in 1996, and is on track to $150 million in 1997.

The original construction division was based on the industrial market with pulp and paper being the cornerstone into the 1970s. Today E C crews are in virtually every paper mill and all the steel mills, plus numerous other plants, maintaining the company as the premier heavy industry electrical contractor in the Northwest.

While rewinding motors and electro-magnets remain a small but important part of the business, diversification has made E C Company a major player in the advanced technology industry, providing customers full service through its six business units.

The experience and leading edge skills of the Specialty Industries Division assure customers expert construction, renovation and maintenance for the advanced technology industry while meeting exact standards on tight schedules, without disruption to on-going business. E C electricians are experts at tool and equipment installation and relocation, facility and systems upgrades, and state-of-the-art mechanical, lighting and control systems.

Examples of projects include: constructing wafer manufacturing plants, clean rooms, assembly plants and complete manufacturing facilities. The division has constructed, installed and maintained such systems as powered hepa filters, scrubbers, acid water reclamation and gas plants; chemical and gas delivery, monitoring and detection; life safety and support; RO/DI; and building maintenance.

The Commercial Division's experienced professionals provide quality, cost-effective electrical construction and renovation ranging from tenant improvements to performing a significant portion of the traffic signal work in the state of Oregon. Hospitals, airports, office and retail space, high- rise buildings, residential towers, light manufacturing plants and institutional facilities use E C's expertise in such areas as: value engineering, scheduling, design-build, fast track, energy management, lighting retrofit, power quality assurance, and uninteruptable power to help construct, renovate and maintain the best possible facilities and programs tailored to their specific operations.

The Voice and Data Division specializes in voice, data and fiber optic network cabling systems. Whether a project is a communications network for new construction, an "adds, move and changes" for a growing company, or an industrial processing and process control system, E C works with clients to determine their needs, clarify options and choose the best installation.

Using expertise in fiber optics, category-5 UTP wiring; high pair riser cabling; and IBM cabling systems, project managers and skilled technicians take responsibility for both power and data installations to assure uniform design and construction while minimizing time and costs. Services include: CAD "as built" drawings, third-party certification, testing and documentation, and 24-hour emergency service.

The Industrial Division specializes in power distribution up to 115KV, substation installations, controls and instrumentation, distributed control systems (DCS), co-generation and line work. Large crews of skilled electricians can be mobilized within hours for emergencies or planned maintenance shutdowns.

Many of the Northwest's largest firms in such industries as pulp and paper, primary metals, chemicals, utilities, printing, and oil/gas have partnering alliances with E C or have made them their "Contractor of Choice." Many have depended for decades on E C for design, engineering, budgeting, scheduling as well as installation and maintenance.

Pairing their extensive team experience with perpetual upgrading of knowledge of new and old materials and techniques enables the Design/ Build Department to conceptualize,

estimate, budget, engineer, design and draft drawings from concept to installation and operation quickly and cost effectively. By identifying common goals, detrimental impact on other systems is avoided, giving clients an effective design that achieves the optimum combination of value and quality.

The Technical & Services group, on-call 24-hours every day of the year, combines fast response with quality, reliable electrical repair when simple or complex equipment falters or the power goes out. E C expertise can move a large computer room over the weekend and provide long-term preventive maintenance of equipment and facilities to complete the circle of services the construction group provides its customers.

Service is the key according to Chief Operating Officer George Adams and Senior Vice President Ray Kelly. They attribute the company's continuing Northwest and world-wide success to the motto, "We Solve Problems." Working as a team with a 'handshake

relationship' based on cooperation, mutual trust and respect, E C has become a key part of each customer's long-term operation. Over 80% of these are loyal repeaters, many for 20, 30 and 40 years.

With the same philosophy, E C Power Systems sells and services engines and generators produced by Ford, Kubota, Kohler, John Deere, Katolight, Gillette, Lincoln and Miller. The division is directed by John McGraw, its president and operates in seven western states. Full-service facilities located in Portland, Seattle, Boise and Salt Lake City serve more than 300 dealers in Alaska, Idaho, Montana, Nevada, Oregon, Utah and Washington.

The growth and success of E C Power Systems is simple: sell quality products and provide the very best customer service.

E C aggressively pursues new methods and technology by training their people to constantly upgrade their knowledge and experience to provide the customer with lasting value.

FRED MEYER

Throughout the land, a routine grocery shopping trip in 1920 required an itinerary and tough shoe leather. There were stops at the baker's for bread, the butcher's for meat, the grocer's for sugar, and probably a visit to the farmer's market for fresh produce. Additional items meant additional stops at specialty stores. A young Portland coffee merchant named Fred G. Meyer wondered why shoppers couldn't be offered all these goods under one roof–his roof.

Meyer's notion of complete one-stop shopping was a new concept in the United States, but the idea caught on, grew and multiplied. We take this and many other Fred Meyer innovations for granted today, but Portland's merchandising pioneer revolutionized the industry, and when he died in 1978 the firm he had founded as a visionary young man in 1922, and personally guided for 56 years, was ranked 45th in sales among Fortune magazine's 50 largest retailing companies.

Frederick Grubmeyer was born in Brooklyn, New York in 1886. At the age of 22 he changed his unappealing moniker to Fred G. Meyer and headed west, settling in Portland after a brief stay in the goldfields of Alaska. There he sold coffee, teas, spices and other grocery items door to door from his horse-drawn wagon.

Meyer soon opened the Java Coffee and Mission Tea companies in the public market at First and Washington, that era's riverside hub of the city. He also became a landlord, subleasing space to others, and as different specialty food operators moved out, he took over their operation. But the city was growing and merchants were flocking uptown to Yamhill Street and 3rd and 4th Avenues. Meyer joined them, but envisioned the town's

Fred Meyer opened the world's first self-service drugstore in downtown Portland.

Here, in 1947, Fred Meyer poses with some of his MY-TE-FINE line of products, which continue as one of many lines of private-label products sold today at Fred Meyer stores to give customers alternatives that are comparable in quality to national brands, but lower in price.

continued westward expansion and took an option on the southeast corner of 5th and Yamhill. Here, he tried something that no one else had ever done. He conceived the idea of a grocery department store–an establishment that would house a grocery department, meat department, fruit department, coffee, tobacco, a delicatessen, and more all under one roof. One-stop shopping was born.

More shocking innovations followed. In the days of weekly or monthly accounts and home delivery, Meyer's new store was Portland's first cash-and-carry grocery. This was coupled with "self-service;" rather than dealing with clerks, signs instructed novice customers to "Serve Yourself and Pay Cashier." Shoppers loved this convenient novelty.

In those days most bulk foods, such as sugar, dry beans, rice and spaghetti, were kept in large sacks or bins. Upon request, they were scooped into sacks, weighed and given to the customer. To enhance the self-service concept at his 5th Avenue and Yamhill store, Meyer weighed and packaged bulk items in advance–a one-pound unit of this, five pounds of that. Meyer supplied self-service shoppers with baskets to carry their purchases, then baskets on wheels, which evolved into today's familiar shopping cart.

Meyer continued expanding in 1923 with his Vista market–a grocery and dairy store he opened at 4th Avenue

and Yamhill. He followed that in 1928 with a remedies, tobacco, and toiletries store nearby in the Alderway Building, which is believed by many to be the world's first self-service drugstore.

During the Great Depression Meyer's longtime policy of buying Oregon products, selling them inexpensively, offering discounts and coupons, plus his entertaining promotions endeared his store to the public. He prospered to the benefit of all, hiring new employees in those troubled years of vast unemployment.

The expansion of Meyer's operation entered a new era in 1931 with the opening of his Hollywood store at N.E. 41st and Sandy Boulevard. As his first suburban store, it offered free parking for automobiles, which were fast becoming an increasing factor in marketing activity. It was also there that Meyer continued to pioneer one-stop shopping by adding general merchandise and apparel products. The innovative Hollywood store was followed by stores in Salem and Astoria.

From 1939 to 1941, Meyer moved into the neighborhoods of Walnut Park and Rose City, as well as uptown with the Stadium branch on West Burnside. Meyer also developed a knack for gauging future transportation corridors, buying property in those areas and building when residents inevitably began arriving. Both the Gateway store and the Burlingame store on

Fred Meyer's original grocery department store on 5th and Yamhill was the first of its kind in the nation and parent store of the present chain serving the Northwest.

Barbur Boulevard were somewhat in the "boondocks" when Meyer bought the land, but then came the Banfield and Baldock freeways which lured residential growth around these stores.

Fred Meyer died in 1978 at the age of 92 and in 1979 noted historian E. Kimbark MacColl spoke of him in his book, *The Growth of a City*:

"Starting with literally no capital and no formal education, he built an empire that should exceed one billion dollars in sales during 1979. He left an estate of more than $125 million, with nearly the entire amount bequeathed to a charitable trust, the income to be used for religious, charitable, scientific, literary or educational purposes."

That one small cash-and-carry store on the corner of 5th and Yamhill has blossomed into a major western retail chain featuring unique one-stop shopping stores that carry more than 225,000 food and nonfood products in stores averaging 150,000 square feet in size. From bananas to circular saws, diamond rings to riding lawn mowers, silk blouses to digital satellite systems, you'll find all those products and much more at a Fred Meyer store.

As of mid-1997–its 75th anniversary year–Fred Meyer had 113 of its large one-stop stores in six western states, plus 112 small specialty stores comprised primarily of 107 fine jewelry stores in malls in 16 states. It also operated a dairy, commercial bakery, and 2.4 million square feet in three major distribution facilities. And it was heavily involved at mid-year in seeking shareholder approval for a dramatic merger with Smith's Food and Drug, a major grocery chain in seven western states, to create an even stronger company headquartered in Portland with combined sales of more than $7 billion and 48,000 employees.

Fruit was just one of many departments under one roof, a new one-stop-shopping concept pioneered by Fred Meyer in 1922.

THE HEATHMAN HOTEL

Constructed during The Roaring 20s, a time of unprecedented growth and development in the city, the New Heathman Hotel turned out to be the last of the grand hotels to debut in downtown Portland. It stands as one of the few large hotels dating from that period which retains its function as a hotel.

The New Heathman Hotel, at the corner of Broadway Avenue and Salmon Street, was completed in December 1927. A ten-story structure constructed of reinforced concrete and faced with brick, its decorative details were evocative of the Italian Renaissance style. Plans for the building were executed by the Portland architectural firm of DeYoung and Roald, including second story and upper floor windows trimmed in stone and decorative lintels and radiating voussoirs at the head of pairs of select corner windows.

KOIN Radio, which had been

founded in 1926 in the basement of the first Heathman Hotel (across the street) had outgrown its studio within a few years and looked to the New Heathman as a place for potential relocation.

The New Heathman Hotel, photo c. 1938.

Mid-1930s view of the mezzanine and KOIN studios.

Between 1933 and 1939, several modifications were made to the hotel's mezzanine level to accommodate the expanding needs of the station. While headquartered at the New Heathman, KOIN had a larger staff of musicians and entertainers than all the other Portland stations combined. Its early audience reach extended from the greater Portland metropolitan area into California, Nevada and Idaho. KOIN occupied its Heathman studios until 1953 when its entry into television required development of substantially larger quarters.

In the 1950s, downtown Portland began to suffer the same fate as many other major cities. Businesses and entertainment began to move into the suburbs, and by the late 1960s, there were not many lights to be seen on once-bustling Broadway. But new city leadership began to turn things around by the next decade as major retail stores were convinced not only to keep their flagship operations in the heart of the city, but even to build new ones. Portland's downtown renaissance had begun, and The Heathman was in the very center of it.

As part of the downtown redevelopment effort, the city of Portland actively pursued efforts to reintroduce music and theater to the Broadway area. Through the cooperative efforts of the city, private investors, and concerned citizens and artists, site development plans and architectural designs for a performing arts center were drawn.

In the spring of 1982, the *Portland Center for Performing Arts Area Development Plan* noted the critical location and development opportunities of the Heathman Hotel, "The Heathman Hotel is located adjacent to the future Paramount/Concert Hall, and its condition is important to the success of that facility." Although other redevelopment projects were available, The Heathman's importance to the neighborhood's revitalization appealed to developers. In autumn 1984, after a two-year, $16 million renovation, the Heathman Hotel reopened.

Portland architect Carter Case and interior designer Andrew Delfino utilized a variety of natural materials including marble, granite and teak to return the original luster to the public spaces. Owner Mark Stevenson's vision for the hotel included painstaking restoration of the hotel's exterior and the eucalyptus paneled Tea Court at the heart of the hotel, which earned the hotel recognition as a National Historic Landmark.

Walls in the lobby feature original dark gum wood wainscot paneling that extends to the mezzanine balcony floor level. A series of tall, arched windows and smaller square-headed clerestory windows flood the area with light.

The mezzanine balcony features five broad pilaster columns along the east wall with decorative acanthus leaves at the capitals. The ornamental

The Heathman Hotel mezzanine today.

acanthus leaf pattern is continued in the deep cove molding along the ceiling edges throughout the mezzanine level. At the south end of the mezzanine arched openings encircle a large meeting room that originally functioned as KOIN's "Studio A."

Guest rooms were furnished in 18th- through 20th-century styles in Regency, Empire, Ming and Biedermeyer. Given its location in the arts district, The Heathman launched a campaign of support for the visual arts that included acquisition of original works as a key component of the hotel's decor. The Heathman's art collection includes 250 original paintings, photographs, and works on paper, with key focus on the creations of leading Northwest and American artists.

Curated exhibits, changed regularly, highlight The Heathman's mezzanine. The mezzanine library houses a permanent collection of editions signed by authors who have visited the hotel, teamed with a lending library that includes a broad collection of books by the same writers. Signed editions include works by Wallace Stegner,

Alice Walker, Calvin Trillin, Joyce Carol Oates and Norman Mailer, among others.

Symbolic of the link between The Heathman and the arts, developers renovating The Heathman discovered a passage leading directly from the hotel's mezzanine into the concert hall next door. They later learned that The Heathman's architects had simultaneously served as supervising architects for the theater and may have cut the door simply to make work on both projects more convenient. The theater opened its doors in 1927 as the Paramount Theatre and was later renamed the Portland Public Theatre (hence the "Portland" on the marquee). It has since been fully renovated and renamed the Arlene Schnitzer Concert Hall, permanent home of the Oregon Symphony and part of the Portland Center for the Performing Arts theater complex. Concert-goers now use the passageway to enjoy refreshments on The Heathman's mezzanine during breaks in the performances.

LEGACY HEALTH SYSTEM

Legacy Health System is a nonprofit healthcare organization formed in 1989 by the merger of Good Samaritan Hospital & Medical Center and HealthLink (which included Emanuel Hospital & Health Center, Meridian Park Hospital, Mount Hood Medical Center, Holladay Park Medical Center and the Visiting Nurse Association). Known nationally as a progressive example of today's healthcare delivery system model, Legacy combines the accomplishments of a rich history with forward, innovative thinking in order to provide a full range of acute and critical care inpatient, outpatient, emergency, home health and community health education services.

Good Samaritan

On October 9,1875, when the doors to Good Samaritan Hospital first opened, the concept of a coordinated network of healthcare services—with an overall mission to enhance the health of an entire community—was still more than a century away. Founded as the Episcopal Hospital of the Diocese of Oregon by Bishop B. Wistar Morris, Good Samaritan's mission was basic, but no less significant: to provide medical care "to all, regardless of race, color, creed or religion."

One of the oldest hospitals in the Pacific Northwest, Good Samaritan began operation with 50 beds and a staff of five. Even in strained economic times, the hospital's policy according to Bishop Morris was "one-fourth of its work must go to the poor and needy." Throughout the years, Good Samaritan became known for a series of "firsts" in Portland: the first maternity hospital (Wilcox Maternity Hospital), the first EKG machine, the first EEG machine.

Good Samaritan School of Nursing, the first formal school of nursing in the Northwest, was established in 1890 by Emily Loveridge. In its 95 year tradition, the school has graduated more than 4,000 nurses. The school is now known as the Good Samaritan-

Linfield School of Nursing.

If Bishop Morris were alive today, he would certainly marvel at the seemingly miraculous advancements made in medical technology during the past century. He would also beam with pride to see that the hospital he founded not only still exists, but thrives. As a member of Legacy Health System, Legacy Good Samaritan Hospital & Medical Center has woven itself into the fabric of the community; changing and growing with the neighborhood, and responding to the needs of its citizens.

Emanuel Hospital

Legacy Health System also includes Legacy Emanuel Hospital & Health Center, founded by Rev. Carl J. Renhard in 1912. A Lutheran affiliated hospital, Emanuel began in a three story "gingerbread house" located at S.W. Tenth Avenue and Taylor Street, formerly known as Pacific Hospital. Medical equipment and accommodations for 28 patients were housed on the first two floors. Nurses lived in a dormitory on the third floor. The first class of the Emanuel Hospital School

Founded by Bishop B. Wistar Morris, Good Sanaritan Hospital opened its doors on October 9, 1875 with 25 beds and a staff of five. The first patient was a 40 year-old miner from Oswego. The Good Samaritan Hospital of the 1870s was "in the belt of timber which skirts the city and only reached by a circuitous route of a small path through the woods." Circa 1875.

of Nursing, established by Sister Betty Hanson, graduated in 1914.

The new hospital soon outgrew its original building. The first building at the hospital's present site in the Albina section of Northeast Portland was completed in December 1915.

By 1919, Emanuel Hospital was a major medical facility serving nearly 3,500 patients and providing care for more than 500 newborns. A Nurses Home housed 60 nursing students. Construction on the main hospital building began in 1925.

The Emanuel Hospital of today bears little resemblance to its original facility. A vital contributor to the community, Emanuel provides state-of-the-art care in trauma and emergency services. It is also the home of Legacy

Emanuel Children's Hospital, one of the region's leaders in family-centered care, and the Oregon Burn Center, the only burn unit between Seattle and San Francisco.

Visiting Nurse Association

Another contributor to Legacy's rich history is the Visiting Nurse Association, founded in 1902. As both teachers and caregivers, visiting nurses were trusted friends in Portland's neighborhoods. They emphasized the unprecedented notion that cleanliness and hygiene were essential weapons for preventing and fighting infectious diseases. During the economic strain of the Depression, visiting nurses assumed greater responsibility for a family's general welfare by making referrals to social agencies.

Today, Legacy's visiting nurses still uphold that responsibility, committed to bringing dignity and independence to individuals who otherwise would face hospitalization or long-term institutionalization.

Mount Hood & Meridian Park

Legacy's suburban hospitals serve two of the region's fastest growing areas. Mount Hood Medical Center, located east of Portland, was established in 1922 as Gresham General Hospital. Specialty services include a Family Birth Center, chemical dependency and dual diagnosis treatment services. The hospital's Mountain Medical Clinic provides medical care at Mt. Hood Meadows ski area during ski season.

Legacy's newest hospital is Tualatin's Meridian Park Hospital, established in 1973. The name Meridian comes from the fact that the hospital is situated on the county line between Clackamas and Washington counties. Meridian Park has expanded its services significantly in recent years to meet the needs of its rapidly growing community.

With the support of its rich history, Legacy's priority commitment is to continuous, measurable improvement in the quality of its service to patients and other customers, in order to provide effective and affordable healthcare to everyone in need. Collaborating with other healthcare providers, schools, employers, government, religious organizations and community groups, Legacy encourages and assists individuals to become more involved in achieving their optimal personal health and wellness.

Student nurses pose with Rev. Carl J. Renhard (back row, far right), founder of Emanuel Hospital, at the entrance of the original three story "gingerbread house" hospital located at 209 S.W. Tenth Street. Medical equipment and accomodations for 28 patients were housed on the first two floors. Nurses lived in a dormitory on the third floor. Students were paid $10 a month, out of which they had to purchase their floor-length blue-and-white striped uniforms, aprons, black hosiery and high-button shoes. Circa 1913.

McCORMICK & SCHMICK RESTAURANTS, INC.

The talents of two very different, but compatible men have merged in a chronology of events that have evolved into a multi-faceted enterprise encompassing eighteen restaurants, catering services, gourmet food products, cookbooks and logo'd fine quality clothing.

The odyssey started in the early 1960s when Bill McCormick was working for a New England bank. In 1965, a boyhood friend, visiting from California, persuaded him to try his luck on the West Coast and he began working for Connecticut General in San Francisco.

McCormick's first venture into what was to become a love affair with the preparation and presentation of fine food came when he started the Cooperage Restaurant and Bar in San Francisco in 1966. It was tremendously popular and he sold his interest in 1969, becoming a partner in the rapidly expanding chain of Refectory Steak House Restaurants.

In 1970 Bill McCormick arrived in Portland and took a gamble that would have a great impact on his career and the many communities his future businesses would touch. Jake's Famous Crawfish Restaurant had been serving patrons in Portland since the 1890s. Its basements were full of

Jake's Grill with patrons at the bar.

crawfish ponds and its walls were hung with a vast collection of nineteenth century paintings. But most of its patrons had long since abandoned the place when ebullient Bill McCormick purchased the restaurant in 1971 and brought it back to life. The decision to feature seafood, coupled with hard work, replaced a restaurant that had hit skid row, to one with a line out Jake's door inside of a month. Within a year Doug Schmick entered the picture.

Doug Schmick grew up in Colfax, Washington. After graduation from Idaho University, he and his wife Melanie took to the road in a V.W. Bus to write The Great American Novel. With a baby on the way in 1972, the novel was put on the shelf and Doug became a management trainee at Jake's Famous Crawfish Restaurant. He then moved to a management role at the Refectory in East Portland. In 1973 he returned to Jake's after Bill McCormick purchased it.

Bill McCormick and Doug Schmick founded Traditional Concepts, a restaurant management organization, in 1974. Over the next two decades

they established fourteen restaurants up and down the West Coast including McCormick and Schmick's Seafood Restaurant in 1978. Today there are restaurants in Portland, Seattle, San Francisco, Corte Madera, Pasadena, Irvine, Los Angeles, Manhattan Beach, Beverly Hills, Denver, Washington, D.C. and Reston, VA.

This growth rests upon the innovative corporate structure of McCormick & Schmick Restaurants, Inc. which was founded in 1980. It supports the philosophy of providing the highest

Doug Schmick

Bill McCormick

Bartenders at Jake's famous Crawfish

level of service and product in an atmosphere of tradition and comfort. Unlike the typical pyramid with multiple layers of authority and transfer, each restaurant operates with considerable independence as a profit center. Its manager reports directly to top management, but functions as an entrepreneur running a multimillion dollar business of providing patrons, night after night, with food and service they love.

The company's highly successful restaurant and bar operation is complemented with extremely profitable products and catering operations. Jake's Famous Products merged with another specialty food company, Trailblazer Foods, and popular favorites include gift packaged clam chowder, gourmet smoked seafood in a retort pouch, and Jake's World Famous Chocolate Truffle Cake.

The operation continues to expand with the latest product being Jake's Famous Chocolate Truffle Cake Ice Cream, produced in pint sizes and distributed once a year by Danken's Gourmet Ice Creams of Seattle.

McCormick & Schmick Restaurants, Inc. also has catering and banquet

services and facilities. Jake's Catering at the Governor Hotel provides quality food and professional service in the exquisite banquet rooms. Off-premise catering also is available. In Seattle, McCormick & Schmick's Catering at the Museum of Flight offers unique meeting and banquet rooms at Boeing Airfield's renowned Museum of Flight. In addition, McCormick & Schmick Catering is the exclusive caterer at the historic Smith Tower Building, in the Chinese Room; and offers off-premise catering at numerous other locations. In Denver, McCormick's Catering at the Oxford Hotel is considered one of the finest banquet facilities and caterers in the city. Banquet services are offered in Washington, D.C., San Francisco, Southern California and in the respective locations in Seattle and Portland.

McCormick & Schmick Restaurants, Inc. also published its own cookbooks. *Jake's Seafood Cookbook* and *McCormick & Schmick's Seafood Cookbook* are available at all McCormick & Schmick's restaurants. They also are distributed by Chronicle Books of San Francisco.

The "Bait Shop" at each McCormick & Schmick restaurant

features logo'd fine quality clothing and accessories.

Pacific Northwest cuisine is based on the bounty of the Pacific Northwest's sea and country. It is featured in each restaurant's menu and includes such delicacies as Albacore Tuna, salmon, Freshwater Sturgeon, Dungeness Crab, oysters, wild mushrooms, hazelnuts, wild and farm raised game, berries, apples and pears, asparagus, mint peas, hops, cherries, Walla Walla onions and other locally caught and grown foods. McCormick & Schmick's chefs explore the rich possibilities inherent in this natural bounty by preparing it imaginatively so that all the natural flavors are enhanced. Three McCormick & Schmick's chefs were named America's top rated Chefs 2000 by the Chefs in America Awards Foundation.

Each restaurant welcomes special interests by hosting special events. Cigar Night is a monthly favorite (excluding summer months) at McCormick & Schmick's in Portland. Brewmaster Dinners showcasing microbrew ales attract diners to the Pilsner Room in Portland. In Denver, the chefs' cooking classes are a popular feature. In downtown Los Angeles, the restaurant has hosted variations of winemaker and brewmaster dinners. On Valentines Day, some restaurants feature dinners prepared with aphrodisiacs.

McCormick & Schmick Restaurants, Inc. makes a point of giving back to its communities by supporting dozens of programs and organizations. These range from Oregon Special Olympics and SMART to the Citizens Crime Commission; Shamrock Run, a fund raiser for Doernbecher Children's Hospital, the Portland Art Museum's After Hours and San Francisco's Black and White Ball. "Giving back to the community is a fundamental part of our philosophy," says Bill McCormick.

MEIER & FRANK COMPANY

If you were able to go back and visit the Portland of 140 years ago, a lot would be different from the Portland of today. There wouldn't be high-rises and bridges. There wouldn't be waterfront parks and condominiums. There wouldn't even be paved roads. But there would be Meier & Frank. Founded two years before Oregon became a state, Meier & Frank remains a retail institution in the heart of downtown Portland and throughout the Willamette Valley—from Vancouver, Washington to Medford. But it wasn't always easy.

Aaron Meier, a 26-year-old German immigrant, came to Portland from the rugged gold camps of California in 1857. In this raw village called "Stumptown," Meier founded a retail store in a modest frame building near the intersection of Front and Yamhill Streets. Meier struggled for several years, stretching his credit to the limit as everything seemed to go wrong.

"Those were trying times," his widow, Jeanette Meier, recalled in 1920. "Mostly, I was fearful that Father would break down. But he never did. He always said, "Someday, Mother, we will have the greatest store in the Northwest." Sure enough, he was soon moving into larger quarters.

In 1873, 23-year-old Sigmund Frank arrived in Portland. Meier was immediately taken with the young man's business savvy and made him a partner. Business went well for Meier & Frank until the worst fire in Portland history reduced twenty square blocks of the city's central business district to ashes in August, 1873. The partners quickly rebuilt. In 1885, the Meier & Frank Company moved into a new two-story building on Taylor Street between First and Second Avenues. Here, they took dressmaking out of the home by introducing ladies' ready-to-wear to Portland. Disaster struck again when the Great Flood of 1894 inundated the first floor to a depth of over three feet. The store,

Meier & Frank was located on Taylor Street between First and Second from 1885 to 1898. The great flood of 1894 inundated the first floor of the store and the water reached a depth of over three feet.

however, stayed open for business. False raised walks and counters served customers in rowboats.

That flood may have prompted the move of Meier & Frank to higher ground "way up" on Fifth Avenue in 1898. In the store's new five-story, half-block building, the enterprise emerged as "One of America's Great Stores," boasting two elevators and many mechanical innovations never before seen on the Pacific Coast. In 1909, a ten-story annex was added to the store, and in 1913, the five-story structure on Fifth Avenue was razed to make way for a new sixteen-story building, Portland's first skyscraper and the largest department store west of Chicago.

Meier & Frank not only survived the Great Depression of the 1930s, it helped guide Oregon through those grim times when company president, Julius L. Meier, was elected governor of Oregon, serving two terms. During World War II, Meier & Frank's war bond drives were cited as the "most outstanding of any department store in the United States" by the U.S. Treasury Department. Improvements continued after the war, and in 1950, the store installed the longest escalator system in the world.

Although Meier & Frank ceased

being a family operation in 1966 when it joined the May Department Stores Company, the firm remained very civic minded. Each year the store sponsors and promotes the Thanksgiving Holiday Parade, provides support to the Portland Symphony, the Portland Ballet Company and the Portland Art Museum, assists in children's charities, and in 1985, even provided the land for the Pioneer Courthouse Square, dubbed Portland's Living Room. 140 years later, Meier & Frank is still the Portland good neighbor Aaron Meier always insisted it be.

The current Meier & Frank building before construction of the transit mall. The left corner of the structure was added to the original facility during the Depression, filling in the entire block.

MUNNELL & SHERRILL

In 1915, when Chicago Leather Belting Co. decided to close its Portland branch since it was too far from the Chicago home office, a series of very improbable events evolved into 1997s Munnell & Sherrill. E. J. Munnell, the branch bookkeeper, knew that the timber and sawmill customers would continue to need belts to connect the drive shaft of their central engine to the various pieces of equipment plus hoses and related products. So he and A. J. Sherrill pooled their $200 savings; A. J. borrowed an additional $2,000 from a friend for ten days, and Munnell & Sherrill was born when they bought the inventory.

From its building at S.W. 1st Avenue and Stark Street, the business prospered. Munnell died Dec. 26, 1933 and Sherrill carried on until 1944 when he confided to Joe Wreisner, a future company president, as it developed, that he wanted to sell the business since he was feeling his advanced age precluded him from running the company.

Wreisner's suggestion that the employees buy the business precipitated extended negotiations and a search for money. Bankers and businessmen were reluctant to believe that a twelve-man partnership could work but the employees perservered and bought the firm in 1945.

A system was established that continues to work today. During the working day everyone was an employee doing his or her job in the office, warehouse, shipping department or out on the road. Suggestions and complaints were saved for the regular partnership meetings. When they could afford to become a corporation in 1947, the same procedure was maintained.

This philosophy of people working with people was also applied to "customers" and resulted in rapid growth. A major component of the business at that time involved "salesmen" bringing the latest fire-fighting equipment, everything but the truck, to the attention of municipalities and fire departments, then assisting them to get the best possible protection with their limited funds.

Over the years, additional product lines and services have been added to meet client's needs in such industries as wood, sand and gravel, food processing and for any type of "wear" application. A prime example is Munnell & Sherrill's 1967 introduction of "UHMW" polyethylene to a lumber mill in McCloud, Northern California. This Ultra High Molecular Weight plastic, originally designed for Eastern U.S. textile mills, replaced the low grade steel wear bars and strips. Friction was reduced requiring less horsepower to drive the welded steel chains which ran smoother and lasted longer. That small application grew dramatically to approximately 40,000 pounds a month used today in a variety of operations.

When the new Morrison Bridge approach wiped out the old 1st and Stark office in 1956, the main office moved to 1163 NE 63rd Avenue off the Banfield Freeway.

Today, Munnell & Sherrill has six main product lines. It is a full-line distributor of Goodyear Tire and Rubber Co., Foot-Jones Gearing, Jeffrey Welded Steel Chain, Poly Hi, Continental Con-veyor, and Arch Environmental. A very unique triple combination of activities includes serving as a full-line power transmission house, an industrial distributor and a plastics distributor.

These products and services are rapidly available through stores in Portland, Coos Bay, Eugene, Klamath Falls, Medford, Bend, and Roseburg all in Oregon, as well as Arcata, Redding and Ukiah, California and Tacoma, Washington. All "salesmen" drive 3/4 ton trucks to provide 24-hour-a-day pick-up and delivery right to the end user. Any company person, even when called at their residence, will drive 200 or more miles to keep a client's operation functioning.

Sam Mangone, current president, attributes Munnell & Sherrill's steady growth to this caring attitude. "We are employee owned and our employees care. We try to be family and make every effort to treat those who use our products and services as part of our family—not just as customers. We keep in touch even when they retire."

"Munnell & Sherrill should have a bright future since we are self-perpetuating," Mangone explained. "As a closed-end corporation, each employee sells his stock back to the company when he or she retires or leaves. Newcomers earn the right to purchase it. We do not worry about the company passing on to relatives who might not know the business. Everything comes from within; even my replacement is on board. With this solid foundation, the company should continue to grow and probably expand in Northern California and into Washington and Idaho."

NEIL KELLY COMPANY

Neil Kelly Company is celebrating its 50th anniversary this year. The company was founded by Neil Kelly in 1947 when he bought a roofing and siding company for $100.00 and expanded the services offered to include general home remodeling. In those early years, Neil's wife, Arlene, served as the office staff and bookkeeper and a small crew of carpenters was kept busy. Neil Kelly Company now employs 115 people in three divisions: residential remodeling, home repairs and small jobs, and cabinet manufacturing. The company is one of the largest residential remodeling firms in the country, and its work is often published in national magazines. Neil Kelly was actively involved in the business until 1980 when his son, Tom Kelly, became the company's president. Neil continued to be very involved in the remodeling industry, going on to serve the National Association of the Remodeling Industry as its president for two terms in the 1980s.

The original Neil Kelly Company office was in the basement of the Kelly family home on the corner of Northeast 31st Avenue and Couch Street; moving to its present headquarters location of North Alberta St. and Albina Ave. in 1966. The "Columbus Day Storm" of 1962 gave Neil Kelly Company the opportunity to provide quality remodeling and home repair services to a large number of Portland families. Many of those families have been regular customers over the years. The firm is now remodeling homes for the grandchildren of some of their first customers. Additional sites include a sales office in the Parkside Business Center in Beaverton and a cabinet manufacturing shop on Northeast Martin Luther King, Jr. Blvd. in Portland. Remodeling and home repair crews work all over the greater Portland/Vancouver Metropolitan area and their cabinets are sent to customers across the country.

Neil Kelly prided himself in being a good community citizen and he founded his business on that principle.

Our 50th anniversary logo includes the company's advertising symbol from the 1950s, Neil Kelly's three year-old twin sons. Current president, Tom Kelly, is on the left.

Many of the company's employees have, over the years, been active community volunteers in programs such as Habitat for Humanity, Meals on Wheels/Loaves and Fishes, Business Youth Exchange, Volunteers of America, and the St. Andrew Community Center located near their North Portland offices. In both 1995 and 1996, Neil Kelly Company was named to the Oregon Business Magazine's 100 Best Places to Work in Oregon with one of the attributes being the company's community involvement. In addition to civic and charitable efforts, Neil Kelly employees are active, and have served in leadership positions, in Rotary International, Business for Social Responsibility, and both local and national trade associations including the Oregon Remodelers Association, the National Kitchen & Bath Association, and the National Association of Home Builders. Tom Kelly served as Chair of the State of Oregon Construction Contractors Board.

Over the years, the Neil Kelly name has come to represent high quality design and construction, and excellent customer service. The firm's kitchens and bathrooms are often noted in local real estate advertising as a special selling point for Portland area homes and they have won numerous regional and national awards for their work. The company's designers, project managers, carpenters, and cabinet makers work very hard to build on the reputation Neil began. In 1996, Neil Kelly Company was one of three companies in the country to win a coveted National Association of Home Builders Remodeling Quality Award, given for business practices and principles. They are very proud of that.

The future looks bright for Neil Kelly Company. Portland's healthy downtown and vital suburbs create a strong environment for quality remodeling and repair services. Their Home Repair Team and Neil Kelly Signature Cabinets are growing and earning their own reputations for excellence.

The company believes that their success is built on the Neil Kelly people, on the care and craftsmanship they bring to each project. Neil Kelly founded his business on belief in the people he hired and on their ability to learn and excel. That tradition continues today. They believe in their motto, "It's the way we care." Current President Tom Kelly says " We care about our clients, our colleagues, and our community."

Our founder, Neil B. Kelly.

NORTH PACIFIC INSURANCE COMPANY

Today Americans sue with bee swarm frenzy. Both legitimate and frivolous lawsuits overwhelm court dockets. We fixate on shocking jury awards, the spate of product warnings and a mountain of legislation aimed at the negligent, careless or indifferent among us.

Can we understand that time when pedestrians, horsemen, wagoneers or drivers of carriages drawn by horses first craved relief from late nineteenth century technology, the sputtering, infernal (and horseless) machines careening down dusty or rutted roads, seemingly bent on mayhem? Perhaps we smile, imagining those halcyon times when on Portland's few paved streets a speed limit was eight miles per hour. An *Oregonian* editor, in harmony with the opinions of many, proclaimed that "Horses existed before automobiles and are in the vast majority."

How could sufferers be protected from agents of suffering?

In 1926 this question was still new. Oregon Automobile Insurance Company was formed to answer it and has done so successfully ever since. Like other visionaries and pioneers who understood opportunity, founder Arthur M. Eppstein envisioned the automobile's essential contribution to business and personal lives. He created a network of loyal northwest insurance agents to service that purpose.

As of 1924, few states required that auto accidents be reported. Only 17% of Oregon drivers carried automobile liability insurance. Street corners more likely had banks, not service stations. Then, as now, safety could be an afterthought; citizens drove first, then learned how the new-fangled gizmos worked; legislators wisely considered drivers' financial responsibility for their actions. Oregon Automobile collected $350,000 in premiums in 1927 and, comfortable with America's sustained love affair with the automobile, has grown and prospered.

In the 1930s, Mr. Eppstein toured Oregon each year to make personal

With the oil painting of Mr. Eppstein in the background, Mrs. Eppstein is receiving the first copy of "The First 40" from W. A. "Pete" Brooks, the anniversary book prepared at the time of the 40th anniversary of North Pacific Insurance Company.

calls on an ever-growing cadre of insurance agents representing the company. His attention to agent needs for meaningful insurance products and consistent presence in a very competitive marketplace still distinguishes the company today. Add to this the importance always placed on claim service and you have the modern formula for continued success that Mr. Eppstein envisioned.

Through the intervening seventy years, Oregon Automobile Insurance Company has expanded beyond Mr. Eppstein's original vision of an Oregon company for Oregonians. Formed as a subsidiary, then principal operating entity, North Pacific Insurance Company has further enlarged it. NPIC is a multiline personal and commercial insurance company operating in two additional northwest states, Washington and Idaho, and in one Rocky Mountain state, Utah. Since 1986, both companies are wholly owned subsidiaries of General Accident Insurance of America, with all the business and financial strength that such a relationship implies.

Led by a series of distinguished

presidents, including Arthur Eppstein, Max Unger, Pete Brooks, Lou Wilson and, currently, Ken Horner, NPIC has earned a reputation as a formidable regional presence and good corporate citizen and advanced the computerization of insurance programs, all while filling the insurance needs of about 200,000 policyholders. In 1996, North Pacific/Oregon Auto collected almost $185,000,000 in premiums from its four state operation in multiple lines.

As with many similar events over 70 years, the winter storms of December, 1996 produced snow, rain and massive runoff that resulted in concerned Oregon and Washington customers reporting about 2,000 claims by January 2, 1997. North Pacific's claims and support units fulfilled the promise of its customers' insurance policies with prompt payment of about $10,000,000. Mr. Eppstein, long ago chauffeured off to the land of large numbers, would be proud.

NORTHWEST NATURAL GAS COMPANY

Gasco's familiar Linnton Plant as it looked in October 1923. One of these buildings still stands in Portland's Northwest Industrial Area.

Pounding hooves in the night kicked sparks from cobblestone streets lined by glowing gas street lamps as horsedrawn fire engines rolled full tilt to fight a roaring blaze. Water for steam to drive the engine's pump was preheated by manufactured gas, and the streets were also illuminated by the fuel. The gas came from the waterfront plant of the Portland Gas Light Company, franchised by the Territorial Legislature in January 1859, five weeks before Oregon became a state. The pioneer utility now distributes natural gas—as indicated by its modern name, Northwest Natural Gas Company—and in 1999 observes its 140th year of service.

Two Astoria merchants, H.C. Leonard and Henry D. Green, came to Portland to build a "gas manufactory." The first such plant in the Pacific Northwest, it was located on the west bank of the Willamette River near the foot of Flanders Street in 1859. Within a year flickering yellow gas lamps began brightening Portland's dark, rain-slick streets. This early gas was produced by heating coal imported as ballast on windjammers sailing into the river from Australia and Canada. Portland Gas Light Company was just that; in the earliest days of the firm lighting was the only use for the combustible vapor. Then came the preheating of water for those fire wagons and other new uses for gas, and when the firm was sold to a group of local businessmen in 1892, its name was shortened to Portland Gas Company.

By this time service had expanded throughout the city and pipes were carrying gas on the east side of the Willamette, as well as the west. But the new owners soon experienced a temporary setback—the great flood of 1894, which put the gas works out of commission. The company's only complete service interruption, the flood prompted it to move its plant to the higher and drier ground of Everett Street.

In 1906 low-cost surplus California oil encouraged a conversion from coal-gas to oil-gas manufacture. This was also about the time gas appliances were developed—gas ranges, water heaters, and home furnaces. The West Coast's first gas furnace was installed in the home of company president C.F. Adams.

A 1910 reorganization of the utility resulted in the familiar label, "Gasco," a contraction for the new Portland Gas and Coke Company. Demand for gas had burgeoned by 1913, and the larger plant was constructed at Linnton along the Willamette about seven miles north of Portland.

In 1955 natural gas became available to replace manufactured gas, and the next year Gasco converted its entire system to this new resource, resulting in a 17-percent rate reduction for customers. The name Northwest Natural Gas replaced Portland Gas and Coke in 1958 to reflect the change.

Northwest Natural Gas serves about 450,000 customers in a rapidly growing service territory in Northwest Oregon and Southwest Washington. The company has one active operating subsidiary, Canor Energy Ltd., which owns oil and gas properties in Alberta and Saskatchewan, Canada. Northwest Natural also operates an underground storage facility in Columbia County, Oregon, as well as two liquefied natural gas plants in Oregon.

This 1929 repairman advertises on his tool box the health benefits of Gasco's products.

OREGON HEALTH SCIENCES UNIVERSITY

Oregon Health Sciences University's fundamental aim is to improve the health of all Oregonians. OHSU educates health professionals and biomedical researchers in a variety of fields, and it undertakes the indispensable functions of patient care, community service and biomedical research. It touches the life of everyone in Oregon.

The institution can trace its beginnings back to the 1800s and the dreams of several generations of Oregonians. The medical and dental schools were born just before the turn of the century. Nursing education arrived in the early 1900s. Soon after that a hospital was built on campus, and then the state's first full-service children's hospital—Doernbecher Children's Hospital—came into being. The Child Development and Rehabilitation Center emerged in the 1950s. These entities combined in 1974 to form an independent institution within the Oregon State System of Higher Education.

That independence increased when the Oregon Legislature converted OHSU to a non-profit public corporation in July 1995. While the university's academic programs still are coordinated with the state's higher education system, OHSU no longer is governed by OSSHE. Today, the university is governed by a single board of directors appointed by the governor and confirmed by the Oregon Senate. This governance model has replaced several layers of state government oversight and regulation.

While OHSU no longer is a state agency, it retains its public obligations to heal, to teach and to discover. The new, simpler structure merely allows OHSU to make changes appropriate to today's market with greater speed, agility and efficiency.

OHSU today is structured like a private sector corporation except that it is not owned by stockholders. Its land and buildings are owned by the citizens of Oregon. The physical facilities are operated through an agreement similar to a long-term lease.

OHSU sits atop Marquam Hill on a 116-acre campus overlooking Portland. The institution encompasses more than 30 buildings on campus and dozens of facilities at other sites throughout the region. Its programs and services extend across the state's entire 96,000 square miles and even reach into neighboring states.

Healing, teaching and research are the pillars of OHSU. In fulfilling these missions, the institution makes another contribution to Oregon's well-being. As Portland's largest employer—and the seventh largest statewide—OHSU also plays an important role in keeping Oregon's economy healthy.

OHSU provides jobs for more than 8,300 people. This means it employs more people than the City of Portland, Multnomah County or the Portland Public Schools—more than any other hospital, health care system or university in Oregon. OHSU employs more than just clinicians, teachers and researchers. Today, you'll find systems analysts, information specialists, accountants, architects, engineers, electricians, plumbers and many others working as part of the institution to respond to the needs of the region.

With an annual budget in excess of $520 million, OHSU's impact is felt well beyond its ability to teach, heal and discover. Economists conservatively estimate that its activities generate approximately 32,000 jobs in Oregon communities. OHSU, its students and employees spend millions of dollars each year buying goods and services, fueling nearly $2 billion in regional economic activity.

OHSU has evolved into one of America's top academic health care and medical research centers. It has a well-earned national reputation for its expertise, leadership, and commitment to service and education. It is widely recognized for its distinguished faculty and innovative research endeavors. OHSU's many top-ranking professionals have helped place the institution at the vanguard of biomedical advances for decades. The institution continues to be a magnet for attracting practitioners, faculty and researchers who are national leaders in their fields. Top-ranking students from throughout the country vie for the opportunity to attend OHSU. The best and the brightest professionals are the heart of the university.

PACIFICORP

No insurance company would underwrite her maiden voyage from New York to Portland, and all the experts of the day predicted that she would be incinerated at sea, but in August 1880 the world's first electric ship, Henry Villard's steamship *Columbia,* cruised safely past the "Graveyard of the Pacific" and entered the Columbia River. On board were 115 incandescent lamps sparkling throughout the ship—the first electric lights ever installed outside of Thomas Edison's Menlo Park laboratories. Henry Villard, Northern Pacific Railroad baron and president of the Oregon Railway and Navigation Company, had scored another coup in his incessant effort to publicize both Portland and the Northwest.

Those first twinkling globes inspired the spread of electric power production in the Northwest, and by the end of the 1880s small power plants were operating in Astoria, Pendleton, The Dalles, and Walla Walla. These scattered companies joined together in 1910 to form the nucleus of the Portland-based Pacific Power & Light Company.

It started back in 1909, when Seattle's Sidncy Z. Mitchell, president of thc New York-based Electric Bond & Share Company, organized Amcrican Power & Light Company to consolidate several small power companies in Kansas, but his real interest remained in the Pacific Northwest. Mitchell had been involved in the region since the 1880s, and in 1885 was granted exclusive agent rights for Thomas Edison's products in the Northwest.

Twenty-five years later Mitchell's interest returned to the Northwest, and in 1910 four scattered rural power companies struggling to stay in business were brought together by his firm to create Pacific Power & Light. Guy W. Talbot was named president of this combination of the Yakima-Pasco, the Walla Walla-Pendleton, The

Dalles, and the Astoria systems. This gave PP&L 10,780 customers in fourteen towns and rural areas of Washington and Oregon, but during its first year of operation the firm had to build 200 miles of transmission lines to link together its scattered holdings.

It was recognized that the success of the company was linked to the prosperity of agriculture in its region, and the company's farm agents drove many miles on the dusty roads of eastern Oregon and Washington's Palouse to help farmers build electric brooders and pump-irrigation systems. One circuit was long known as the "Moo

This rugged Pacific Power & Light Company line crew used hand-operated gear on an early line truck, helping to bring electric service to customers.

Cow" line because it powered some of thc first electrified dairy barns in thc nation. In small towns, meter readers carried newfangled gadgets called electric irons under their arms to demonstrate the invention's convenience to skeptical housewives.

The acquisition of small electric companies throughout the hinterlands of Oregon and Washington continued well into the 1920s, but the metropolis of Portland, the company's headquarters, remained outside the power realm of PP&L. This changed in 1925, when Northwestern Electric Company joined Pacific Power as part of American Power & Light, a holding company. Northwestern Electric was a small utility operating in the Columbia River Gorge when, in 1913, it obtained a 25-

year franchise to operate in the city of Portland and buck heads with the Portland Railway, Light & Power Company. The first inroad was made by running a 66,000-volt transmission line from Camas, Washington, across the Columbia River, and down the south bank to Portland.

By 1925 Northwestern Electric had 34,500 kilowatts of generating capacity at three locations, including two in Portland—the Pittock steamgenerating station downtown and the Lincoln steam plant on the Willamette River just south of city center. It served one-third of Portland's customers and businesses.

With all of its plant additions over the years, Pacific Power was in a good position to serve new loads, but new markets for electricity now had to be created. At a 1925 sales and service convention, president Guy W. Talbot and vice-president and general manager Lewis A. McArthur spoke on the growing necessity for sales activity on the system due to the firm's increasing power surplus. Vacuum cleaners, ranges, washers, and irons were discussed. However, the device that caught everyone's fancy was demonstrated by the Electro-Kold Corporation, which promoted household refrigeration units to convert domestic iceboxes to electric operation. The firm claimed that an electric refrigerator saved enough in what would have been paid for food spoilage and ice to pay for itself. Sales were slow at first, but in 1929 over 900 were sold as the idea began to catch on.

Through the increasing sales of electric appliances, the number of kilowatt-hours used by the average home doubled in five years, reaching 997 in 1929 and 1,170 in 1930. This was a far cry from the days in 1910 when some companies provided a home with only a single sixteen-watt bulb and kept it lighted for seventy-five cents a month. A globe for the front porch cost an additional twenty-five cents.

Getting a fifty- foot pole into a hole was accomplished with muscle in the earlier years–a job now done by a power truck.

The expanding company was on the rise, and by 1925 was experiencing growing pains. Pacific Power had shared leased offices in the Failing Building with Portland Gas & Coke since 1918, and newly acquired Northwestern Electric's offices were squeezed into the Pittock Block. This need for more space led to the decision to construct what was to become the Public Service Building. Within a year distinguished Portland architect A.E. Doyle had perfected the building's plans and construction had begun. The day before the building's January 3, 1928, formal opening, a Portland *Telegram* headline read: "New Edifice Enchanting to Visitor's Eye."

For many years the red-capped stately white tower ranked as the tallest building in Oregon. This Portland landmark later was crowned by a flashing red and green Pacific Power

sign visible at night for several miles. Airplanes flying into Portland used the lighted building as a beacon to the Swan Island Airport, and the structure was so well known that Pacific Power superimposed the building's image on photos of the company's dams to give people an idea of how high the face of a dam was.

Three of Pacific Power's most significant hydroelectric dam projects were built between the years 1929 and 1956, during the utility's development of the Lewis River in south western Washington. These dams not only generated power and controlled flooding; the lakes formed by their backwater have become prime fishing, boating, picnic, and swimming spots

The Public Service Building in downtown Portland has long been the headquarters for Pacific Power. The lighted sign on the top, no longer in place, was once a well-known landmark.

Oregon and northern California.

In 1989 a merger with Utah Power was concluded pushing total customers served to 1.3 million. It was the first merger in decades between two major owned utilities in the U.S, plus greatly expanded the presence of the company in the West.

Paul B. McKee, head of PP&L from 1932 to 1952, is symbolic of the firm's leadership. McKee personified the spirit of entrepreneurship and the private enterprise system but was always realistic. Even with the public power overtones in connection with the federal government's proposal to construct the Bonneville Dam and other dams on the Columbia River system, McKee's realism made him a supporter of the laudable system of river improvements and helped make the dams on the Columbia possible. McKee's contributions to the community also included being one of the founders of both the Community Chest and the United Fund. Former chairman of the board Glen Jackson is offered as another "prime example of unselfish efforts for this community and region," and an "example rather than an exception" of the role PP&L's leadership has played in the community.

In the years since, the firm has grown from generating only 10,600 kilowatts in 1910 to a worldwide supplier of energy and related services, with operations now in Australia and other points around the globe. The company born in the white heat of Edison's genius has re-invented itself. Now part of Pacificorp, Pacific Power and its 1989 merger partner Utah Power & Light, have a commanding presence in the generation, distribution and transmission of electricity in the United States.

for thousands of Portland-Vancouver residents. These pastimes have been encouraged by the development of Pacific Power's recreation areas, which provide facilities for the public, including a salmon fishery enhancement program and hatchery.

Beginning in 1947 a series of mergers led to a phenomenal growth for the company. That year Pacific Power & Light formally merged with Northwestern Electric, which provided direct access to the Portland market. As a result of the process, Portland remains the only city in the United States to be served by two investor-owned power companies.

Another merger occurred in 1954 with the Mountain States Power Company, an acquisition which added a vast amount of territory from Montana to the Pacific to the PP&L

system. Included in this transaction were two local telephone operations.

With that merger also came service territory in Wyoming, where Pacific Power built its first coal-fired power plant. The first unit was completed in 1958. In preparing for its new role as a user of coal, the company began in the mid-1950s to acquire coal reserves in Wyoming and Montana as future fuel sources. The size of the coal reserves and the increasing interest in coal as an energy source gave birth to Northern Energy Resources Company (NERCO) in 1977 as a wholly owned subsidiary of Pacific Power (now PacifiCorp). It was sold in the early 1990s.

In early 1961 shareholders approved the merger with the California Oregon Power Company, which then served 93,000 electric customers in southern

R. M. WADE & COMPANY

The covered wagons of over 6,000 pioneers rolled along the Oregon Trail to The Dalles in 1850, and one of those immigrants was seventeen-year-old R. M. Wade, who settled with his family at The Dalles. A restless lad, Wade later crossed the Cascade Mountains via the torturous Barlow Road. Moving south, Wade courted and married Anne Williams of Lookingglass, Oregon, and the young couple journeyed by stage to the goldfields of California, settling in Yreka. Here, Wade opened a hardware store to outfit miners.

In 1865 Wade moved to Salem, Oregon, and founded R. M. Wade & Co., selling hardware and farm implements. R. M. Wade & Co. was the ninth company to receive *The Oregonian* 100-year-old recognition and is the only one of the nine that is still owned and run by the same family, making it one of the state's most venerable businesses.

In 1883 the company moved its headquarters to Portland, operating from a building on S. E. Hawthorne Avenue amd Water Streets. The firm acquired a manufacturing plant, Multnomah Iron Works, in 1920, and a principal product of this factory became a gasoline-driven drag saw, an early power saw for loggers introduced by R. M. Wade in 1914. In 1936 the factory designed and manufactured one of the first farm sprinkler irrigation systems, and today is a worldwide leader in all

types of farm irrigation.

A nineteenth-century pioneer in its field, Wade has linked its programs to two crucial aspects of the nation's growth: America's western development and the agricultural revolution in soil tools and methods of crop harvesting.

R. M. Wade & Co. has three divisions. One is Wade Mfg. Co., which manufactures and distributes sprinkler irrigation throughout the world under the brand name "WADE RAIN." Headed by Edward Hall Newbegin, great-grandson of R. M. Wade, the division is located in a modern factory on fifteen acres at Tualatin, Oregon.

R. M. Wade Farm & Garden is a wholesale distribution company selling farm equipment and outdoor power equipment of U.S. and foreign factories to dealers throughout Oregon, Washington, Idaho, Utah, Nevada and Alaska. The manager of this division is Mike Bechtolt. Wade Credit Corp. is

Farm equipment and outdoor power equipment are shipped throughout the West from the R. M. Wade Farm & Garden Division in Beaverton.

the financing arm of the distribution division.

The Corporate Division is headed by Edward Hall Newbegin, chairman of the board and president of R. M. Wade & Co. It is the financial center for the firm.

R. M. Wade is a closely held enterprise with all ownership in the Newbegin family. Edward Newbegin married R. M. Wade's daughter, Susan, and was president of the company from 1915 to 1929. Wade Newbegin, Sr., grandson of R. M. Wade, was president of the corporation from 1929 to 1982, assuming position of chairman of the board until 1989. Edward Hall Newbegin became president of the firm in 1982 and chairman in 1989. Wade Newbegin, Jr. is vice president and Susan Newbegin Russell is secretary of the company. Edward Hall Newbegin, together with Wade Newbegin, Jr. and Susan Newbegin Russell, comprise the fourth generation in the business.

R. M. Wade & Co. established the R. M. Wade Foundation to honor its founder and has used the foundation income to aid agriculture education and experimentation in the Pacific Northwest.

Wade Mfg. Co., a division of R. M. Wade & Co., is located in this up-to-date facility on five acres near Tualatin.

PENDLETON WOOLEN MILLS

The Friendly Scout, an artist's rendering, reflects Pendleton's early trade with the tribes of the West.

The Pendleton story is one of pioneer heritage. It's a story as old as the Oregon Trail and as modern as the Company's state-of-the-art mills.

In the mid-1800s several small woolen mills had been built in the Willamette Valley, where sheep thrived on the abundant grasses and the availability of high quality wool, soft water for processing and small streams for water power encouraged woolen manufacturing. Thus, the stage was set for a young Englishman named Thomas Kay, who had ventured forth from his native Yorkshire county in England to America to fulfill a lifelong dream. In 1863, Kay was hired to help establish one of Oregon's first woolen mills in Brownsville as boss weaver, setting in motion the course of events that would lead to the founding of the Pendleton Woolen Mills.

Originally built in 1893 as the region's first scouring plant, the Pendleton Mill was expanded in 1895 to include yarn and fabric capabilities. Unfortunately, with limited successes and frequent reversals, the mill finally collapsed under the weight of the recession of 1907. By 1908, the once-ambitious Pendleton Mill had become an idle facility with broken-down machinery and a leaky roof.

This was just the opportunity Thomas Kay's grandsons, Clarence, Roy and Chauncey, had been preparing for. As boys, they had grown up in their grandfather's woolen mill in Salem, as well as working in the family clothing store. Additional experience and knowledge had been gained through college, advance courses at the Philadelphia Textile School and by working in mills throughout the east, south and west.

So in 1909, the Pendleton Woolen Mill was incorporated under the ownership of the Bishop family and production began under the guidance of a family skilled in the textile business.

Production of blankets, Indian robes and shawls resumed, with the brothers handling every facet of the business. Using the finest 100% virgin wool and with a commitment to unmatched quality, the business grew. The best customers were the Native Americans themselves, who appreciated the beautiful colors and outstanding quality. Through the years, Pendleton blankets and robes came to be considered a standard of value among the settlers and Indians throughout the West—a standard which continues to this day.

Under Pendleton's new and energetic owners, business continued to expand with the addition of new facilities. In 1912, a weaving mill in Washougal, Washington was acquired, which broadened the company's capability to produce a variety of woolen fabrics.

In 1918, Roy Bishop left the company to concentrate his energies on the Multnomah Mohair Mills, which he had purchased and renamed Oregon Worsted Company.

After World War I, Pendleton opened an office in Portland on the first floor of the Oregon Building at Southwest Fifth and Oak streets, which served as both a showroom and an office. Expansion included the incorporation of the Coast Mills Wool Company, a wool scouring facility.

The 20s were a decade of significant change for Pendleton. A major fire at Washougal gutted the main building, and extensive improvements were needed. In 1924, Pendleton headquarters were established at N.W. Ninth and Flanders, where a building with 15,000 square feet was leased. This space was soon outgrown however, and arrangements were made to lease a Meier & Frank warehouse at Second and Jefferson.

Then in 1927, Chauncey was killed in a hunting accident, which left the responsibilities of Pendleton solely to Clarence.

Wool shirts for men, in the early 20th century, were a utility item. In the damp Pacific Northwest, they were appreciated for their durability, warmth and comfort—but not their attractiveness.

Clarence Bishop saw an opportunity. And in 1924, Pendleton began making wool shirts from the finest 100% virgin

Clarence Morton Bishop, grandson of Thomas Kay and founder of the Pendleton Woolen Mills.

wool, in vivid colors, and with meticulous attention to tailoring detail. Shirts that were "warranted to be a Pendleton", assuring the finest quality and craftsmanship. By the end of the decade, an extensive line of men's 100% virgin wool sportswear included jackets, sport coats, sweaters, slacks, robes and accessories.

The Great Depression was another critical time for the company. Business was stagnant, shipments were returned unpaid and it became a necessity of survival to sell finished goods directly to the public. A strong consumer response enabled the firm to weather this difficult period.

After World War II, business prospered in the thriving economy and Pendleton introduced a line of branded virgin wool womenswear. One garment, the 49'er jacket, captured the attention of women across the country. Its casual, comfortable simplicity met the needs of women who were part of the new move to suburban living.

By the time Clarence M. Bishop passed away in 1969, a fourth generation of family management was well established. Sons, C.M. Bishop, Jr., and Broughton Bishop had both grown up at Pendleton and were well prepared to continue the family tradition. At the time, Pendleton Woolen Mills had grown from eight employees and 40,000 square feet of space in 1909, to eight manufacturing facilities, over 2,000

employees and one million square feet of plant space.

Under Brot and Mort's guidance, the apparel and mill divisions thrived. Responding to a consumer need for non-wool garments to complement its fine woolen coordinates, Pendleton became a year-round sportswear resource in 1972, with distinctively styled menswear and womenswear in lightweight fabrics for spring and summer.

A Pendleton products store was opened in Chicago's Palmer House in 1930, where it continues to this day. In the 1980s, Pendleton applied its considerable retail experience to

Pendleton's blue and gold label has been an assurance of quality and craftsmanship since 1909.

building a retail division that encompassed both company and privately owned specialty stores. A direct mail retail catalog was introduced in 1995.

In the 90s, two major shifts in the apparel industry were to have a significant impact on Pendleton. Increasing consumer demand for lesser priced apparel had expanded public acceptance of global sourcing. And, with the passage of NAFTA in 1996, access to production sources in Mexico became an economic reality.

Historically, the company's vertical operation had assured the ability to control each step in the manufacturing process. After much soul searching, Pendleton began testing limited production in Mexico. This capability has enabled the company to continue manufacturing most of its products domestically by averaging in off-shore production, while maintaining its exacting quality standards on all garments, regardless of origin.

In 1990, the Pendleton office returned to its Northwest Portland roots. New headquarters were established in the old town district on N.W. Broadway — not far from the original showroom and office on N.W. Ninth and Flanders. This move consolidated all divisions under one roof, and in June of 1997, also included computer grading and pattern making.

Pendleton continues to evolve to meet the changing needs of the retailer and consumer. Currently, the company is undergoing an extensive information systems conversion that will significantly streamline order processing and speed information access. In addition, Pendleton's continuing commitment to environmentally-friendly manufacturing has been a primary factor in the multi-million dollar upgrades throughout the company's mills.

As Pendleton continues to position itself for the next century, a fifth generation of family management has assumed administrative roles in the company. C. M. Bishop III is manager of the womenswear division, while John and Charles Bishop are both involved in mill production and sales and financial management. Peter is a merchandiser for the menswear division, thus assuring the continuation of the family tradition—with a sixth generation in the wings.

Today, Pendleton's product line meets a variety of consumer needs, with the same commitment to quality that has been the company's signature for over five generations.

SCHLESSER CO., INC.

Schlesser Co., Inc., is the latest of several family businesses located in the Kenton and St. Johns districts of Portland.

The first enterprise, Schlesser Brothers, a slaughterhouse, was started in 1908 by Edward E. Schlesser and his brother, Curtis C. Schlesser. With the rudimentary act of killing a cow underneath a tree and selling its parts, the business began at the same location now inhabited by Schlesser Co., Inc.

The Schlesser Brothers chain-driven Mac Truck is depicted in the Oregon Public Broadcasting production of the history of the Columbia River. This meat business was sold to Armour in 1941.

E. E. Schlesser's son, Edward, founded Mankind Dog Food, and later Schlesser Sales Company, which shifted the family enterprise from meat to wood products.

Edward Schlesser bought and sold birch door skins, lumber, and plywood in the 1950s. Eventually, Schlesser Sales Company grew into Schlesser Co., Inc. and featured prefinished mouldings for the manufactured housing industry. In 1972, Schlesser purchased part of the property originally owned by his father and uncle and built the moulding prefinishing facility still in operation to this day.

Edward Schlesser has been joined by his son, Steven, in running the family business, thus extending the tradition of Schlesser businessmen in North Portland.

Schlesser Co., Inc. manufactures a variety of products, including hemlock, alder, oak, maple, fingerjointed, agathis, painted, printed, paper-wrapped and MDF mouldings as well as oak and alder cabinetry components, picture frames, wood door jambs, MDF door jambs, window sills, wood drawer sides and closet poles.

A few reminders of the old days of the meat business still remain. A photograph belonging to Edward Schlesser's grandfather, John Schlesser, depicting two Schlesser Brothers employees rounding up wild horses, is still displayed on the walls of the offices of Schlesser Co., Inc.

STEINFELD'S PRODUCTS COMPANY

The Steinfeld family has been associated with Portland for over seventy-five years. European immigrants Henry and Barbara Steinfeld were wed in Winnepeg, Canada, in 1909 and honeymooned in Portland. The newlyweds were so taken by the Rose City they moved there in 1909. The vegetables grown on the Steinfeld's North Portland family farm were sold in the old, fragrant Farmers' Market along Southwest Yamhill Street until a surplus remained of cucumbers and cabbages in 1922.

With the surplus vegetables and some recipes she had brought with her from Canada, Mrs. Steinfeld and her daughter, Elsie, made two 48-gallon wooden crocks of pickles and one of sauerkraut in the back of the family garage. Introduced downtown, the Steinfelds' pickles and sauerkraut immediately caught the fancy of Farmers' Market shoppers.

Their experimenting with cucumbers and cabbages grew to become Steinfeld's "Western Acres" Products, and today is the only major sauerkraut packer west of the Mississippi producing more than 8,000 tons a year. However, cabbage for sauerkraut is only a part of the forty-five million pounds of locally grown cucumbers,

Henry Steinfeld (center) stands behind his prize-winning sauerkraut. Introduced in his downtown vegetable stall in 1922, Steinfeld's pickles and sauerkraut immediately caught the fancy of Farmers' Market shoppers.

cauliflower, and other vegetable products Steinfeld's ships annually throughout the West, around the Pacific Rim, and to the Middle East.

The Steinfelds' pickling business grew up around their home in St. Johns on North Allegheny. Sons Victor and Raymond grew up with it. They began working when they were old enough to pull weeds, and later lugged 100-pound sacks of cucumbers to the 5,000-gallon vats. Years later, after their father retired from the

business in 1942, the two sons' intimate knowledge of the entire process made the family business what it is today.

In 1951 the company bought a Scappoose, Oregon, plant that was transformed into Steinfeld's major sauerkraut facility. Today the site is one of the most modern manufacturing operations handling sauerkraut, relying on state-of-the-art equipment.

Steinfeld's Products Company has experienced continual growth throughout the years in spite of a disastrous fire in 1978 which destroyed the St. Johns facility. The company rose from the ashes the following year when a manufacturing plant was dedicated in South Rivergate Industrial Area.

Steinfeld's prides itself in blending improved technology and equipment with the old, proven methods of processing. It continues to make genuine dill pickles cured the old-fashioned, natural way, using good local produce and fresh spices, the way Mrs. Steinfeld did in 1922.

Seventy-five percent of the vegetables used by Steinfeld's are grown within a thirty-mile radius of its two Portland-area plants. Over $2.5 million in vegetables were purchased from the local agricultural community in 1996. Steinfeld's wishes to continue growing with the community, and is one of the nation's few family-held pickle-producing companies able to boast of doing just that. Third-generation Steinfeld's Richard, Ray, Jr., Jim, and Jane now guide this local pickle family towards continued prosperity, while contributing to Portland's growth.

Steinfeld's extends beyond the immediate family. Many of the firm's dedicated employees have worked over twenty-five years for Steinfeld's. In fact, three generations of other families have been employed, making Steinfeld's a truly Oregon family business.

The first two generations of Steinfelds in the early 1920's. In the front row Henry and Barbara Steinfeld flank son Raymond, while standing (left to right) are William, Elsie, and Victor.

STANDARD INSURANCE COMPANY

Leo Samuel (1847-1916), founder.

Standard Insurance Company, one of the oldest life insurance companies in the West, has built its reputation on financial strength, excellence and growth. More specifically, Standard is in the business of helping families and businesses achieve financial security and has done so for more than 90 years.

Roughriding President Theodore Roosevelt was in the midst of breaking up the monopolies and unbridled energies of the nation's "robber barons" in 1905, when Leo Samuel returned to Portland from New York a changed man.

Samuel was the agent for Equitable Life in Oregon and Idaho, but early in the century an investigation by New York State's Armstrong Commission found problems with some insurance companies. Why, he asked himself, should Oregonians insure themselves with Eastern companies whose distance meant that it often took months to get a claim settled? Why not a Western company? Indeed, why not an Oregon company?

Samuel's musings led to the chartering of the Oregon Life Insurance Company in 1906. Over the years the firm grew to become Portland-based Standard Insurance

Company. The firm, which celebrated its 90th anniversary in 1996, now has assets in excess of $4.3 billion.

Thirteen-year-old Leo Samuel arrived in the United States from Germany in 1860 with an uncle who promptly deserted the boy, leaving him "one dollar and good wishes." But young Samuel also had a dream to one day publish a magazine.

He began by hawking papers on the streets of New York on the eve of the Civil War, and in 1861 moved to Sacramento, California, to peddle Western newsprint, sell advertising space, and eventually publish a traveler's guide for steamboat passengers. In 1871, the 24-year-old publisher moved to Portland and began publishing a lavishly illustrated and widely read regional magazine called *The West Shore*. After 20 years of successful production, and with a childhood dream fulfilled, Samuel ceased publication to look for greener pastures.

After having both published and sold everything from postcards to city directories, Samuel's proven sales ability and regional contacts made him the logical choice to be Equitable Life's general agent in the area. He performed this new task with predictable success for 10 years, until he decided to establish a life insurance company of his own.

In 1905 Samuel unveiled his plan to establish the Northwest's first life insurance company to Abbot Mills, a friend and one of Portland's most successful businessmen, who gave Samuel his wholehearted support. Samuel went on to found the pioneering Oregon Life Insurance Company with the intent of making it a mutual company which serves its policyowners, not anonymous shareholders. But at the state capital they encountered a barrier to their bold plan. State law required the company to show a reserve fund of at least $100,000 before it could be licensed to insure a single life.

Undaunted, Samuel and Mills returned to Portland to build the required reserve. Within weeks they had secured a list of 81 "guarantors" from among the most prominent citizens of Oregon, each of whom understood that they would receive no profit from their investment outside of simple interest.

With this base the company became a reality in February, 1906. When the company paid back the guarantors and became mutual in 1929, the *Oregon Voter* was moved to write, "We doubt whether policyholders or the community as yet comprehend the moral grandeur of the sacrifice made by the holders of the $100,000 capital stock of our own Oregon Life Insurance Company in giving up all possibilities of speculative profit such as have inured to the benefit of successful life insurance company stockholders generally throughout the world."

During its first 23 years the company grew slowly but soundly under the guidance of some of Portland's leading citizens and financiers. By 1916 Oregon Life had $10 million of life insurance in force and $1 million in assets. Expansion followed, and the company entered Idaho in 1920 and Washington the following year. In

Since 1929 "The Will to Achieve" medallion has symbolized the company's pioneering efforts in providing insurance for western families.

1929, the year of mutualization, the company (now called Oregon Mutual Life), entered California. The solid foundation of the firm allowed it to weather the Great Depression of the 1930s and even boast $10 million in assets one year after the crash on Wall Street. Oregon Mutual began ranging far from its webfoot base when it entered its fifth state, Utah, in 1944. Its name was changed to Standard Insurance Company in 1946 to reflect its broadened operation.

Group insurance products were added in 1951 when Standard issued its first group insurance contract by signing the Oregon State Penitentiary Guards and the Oregon State Police. Throughout the 1960s, '70s and early '80s, group insurance sales increased steadily, but nearly all of those sales were west of the Rockies. A joint venture with Connecticut Mutual in 1985, called GroupAmerica, merged Standard's group long term disability product with Connecticut Mutual's sales force and introduced Standard to the Eastern Seaboard.

After two years Standard sold its interest in GroupAmerica to Connecticut Mutual for a handsome gain and signed another joint venture with Northwestern Mutual Life which is still in force. The company then launched a massive campaign to expand its group products nationwide by obtaining licenses and product approvals in 30 states between 1986 and 1989.

Today, Standard is licensed to do business in 49 states and the District of Columbia and has group sales offices throughout the country. In New York, the company is licensed for reinsurance only. By 1996 sales of group products were evenly distributed by geographic area: the Central, Eastern and Western offices each provided one-third of the company's group sales revenue.

Standard reached $1 billion in assets in 1983, $3 billion in 1993 and $4 billion in 1996. The company continues its stewardship of several

The Standard Insurance Center.

hundred acres in Portland's Sunset Corridor, selling and leasing property in the development of a planned self-contained community.

In 1990 Standard formed a Retirement Plans Division. With the aging of the baby boomer generation and the emphasis on planning for retirement, individuals and their employers alike are looking for effective ways to increase retirement savings. Standard's line of group and individual retirement products was designed specifically for this growing market and by the end of 1996 the Retirement Plans Division had $1.66 billion under management.

With more than 9,000 producers marketing Standard's products nationwide, the company has more than $75 billion of group and individual life insurance in force and serves more than four million people. The Portland Chamber of Commerce recognized Standard's significant growth in sales and employees with one of its Top Ten Growth awards in 1996. Standard has been meeting the financial needs of its customers since 1906 and is well positioned to do so for generations to come.

STOEL RIVES LLP

The Portland law firm of Stoel Rives LLP grew up with some of the Pacific Northwest's earliest railroads and electric utility companies. Having gone through many name changes over the years, the current firm is the product of a 1979 merger of two important local law firms–Davies, Biggs, Strayer, Stoel and Boley and Rives, Bonyhadi and Smith. This merger brought together Portland's largest law firm, with a broad corporate, business and litigation practice, and a medium-size firm, with the largest utility practice in the state.

The older firm of Davies, Biggs, Strayer, Stoel and Boley traces its roots back to 1883, the year the Northwest's first transcontinental railroad was completed with Portland its terminus. That year Charles H. Carey began a long career of practicing law in Portland and represented the Northern Pacific Railroad as its Oregon counsel. Carey, who later penned the still popular *General History of Oregon,* formed a partnership with James B. Kerr in 1907.

In 1905, Kerr came west from St. Paul, Minnesota, to represent the Northern Pacific Railroad when it joined with the Great Northern Railroad to construct the Spokane, Portland & Seattle Railroad (SP&S) line along the north bank of the Columbia River, providing both railroads access from Spokane to Portland. Kerr went on to become one of the great land lawyers in the region and continued to handle the Northern Pacific's tangled land grant problems. Thomas B. Stoel joined the Davies firm in 1937. He became a nationally recognized corporate and tax lawyer.

The firm of Rives, Bonyhadi and Smith grew from the partnership of Laing and Gray, formed in 1935. John A. Laing came west from New York in 1910 to represent Electric Bond & Share, which had acquired several small electric utilities in the Northwest. When these companies were merged into the predecessor of Pacific Power & Light (PP&L), Laing served as vice president and general counsel

and was joined by Henry Gray as part of the house counsel office.

In 1935, Laing and Gray formed an independent law firm but continued to represent PP&L while building a broader client base. The firm also has represented Northwest Natural Gas since the 1950s.

When PP&L's first rate case was initiated in 1958, the firm engaged George Rives to handle the matter; he did so successfully and was invited to join the firm in 1963. Rives brought with him a belief that the venture should further broaden its client base and reduce its dependence on PP&L. During the next 15 years its representation expanded into business litigation, corporate representation and antitrust work.

The 1979 merger of the Davies and Rives firms brought together more than 100 lawyers. In 1987, the Portland firm merged with the Seattle firm of Jones Gray Bailey. In 1991, the firm opened an office in Boise, Idaho, and in 1992 it expanded to Salt Lake City, Utah. Today the firm has over 200 attorneys in seven offices.

Thomas B. Stoel, left and George D. Rives, right.

UNITED FINANCE CO.

Personal service is more than just a slogan for United Finance Co., as it celebrates seventy-five years of continuing to meet its customers' needs in 1997. It all started when Ralph C. Parker founded Automobile Securities Co. in 1922. He enjoyed immediate prosperity by helping families to acquire their first automobiles, a purchase that very few lenders anywhere would finance at that time. This ability to serve the customers and build trust from one generation to the next has remained the foundation of the company's consistent growth and stability.

In 1944 Ralph joined forces with Doug Gerow at United Finance to meet the growing demand for loans generated by the multitude of new and improved consumer goods available as WW II drew to a close. When Ralph brought his son, Dick, into the business the next year, the largest loan available was $300. By 1956 the loan limit was $1,500 and in 1971 it reached $5,000. The year 1973 saw all loan caps lifted. Ralph Parker died in 1964 after spearheading forty-two years of growth.

Dick had been named president in 1954 and served in that position until 1981. Now Chairman and Chief Financial Officer, he recently celebrated his 50 year anniversary with United.

Third generation Richard H. Parker, Jr. began preparing to enter the family business graduating from Santa Clara University and joining United California Bank (Wells Fargo Bank) in San Francisco where he advanced to assistant branch manager. He then joined his father at United Finance Co. in 1973 and has served as President and Chief Executive Officer from 1981 to the present.

Having survived the early 1980s wave of acquisitions, closures and a 22% prime rate, United Finance Co. is today one of the Pacific Northwest's oldest and largest independently owned finance companies with 21 branches. The growth has been soundly based on earnings instead of upon the overextended debt like many of United's competitors, whose leverage tactics were battered when interest rates rose sharply.

The earnings came from continuing to meet customer needs with such personal service as money-on-the-same-day direct consumer loans whenever possible; credit life and health insurance, and investment certificates. The latter now provides over $27 million of the company's funds.

Another facet of the company's growth is the purchase of retail installment contracts from dealers. Currently United Finance Co. assets total over $42 million with stockholders' equity in excess of $7 million.

The fourth generation, Richard H. Parker III, recently joined the firm after graduating from Regis University and working for First Interstate Bank

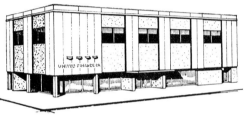

Above, top:
United Finance Co. buillding in the 1930s.

Above:
United Finance Co. building today.

and Norwest in Denver. He is assistant manager at the Vancouver branch and echos his father's sentiments who once stated, "When you eat it and live it day in and day out, your kids begin to think it's a good business. It becomes a part of you when you are growing up. It is a challenge to pass onto the next generation that you don't want to let down." The continuity has been what has kept the company going. Not many companies are passed through three and hopefully four generations with the success of United Finance Co.

Dick Parker and Richard H. Parker, Jr.

THE OREGONIAN

It is hard to imagine Portland without *The Oregonian*. The city and its newspaper have grown up together since *The Oregonian*'s first issue on December 4, 1850. Back then, both the city and its many newspapers were "wide open," reflecting the rollicking early West. This was an era when newspapers were vehemently partisan. It was not unusual for an editor to publicly assault another newspaper editor from a competing paper after a scathing editorial. At this time, *The Oregonian* stood alone among several weekly newspapers—it was "that damn little Whig paper" in a Democratic stronghold.

It was in this atmosphere that Thomas J. Dryer, loyal Whig party member, founder, publisher, editor and not-so-successful entrepreneur, "sold" *The Oregonian* after 10 years. Dryer had come to Portland and started *The Oregonian* after first following the California gold rush west from New York. His destiny, he learned a bit later, was to be appointed governor of the Sandwich Islands by Abraham Lincoln. *The Oregonian*'s new owner,

20-year-old Henry Pittock, was hired originally by Dryer as a printer. He took the small weekly newspaper as well as Dryer's sizable debts in return for back wages.

As the new owner Pittock became publisher, a position he held for the next 60 years. He succeeded, even as many other local newspapers failed, due to his keen business sense. Pittock added new technologies for gathering the news. This included adding pony express service from the nearest telegraph in Yreka, California— bringing the news to people in Portland weeks earlier than before. Pittock saw that *The Oregonian* was one of the first newspapers to subscribe to a fledgling wire service, the Associated Press, in 1880. He also continued to invest in new and more efficient printing presses, and he continued to expand circulation.

But it was in 1865 that Pittock made his best business decision when he hired the city librarian, Harvey W. Scott, to be editor. This began a 40-year publisher-editor partnership that changed and

Above: Harvey W. Scott

Below: The Oregonian *has evolved continuously over the years with each new publisher and editor finding new and better ways to provide information readers need.*

1860   1899   1980   1997

improved nearly every aspect of their newspaper.

Harvey Scott was trained in the classics and had a mastery of the English language. He changed the way newspaper stories were written—not just in Oregon, but throughout the nation. He threw out the traditional, long flowery prose of the time and presented readers with a direct writing style that reads easily today. Harvey Scott enjoyed a national reputation and was regarded among journalists such as Joseph Pulitzer and Horace Greeley. Together Scott and Pittock produced a relevant newspaper that gave Portland the local, national and international news. It also openly promoted everything they believed in—including free trade, sound money and the Republican Party.

In 1950, the Pittock and Scott heirs sold *The Oregonian* to S.I. Newhouse, owner of a national group of newspapers. Eleven years later, Newhouse also bought Portland's other remaining daily, the *Oregon Journal*. Both newspapers

operated independently until 1982 when *Oregonian* publisher Fred A. Stickel consolidated the news and editorial staffs of both to create an expanded *Oregonian*.

But *The Oregonian* in the 1980s wasn't just a larger newspaper. Editor Bill Hilliard sponsored a populist approach to the news, addressing reader interests and reaching out to people and groups throughout the community. He also developed a news staff that more closely resembles all people in Portland with women and ethnic minorities holding positions throughout the news department.

In the 1990s, as the Internet and other traditional media produced an information explosion, Portland's population skyrocketed with people of different backgrounds and interests. In this more competitive, more segmented era, *The Oregonian* went against a national trend of downsizing newspapers. Under the leadership of Publisher Fred A. Stickel and Editor Sandra Mims Rowe, *The Oregonian* added new features devoted to readers' interests, including expanded sections on food, automotive, arts & entertainment, homes & garden and books. Rowe also expanded local coverage, reorganizing the news staff into teams to cover topical areas such as families and education, growth, health and medicine, and public safety. Circulation increased, keeping pace and outstripping the expanding population base.

Inside Line, a voice information system, was launched to provide news, weather, sports and other features by telephone 24-hours a day, as well as provide a new way for businesses to advertise. *The Oregonian* also expanded its capacity for delivering preprinted

inserts to meet the needs of advertisers. More than 3,000 "preprints" are directed at targeted buying groups every year.

Today, *The Oregonian* is several newspapers. Geographically zoned editions cover city neighborhoods, suburbs and nearby towns. Each zone has its own bureau and reporters follow local issues and concerns. Advertising sales representatives help local businesses reach their customers efficiently. Even as Portland's population grows with new people with different backgrounds and interests, this new role helps *The Oregonian* continue to give readers the information they need to form educated opinions and to make intelligent decisions. And as the readers, the marketplace and technology change in the years to come, *The Oregonian* will continue to evolve, providing people with the information they need to lead better lives.

Fred A. Stickel, Publisher

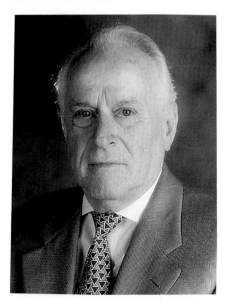

Sandra Mims Rowe, Editor

WACKER SILTRONIC CORPORATION

Historians have divided the development of mankind into eras and have named those eras after materials–the Stone Age, the Bronze Age, and the Iron Age–the use of which has greatly influenced and impacted the progress of our society. However, no other material has influenced and changed our modern life more dramatically than silicon. Silicon is the key chemical element out of which our future is made. No doubt, future generations will teach and tell their children about the "Silicon Age."

Wacker Siltronic Corporation's silicon wafer manufacturing plant site in Portland, Oregon.

The end of the last century saw the development of a technical process for the production of acetylene from carbide. Acetylene was much in demand for lighting, but was soon replaced by the electric light bulb. Dr. Alexander Wacker recognized early on that acetylene may have other uses. In 1896 he founded a laboratory for the development of processes for the chemical utilization of acetylene at Schuckert AG in Nuremberg, Germany. This led to the creation of the Consortium for Electrochemical Industry Ltd. in 1903. Basic research on acetylene chemistry was carried out there and, this work led to the formation of Wacker-Chemie GmbH in 1914. The company is now headquartered in Munich, Germany.

Later on in its development, Wacker also became aware of the significant importance of silicon especially in its monocrystalline form. In 1953, Wacker produced its first monocrystalline silicon ingot, not only opening the door for a new Wacker business venture, but also helping to introduce a material which is now the foundation for today's multibillion dollar electronics industry.

In the early sixties it became very clear that Wacker would have to show a local presence if it wanted to gain a significant foothold in the fast growing U.S. semiconductor market. Consequently, in 1965 Wacker bought a small company in Los Angeles, which

specialized in semiconductor silicon. The firm operated there under the Wacker name for 15 years. Then a decision was made to build a new factory in the United States: Wacker Siltronic Corporation.

In 1978, the cornerstone of Wacker's silicon production plant was established in Portland, Oregon, celebrating its inauguration in 1980. The new facility, located in Northwest Portland on the banks of the Willamette River, soon proved to be the ideal choice with an international harbor and airport nearby, an extensive road network, an economically sound industrial infrastructure, good schools, and, last but not least, a qualified, dependable and committed work force. Since 1980 Wacker has invested

significantly in modern equipment and facilities at this location in order to operate Wacker Siltronic as one of the most modern and efficient silicon wafer plants in the world today.

During the last several years, electronic equipment markets have grown rapidly and to meet the challenging demand, Wacker decided in October of 1994 to expand its Portland wafer capacity. This expansion represents the greatest investment the company has ever made on any single project.

In July of 1996, Wacker celebrated the grand opening of this new "state of the art" Fab 2 facility for the production of 200mm wafers. This investment is just another step to further Wacker's growth in the extremely

Wacker's new Fab 2 "state of the art" 200mm silicon wafer production facility.

competitive world of semiconductor wafer manufacturing. It demonstrates Wacker's long-term commitment, not only to the highly competitive silicon industry but also to the region and the City of Portland and its continued economic growth.

Today Wacker Siltronic represents a milestone in the city's vision for the development of the "Silicon Forest." The company is proud of its role in helping the Portland Area become an important participant in this new "age of silicon."

SELECTED READING

The history of Portland has been well-served by several studies that place the development of the city within the growth of the Pacific Northwest. Dorothy Johansen and Charles Gates, *Empire of the Columbia* (New York: Harper and Row, 1967) and Earl Pomeroy, *The Pacific Slope* (New York: A.A. Knopf, 1965) are regional surveys. Gordon Dodds, *Oregon: A Bicentennial History* (New York: W.W. Norton, 1977) is the most recent state history. Samuel Dicken, *The Making of Oregon* (Portland: Oregon Historical Society, 1979) gives a geographical perspective, while a number of the essays in Thomas Vaughan, ed., *The Western Shore: Oregon Country Essays* (Portland: Oregon Historical Society, 1975) deal directly with Portland.

The Native American peoples of Oregon are treated in Stephen Dow Beckham, *The Indians of Western Oregon* (Coos Bay: Arago Books, 1977); Robert H. Ruby and John A. Brown, *The Chinook Indians* (Norman: University of Oklahoma Press, 1976); Robert H. Ruby and John A. Brown, *Indians of the Pacific Northwest* (Norman: University of Oklahoma Press, 1981); and Jeff Zucker, Kay Hummel, and Bob Hogfoss, *Oregon Indians: Culture, History, and Current Affairs* (Portland: Oregon Historical Society, 1983). Joel V. Berreman's "Tribal Distribution in Oregon," *Memoirs of the American Anthropological Association,* 47 (1937) is a useful specialized source.

For early exploration and pioneering, the journals of Lewis and Clark (various editions) are an invaluable starting point. Also see: Fred William Powell, *Hall J. Kelley on Oregon* (Princeton: Princeton University Press, 1932); Eugene Snyder, *Early Portland: Stumptown Triumphant* (Portland: Binford and Mort, 1970); Malcolm Clark, Jr., *The Eden Seekers: The Settlement of Oregon* (Boston: Houghton Mifflin Co., 1981); Howard Corning, *Willamette Landings: Ghost Towns of the River* (Portland: Oregon Historical Society, 1973); and William Bowen, *The Willamette Valley: Migration and Settlement on the Oregon Frontier* (Seattle: University of Washington Press, 1978).

The essential source on Portland's development as a community during the nineteenth century is Paul Merriam's "Portland, 1840-1890: A Social and Economic History" (Ph.D. Dissertation, University of Oregon, 1971). Harvey Scott's *History of the Oregon Country* edited by Leslie Scott (Cambridge: The Riverside Press, 1924) and Joseph Gaston's *Portland: Its History and Its Builders* (Chicago: S.J. Clarke Co., 1911) are records of the city's development by active participants in its history. Thomas Vaughan and Terence O'Donnell's *Portland: A Historical Sketch and Guide* (Portland: Oregon Historical Society, 1984) captures the spirit of the city. Other valuable studies include Glenn Quiett, *They Built the West: An Epic of Rails and Cities* (New York: Appleton-Century, 1934); Arthur Throckmorton, *Oregon Argonauts: Merchant Adventurers on the Western Frontier* (Portland: Oregon Historical Society, 1961); Charles A. Tracy, "The Police Function in Portland, 1851-74," *Oregon Historical Quarterly* 80 (1979); and Malcolm Clark, Jr., ed., *Pharisee Among the Philistines: The Diary of Judge Mathew P. Deady, 1871-1892* (Portland: Oregon Historical Society, 1975). One of the best recent studies is Ruth B. Moynihan, *Rebel for Rights: Abigail Scott Duniway* (New Haven: Yale University Press, 1983).

The physical development of Portland is traced in Thomas Vaughan and Virginia Guest Ferriday, eds., *Space, Style, and Structure: Building in Northwest America* (Portland, 1974); Richard Marlitt, *Nineteenth Street* (Portland: Oregon Historical Society, 1978); William J. Hawkins III, *The Grand Era of Cast Iron Architecture in Portland* (Portland: Binford and Mort, 1976); Al Staehli, *Preservation Options for Portland Neighborhoods* (Portland, 1974); Fred DeWolfe, *Portland Tradition in Buildings and People* (Portland, 1980); Eugene Snyder, *Portland: Names and Neighborhoods* (Portland: Binford and Mort, 1979); and Virginia Guest Ferriday, *The Last of the Handmade Buildings* (Portland: Mark Publishing Co., 1984).

Ethnic minorities in Portland and Oregon are treated in Elizabeth McLaglen, *A Peculiar Paradise: Blacks in Oregon, 1788-1940* (Portland: Georgian Press, 1981); William A. Little and James Weiss, *Blacks in Oregon* (Portland: Portland State University, 1978); Nelson Chia-Chi Ho, *Portland's Chinatown: The History of an Urban Ethnic District* (Portland: Bureau of Planning, 1978); and Tricia Knoll, *Becoming American: Asian Sojourners, Immigrants, and Refugees in the Western United States* (Portland: Coast to Coast Books, 1982).

For the last hundred years of Portland history, an essential starting point is two books by E. Kimbark MacColl: *The Shaping of a City; Business and Politics in Portland, Oregon, 1885-1915* (Portland: Georgian Press, 1976) and *The Growth of a City: Power and Politics in Portland, Oregon, 1915-1950* (Portland: Georgian Press, 1979). Carl Abbott, *Portland: Planning, Politics and Growth in a Twentieth Century City* (Lincoln: University of Nebraska Press, 1983) also covers Portland's growth over several generations.

More specialized books on the twentieth century city include Carl Abbott, *The Great Extravaganza: Portland's Lewis and Clark Exposition* (Portland: Oregon Historical Society, 1981); William Toll, *The Making of an Ethnic Middle Class: Portland Jewry over Four Generations* (Albany: SUNY Press, 1982); Charles McKinley, *Uncle Sam in the Pacific Northwest* (Berkeley: University of California Press, 1952); William W. Pilcher, *The Portland Longshoremen: A Dispersed Urban Community* (New York: Holt, Rinehart & Winston, 1972); and Ellis Lucia, *The Conscience of a City: The History of the Portland City Club* (Portland, 1966). Other specialized studies include Mansel Blackford, "The Lost Dream: Businessmen and City Planning in Portland, Oregon, 1903-1914," *Western Historical Quarterly* 15 (1984); Harvey G. Tobie, "Oregon Labor Disputes, 1919-23," *Oregon Historical Quarterly* 48 (1947); and Kenneth Jackson, *The Ku Klux Klan in the City* (New York: Oxford University Press, 1967).

INDEX

GENERAL INDEX

List of Oregon Historical Society photographs and their negative numbers

No negative numbers for color renderings and some lithographs.